essence

recipes from
le champignon sauvage
david everitt-matthias

*I dedicate this book
to my wife, Helen.
Thank you for being there.*

essence

recipes from
le champignon sauvage
david everitt-matthias

foreword by
gordon ramsay

Absolute Press

First published in Great Britain
in 2006 by

Absolute Press
Scarborough House
29 James Street West
Bath BA1 2BT
Phone 44 (0) 1225 316013
Fax 44 (0) 1225 445836
E-mail info@absolutepress.co.uk
Website www.absolutepress.co.uk

Reprinted 2007, 2008

Publisher
Jon Croft
Commissioning Editor
Meg Avent
Editor
Jane Middleton
Designer
Matt Inwood
Publishing Assistant
Meg Devenish
Photographer
Lisa Barber
Photography Assistant
Cynthia Lin

A catalogue record of this book is
available from the British Library

ISBN: 1904573525
ISBN 13: 9781904573524

Printed and bound by
Oriental Press, Dubai

A note about the text
This book is set in Sabon MT.
Sabon was designed by Jan
Tschichold in 1964. The roman
design is based on type by Claude
Garamond, whereas the italic
design is based on types by Robert
Granjon.

contents

foreword by gordon ramsay

It is a genuine pleasure to have been asked to write the foreword to David Everitt-Matthias' insightful book, *Essence*. I have been a great admirer of David and Helen ever since I first dined at their restaurant in 1999 with my wife, Tana. I was confident then that two Michelin stars were in their sights and it came as no surprise when they were awarded them the following year.

It is a rare pleasure in this day and age to have a husband and wife team making such a huge success of a restaurant. They are admired throughout the industry for their single-minded dedication and passion in striving for and achieving a cuisine and service of rare quality and originality. If only there were more couples like them in our business.

In all the nineteen years that they have been open, David has somehow managed to miss not one single service – a remarkable achievement. I tend to see David as very much Britain's equivalent of the great three-Michelin-star French chef, Pierre Koffman, a culinary genius of similar conviction and focus, in whose kitchen David once worked for a short while and who I know influenced him greatly.

With the publication of *Essence*, a beautiful book filled with David's brilliantly conceived recipes, the keen amateur cook and the dedicated professional at last have a chance to recreate part of the Le Champignon Sauvage experience.

Gordon Ramsay, August 2006

introduction

I have wanted to be a chef ever since my Auntie Pat allowed me to help her in her kitchen. She wasn't a professional, she was a midwife, but she was a very gifted hedgerow cook. I used to spend one evening a week at her home, helping her to make jams, chutneys, wines and many wonderful dishes. She would take me out to the countryside, or sometimes just the local overgrown common, where we would pick all sorts of things: wild garlic for soup, blackberries for her delicious bramble and apple crumble, sorrel for salads, and oak leaves and cowslips for wine.

This early introduction to wild food lay dormant for a long while, and I didn't return to it until I'd been cooking at my own restaurant for 15 years. I began my career as an apprentice at the Inn on the Park in Mayfair. Now called the Four Seasons, it is one of London's most luxurious five-star hotels – a good place to start. For three years while I was there, the head chef was a talented Frenchman called Jean Michel Bonin, who inspired me with a

After stints as head chef at three London restaurants, which helped me develop my own style, I began searching with Helen for a restaurant to buy. We spent our days off visiting premises all over the country and then by chance, in 1987, details of a restaurant in Cheltenham called La Ciboulette appeared in the post. We hadn't asked for it to be sent but there it was, so we thought we would take a look. Needless to say we fell in love with Cheltenham and bought the restaurant.

This was the beginning of the highest of the highs and the lowest of the lows. We set about putting our stamp on the restaurant and redecorated immediately, concentrating on the dining room rather than the kitchen, as we didn't have enough money for both. We opened with a full restaurant and a cooking style that was decidedly fussy. To be honest, I was cooking for the guides, or what I thought the guides were looking for. I carried on in this way for a while, then recession hit. We lost quite a few of our big

I was forced to seek out humbler ingredients... It taught me a whole new culinary idiom, using many 'forgotten' ingredients. It was cheaper for me to butcher things myself, so I learned how to do this, and as a result had to cook the whole animal rather than just the prime cuts.

hunger to learn. At the same time I was studying at Ealing College under Jackie Cotterell and David Foskett, now a professor at Thames Valley University. Both made learning exciting and were always there to help and offer sound advice. I am indebted to the three of them for creating an environment in which I could flourish.

It was while I was at the Four Seasons that two major events occurred. First, I met my wife, Helen, a receptionist at the time and now my partner and manager. Secondly I was sent to Pierre Koffmann's restaurant, La Tante Claire. It was this introduction to restaurant cooking that made me realise it was the life for me: no time in the stillroom making afternoon teas, no more breakfast shifts – just cooking lunch and dinner, day in, day out. Pierre Koffmann had a knack for taking humble ingredients and turning them into intricate gourmet treats. His stuffed pig's trotter is a prime example, a wonderful dish that has been copied by many other chefs. He will always be a major inspiration to me.

company clients and the restaurant became quieter and quieter. I was forced to seek out humbler ingredients: mackerel instead of sea bass, wood pigeon instead of pigeon de Bresse. It taught me a whole new culinary idiom, using many 'forgotten' ingredients. It was cheaper for me to butcher things myself, so I learned how to do this, and as a result had to cook the whole animal rather than just the prime cuts. A rabbit would give me stuffed legs as one dish and the saddle as another, while the shoulders could be made into rillettes. The offal was served with a pea purée as a dish in its own right, while the bones gave us a wonderful, full-flavoured rabbit soup. This became part of my cooking style and remains so to this day.

I was lucky enough to be invited several times to a restaurant called the Manor House in Romsey, owned by the chef, Mauro Bregoli, who specialised in Italian pork charcuterie, including cotechino, sausages, coppa, and some wonderful salamis. On Sundays, when the restaurant was closed, he would arrange charcuterie days for chefs. What made it even better was that

Pierre Koffmann, a good friend of Mauro's, was there as well, doing French charcuterie such as boudin noir, sauçisson, fromage de tête etc. It was a great learning experience for me and I am indebted to them both for sharing their knowledge and time. I stopped cooking for the critics and started cooking what I liked to eat and enjoyed doing. We began to win awards and some acclaim in the guides. In 1995 Helen and I were awarded our first Michelin star. It was an amazing feeling. Other chefs will know what I am talking about. A Michelin star is something you dream of, and it means you are on the first rung of the ladder to greater things. Then in 1996, just after my mother died, I won the National Chef of the Year competition.

This kind of recognition gave me more confidence in what I was doing, and the hunger to go further. I started experimenting with different spicing and flavour combinations, developing my palette

proverbial cat, to an extended, state-of-the-art kitchen with a Moltini stove, often described as the Rolls Royce of stoves. It has given us a brighter environment in which to work.

Inspiration comes to me in many forms: from walking with Helen, and discovering new wild foods; from my love of spices; from eating in some of the greatest restaurants in the world, including La Tante Claire, Restaurant Gordon Ramsay and Pierre Gagnaire; from reading about some of America's great chefs – Thomas Keller, David Kinch, Jean-Georges Vongerichten, Tom Colicchio, to name but a few. But my biggest influence has been the food of France, and indeed France itself.

Helen and I travel to France at least twice a year. At the moment we favour Paris and Normandy and along the way we have eaten in some lovely restaurants, some grand restaurants and some in

I started experimenting with different spicing and flavour combinations, developing my palette of ingredients and bringing it up to date. Wild food began to enter my repertoire – some old things my aunt had taught me, plus new ideas of my own.

of ingredients and bringing it up to date. Wild food began to enter my repertoire – some old things my aunt had taught me, plus new ideas of my own. My style became more solid, with a very masculine feel and unusual combinations that nevertheless made culinary sense. In 2000 we were awarded a second Michelin star. It's hard to explain how wonderful this felt. It meant we had entered an even more select elite and were being rewarded for all the hard work we had done over the years. It was also a recognition of my new style and, more importantly, of our consistency.

Over the years I have seen the team in my kitchen grow from just one second chef – first, Adrian Offley, who came down from London with me, and later Anthony Rush, who was my only help in the kitchen when we gained our second star – to a brigade of myself and three others. My kitchen has changed, too, from a small galley for the first 18 years, with a wedge of foil helping to keep one of the oven doors shut and little space to swing the

the middle of nowhere. The connection is that they all share a passion for food. In France this extends to everyone, not just restaurateurs. You can see it in the way people shop in markets, the way the stallholders, butchers and fishmongers offer advice on what to do with your purchases. I am glad to say that the same passion is starting to appear in a lot of chefs in the UK, especially the younger ones.

Would I recommend people to enter the trade? Well, if you're very motivated and don't mind hard work, the trade will reward you. After all, look at us. We still love it so much.

What's next? To carry on enjoying ourselves.

David Everitt-Matthias, Cheltenham, July 2006

The current team (from left to right): Steve Lyons, Jason Eaves, Ryan Hodson and me.

Front of house: Helen and Ivana.

how to use my book

the building blocks of creating a dish

The recipes in this book are all made up of different components, each of which has its own heading in the ingredients list and the method. That way, if you don't like something you can easily skip it, and maybe take something else from another part of the book. This will help you to create your own dishes.

There are many important stages in creating a successful dish, paramount being the raw materials. If your ingredients are inferior you will only ever be able to make a second-rate dish, so choose the best and freshest you can find, even if they are a little more expensive. Make friends with your suppliers and ask their advice on what is best at the moment. If they make good recommendations, you know you can trust them. If they don't, then simply don't use them again. I have been with my butchers, Mike and Joan Watts, and now Adrian, for 19 years. They know exactly what I require, hang my meats longer for me, and help source some of my more unusual requests. It is this trust that helps both of us, as we both teach each other new things.

When putting a dish together, try to think it through logically. Over the years I have almost learned to taste things in my head. If you use your imagination, you will find yourself doing the same. Looking through this book, you will see that I have tried to encourage the use of other ingredients as replacements. If I use a pumpkin purée in a recipe, then in all probability it will work with carrot, parsnip, beetroot, young turnips and chervil tubers, too. This is because they all have an inherent sweetness. Logically, if a dish works with sweetness, then it will also work with the other end of the spectrum, bitterness – so you could also try ingredients such as chicory, old turnips, radicchio and asparagus.

Substituting ingredients in this way allows you to create dishes that are seasonal. Seasonality plays an important part in composing dishes, for the obvious reason that the produce will be at its prime when it's in season. It will also be readily available and much better value. The seasons can create magical combinations: wild garlic and morels in the spring; rhubarb and strawberries, or gooseberries and elderflowers in the summer. So if you bear seasonality in mind as you plan your dishes, you won't go far wrong. The next thing I look at is the flavour. It is important to me that if I am creating a lemon dessert, for instance, it will taste of an entire crate of lemons – in short, the *essence* of lemon. This theme runs through all of my cooking. When making a base stock I will use as few vegetables as I can, and sometimes none at all, thus creating a very true and intense stock. This in turn will produce a true sauce. Sauces in this book sometimes contain cream, and a few years ago they would have used a lot more, but nowadays I try to incorporate more milk in them to reduce the fat content and, in turn, to make the flavours purer. Sometimes I will add a little purée to help thicken a sauce. Spices and herbs help create myriad different flavours, so I enjoy experimenting with them and trying different combinations.

Besides flavour, I also look for texture in different forms – maybe juicy vegetables like choy sum and pak choy, which give crispness to a dish and also a wonderful burst of water. Vegetables such as Jerusalem artichokes, water chestnuts and crosnes also have a delicious crisp texture. One technique I favour is to take the same vegetable and serve it raw, cooked and puréed in the same dish. This gives three different levels of texture and brings a rounded flavour to the dish. For desserts, texture can be achieved in many forms: tuiles, caramel craquant, dried fruit, or just something as simple as dusting with icing sugar and glazing with a blowtorch to give a crisp finish. Sponge crumbs, pain d'épice crumbs and crushed cooked pastry can also be used to add a texture to desserts, or simply to act as a base for a ball of ice cream or sorbet to stop it rolling off a plate.

Presentation is in many ways the easiest part of creating a dish – most people have some flair for it. When I am presenting a dish I try to visualise a dish within a dish and then keep within these boundaries. I am not one for streaks of things going up the side of the plate, as it tends to look messy. Try using a variety of shapes and moulds and cutting things at different angles. If possible, build up a collection of different plates – they can dramatically change the presentation of a dish.

Try to keep the various elements of a dish in proportion; it is important to have a good match of flavours. There is no point having two complementary flavours if one of them is served in so small an amount that it runs out before the other one has been finished.

Experiment and play, adapt the dishes to your own palate. Have fun in the kitchen and, above all, enjoy yourself.

the classics – looking to the future

To me, the complete chef has a mind that allows him or her to encompass every style of cooking – and in particular to use classic techniques rather than just dismiss them because they are no longer the latest thing. After all, in the past chefs had to know exactly what they were doing, as they couldn't rely on the machines and gadgets we have today. The complete chef should be able to bake well, to make desserts well, to prep fish well, to butcher their own meat, and to pass these skills on. It is vital that chefs share their knowledge. Gone are the days when secrets were kept. In order to progress, there must be an honest exchange of recipes and information. Restaurant kitchens have now opened their doors to stages – free work placements for a couple of days or even months – thereby allowing chefs from all over the world to enter them and gain work experience.

Today, chefs cannot afford to be complacent and rest on their laurels, or to ignore new techniques and ingredients. Everything should be embraced. People such as Ferran Adria at El Bulli in Spain and Pierre Gagnaire at his eponymous restaurant outside Paris have been a major influence over recent years, developing new techniques such as jellies, foams and froths. This has made restaurant food much lighter, and placed a greater emphasis on differing textures. At the same time, chefs such as Heston Blumenthal are pushing forward this new style of cooking and writing books on the science of food. Then there are chefs like Pierre Koffman, Gordon Ramsay and Clive Dixon – naturals with faultless technique, who have an innate ability to cook anything perfectly. There are very few of them around.

a note on ingredients

butter
I prefer to use unsalted butter, as it enables you to be more precise when it comes to seasoning. I buy my butter from a small dairy in Stow-on-the-Wold.

lecithin
Lecithin is invaluable for helping foams become more stable. I get it from my local healthfood shop in the form of soya lecithin granules, which I then grind to a powder in a spice mill. It can be stored like this and used when needed.

rapeseed oil
I use cold pressed virgin rapeseed oil from a local supplier (see page 183). Hamish's oil has a wonderful nuttiness to it and is a lovely light amber colour.

salt and pepper
Salt and pepper for general seasoning have not been included in ingredients lists in this book. I recommend using table salt and freshly ground black pepper unless otherwise stated.

To add texture to a dish I use Maldon salt, which I consider to be the best in the world. It comes from the east coast of England and its fine, delicate crystals give a wonderful finish to terrines and fish dishes.

measurements
Finally, I have given liquid measures in millilitres throughout this book, as most domestic cooks are more accustomed to working in this way. However, I prefer to measure liquids in grams, which is easily done with a set of digital scales. Millilitres and grams are interchangeable when it comes to liquids.

storecupboard

Below are some of the standbys we use in the restaurant kitchen. It certainly makes life easier to have them on hand and you'll find they appear in a lot of the recipes in this book. They can also be used for many other things – the salted lemons, for example, are a must with Moroccan dishes, give a fresh, clean flavour to a couscous salad and make a perfect foil for fatty fish such as mackerel.

If you build up a storecupboard according to your own preferences, it makes cooking for friends who just drop round much less of a hassle. Choose dishes that have a good shelf life or that you know you will use quickly because they are your favourites.

duck confit

I always have some kind of confit in the kitchen; it is one of the most useful tools in my storecupboard. Rabbit confit, duck leg confit, lamb shank confit, pork hand confit – brilliant in their own right, they are also useful in so many dishes. Try them in a pumpkin risotto, perhaps, or as a ravioli filling, or flaked into a long braise.

The word 'confit' comes from the French confire, meaning 'to preserve', and confit used to be kept in the larder for months. We don't tend to store them that long nowadays, but if you make sure the meat is well covered in fat and stored in a sealed container in the fridge, it should easily keep for a month.

This recipe is not set in stone. The salting time will vary depending on the size of the meat being salted – the bigger the piece, the longer the salting time. You could try using different spices. Chinese spices work well, as do Moroccan ones, or why not give it a Thai flavour with chopped lemongrass and lime leaves?

Serves 6

6 plump duck legs
50g sel gris (grey sea salt)
2 sprigs of thyme, chopped
2 bay leaves, chopped
2 teaspoons juniper berries, crushed
1 teaspoon coriander seeds, crushed
1 teaspoon white peppercorns, crushed
2 strips of orange zest
3 garlic cloves, roughly chopped
750g duck fat

Make sure the duck legs are thoroughly trimmed, removing any feather stubble if necessary. Put them in a dish. Combine the salt with all the herbs and aromatics and rub this mixture into the duck legs. Cover and refrigerate for 24 hours.

Remove the salt and herbs from the duck legs by rubbing them with a paper towel or quickly rinsing under cold water, then dry them. In a thick-bottomed pot, large enough to hold the legs snugly in a single layer, melt the duck fat over a low heat. Add the duck legs; they should be completely covered by the fat. Cover the pan and place in an oven preheated to 150°C/Gas Mark 2. Cook for about 3 hours, until the legs are very tender; the meat should come away from the bone easily and the juices should run clear if you prick the meat with a fork.

Place the confit in a container. Strain the duck fat through a fine sieve into a tallish jug to allow the juices to separate from the fat, then carefully ladle the fat over the confit until it is completely covered. Cover with a lid and store in the fridge until needed.

When you want to use the confit, preheat the oven to 220°C/Gas Mark 7. Heat an ovenproof frying pan large enough to hold the duck legs in a single layer. Remove the duck from the fat, place skin-side down in the pan and cook for 2–3 minutes. Transfer the pan to the oven and cook for a further 20–25 minutes, until the skin is thoroughly crisp and golden and the meat is heated all the way through.

duck gizzard confit

Ducks swallow their food whole, so they need something to help break it down internally. This is where the gizzard comes in. Located between the intestines and the stomach, it more or less grinds the food with its strong muscles, before it passes through to the intestine. As the gizzard is pure muscle, once it is cleaned it makes very lean meat. The taste is slightly livery but very ducky.

This confit is great with salads, added to a fish stew, or anything that requires a little texture. We also mince the confit gizzards and put them in stuffed cabbage or stuffed duck neck. A good butcher should be able to get you some gizzards.

Serves 6–8

450g duck gizzards
30g sel gris (grey sea salt)
2 garlic cloves, chopped
1 bay leaf
a sprig of thyme
1 teaspoon white peppercorns, crushed
500g duck fat

First clean the gizzards by splitting them lengthways in half, removing the gritty, greenish-yellow interior, then removing all the hard skin. Prepare the confit in exactly the same way as for the duck leg version above but salt the meat for just 8–10 hours – any longer and the gizzards will be too salty, as they are much smaller than duck legs. Reduce the cooking time to 2 hours, or $2^1/_2$ if they are large gizzards.

Store in the same way. To use, heat a little of the duck fat in a frying pan, then cut each gizzard into 4–5 slices and fry until golden. Season lightly and serve as required.

tomato confit with lemon

This is very easy to make and useful in so many ways. Try it with pasta, salads, oily fish – we even use it with pig's head or trotters to help balance their fattiness and richness. You could replace the basil with rosemary, thyme, lavender or lovage. We add some grated lemon or orange zest for a fresher taste.

1kg ripe plum tomatoes, skinned, halved
   and deseeded
50ml olive oil
50ml grapeseed oil
1 tablespoon sea salt
grated zest of $1/_2$ lemon
3 garlic cloves, finely sliced
15 basil leaves, torn
1 teaspoon caster sugar

Put the tomatoes in a bowl, drizzle a little of the olive oil and grapeseed oil over them and toss to coat thoroughly. Pour the remaining oil on to a shallow baking tray and spread it around evenly. Sprinkle half the salt over it, then the grated lemon zest.

Place the tomato halves on top, cut-side up, and place a slice of garlic and a little basil in each one. Sprinkle with the remaining salt and the sugar. Place in an oven preheated to 120°C/Gas Mark $1/_2$ and cook for approximately 1 hour. Turn the tomatoes over and cook for another hour. They should look wrinkled and be half their original size. Remove from the oven and cool thoroughly.

Transfer to a jar just big enough to hold the tomatoes and their juices, topping up with more olive oil if needed. They should be completely covered. They will keep in the fridge for a good month or so.

salted grapes

This recipe idea came to me one day when we were making tomato confit. I thought the salting and subsequent drying in the oven would heighten the sweet/sour flavour of the grapes. With a reduced verjus sauce thickened with a little butter, or some White Port and Verjus Syrup (see page 21), they make a perfect accompaniment to fish. The secret is to buy the juiciest grapes, with a good acid-to-sugar balance, so get tasting when you go shopping! Another thought – why don't you try this with gooseberries, but increase the sugar a little?

500g seedless grapes, either red or green
20g salt
2 teaspoons caster sugar
30ml grapeseed oil

to store the grapes
50ml grapeseed oil
50ml olive oil

Blanch the grapes in a large pan of boiling water for 10 seconds, then drain, refresh in cold water and peel off the skins. Leave to dry a little, then place on an oiled baking tray and sprinkle with the salt and caster sugar. Place in an oven preheated to 85–110°C/Gas Mark $1/4$ and cook for $2^1/_2$–3 hours, until they have shrunk a little and have become slightly wrinkled.

Leave to cool, then place in a jar just large enough to hold them and cover with the extra oil. Seal the jar and store in the fridge until ready to use. The grapes will keep for several months.

salted lemons

Salted lemons are used a lot in North African dishes. They are quick and easy to prepare, although they do have to be kept for a while to soften before use. They have a good shelf life and can add so much flavour to a dish, making them well worth the effort. You could include a few stalks of lemongrass in the mix, or a few lime leaves. Why not replace the lemons with oranges or limes and add some crushed coriander seeds and cardamom pods? Whatever you choose to do, they bring a freshness to many fish dishes as well as some meats, and are absolutely perfect with chicken.

12 lemons, cut lengthways into quarters,
*   but not quite all the way through*
250g coarse sea salt
2 bay leaves
200ml lemon juice
about 200ml olive oil

Sprinkle the inside of the lemons with the salt and pack a third of them into a large, wide-necked jar. Add the bay leaves and sprinkle with a little more salt. Push down well to release the juices. Repeat with another third of the lemons, pushing down well. Add the final third and pour in the lemon juice. The lemons should be well covered with juice. If necessary, add enough olive oil to cover; this will form a seal that the air cannot penetrate. Wipe the neck of the jar clean and seal. Leave for at least 1 month before use, so the peel will soften. The juice can be used, as can the pulp. To use the peel, just quickly rinse under cold running water first.

salted sardines

I just love salted sardines and anchovies. They make a great storecupboard ingredient because they can be used to brighten up all sorts of fish dishes. They can also be added to daube of beef in the traditional Provençal way, and they are good with game.

You could add different aromatics and herbs from the ones listed below – just try to think of the dishes that you will be using them for. Besides sardines, you could also salt other oily fish, such as red mullet or mackerel.

200g coarse sea salt
2 garlic cloves, finely sliced
8 juniper berries, crushed
1kg sardines, cleaned, scaled and filleted

Sprinkle a fine layer of salt, a little garlic and a little crushed juniper over the bottom of a large, sealable container, such as a Tupperware box. Arrange a layer of sardine fillets skin-side down on top, sprinkle with more salt, juniper and garlic, then add another layer of fillets, this time skin-side up. Carry on like this until all the fillets have been used. Cover with clingfilm, cover with a lid slightly smaller than the container, then add a weight to press it down lightly. Seal the container and store in the fridge for 4 weeks before use. The sardines will keep very well in the fridge; once you start using them, remove the weight and cover the sardines with some olive oil to keep the air out.

salted sardine tapenade

Here I have used my salted sardines to replace the anchovies in the traditional tapenade. Rather than being fishy, it has a surprisingly meaty taste. Tapenade, as you probably know, comes from Provence, but what you may not know is that to be a true tapenade it must contain capers. The Provençal word for capers is tapeno, hence tapenade.

This is good on toasted baguette on its own as a snack but we have also used it in a beef daube, and a little in a sauce with pigeon or venison is outstanding.

250g pitted Nyons black olives, or other
  good, deeply coloured black olives
50g Salted Sardines (see above)
75g baby capers
1 garlic clove, peeled
leaves from a sprig of savory or thyme
2 tablespoons good olive oil, plus extra
  for drizzling
a few drops of lemon juice

Place all the ingredients except the olive oil and lemon juice in a food processor and pulse to obtain a coarse purée. Add the olive oil in a steady drizzle, with the motor still running. Season with lemon juice and black pepper to taste.

Place the mixture in a jar and smooth the top level. Drizzle over a little more olive oil to cover the surface completely, then seal the jar. It will keep in the fridge for a good few months.

soured cabbage

This is one of our most useful standbys in the kitchen. We also make our own sauerkraut, which is fermented cabbage, and while this is not the same it is a much quicker alternative. It can be used in exactly the same way as sauerkraut. It keeps for 2–3 weeks in the fridge and makes a perfect accompaniment to game and some of the meatier fish, for a sort of fish choucroute.

Serves 10

100g duck fat
2 onions, finely sliced
3 rashers of smoked bacon
4 garlic cloves, finely chopped
1 large white cabbage, quartered, cored and sliced as finely as possible
12 juniper berries, crushed
a sprig of thyme
2 bay leaves
150ml white wine vinegar
50g granulated sugar
1 bottle of Gewürztraminer white wine

Melt the duck fat in a large, thick-bottomed pan, add the sliced onions and cook gently until translucent. Add the smoked bacon, garlic and cabbage, then cover and sweat for 5 minutes. Stir in the juniper, thyme and bay leaves, followed by the vinegar and sugar, and cook until the vinegar has reduced to a syrup at the bottom of the pan. Pour in the white wine, bring to the boil and cook until the wine has completely evaporated. Season with salt and pepper, remove the bacon rashers and leave to cool. Store in a sealed container in the refrigerator. When it's needed, just heat up the required amount in a pan.

maury syrup

This is a very simple recipe that may seem expensive but the resulting syrup will last quite a while. Maury comes from the Roussillon area of France and is a strong, sweet red wine (although you can also get a white) that makes a good accompaniment to chocolate and foie gras. It performs just as well in its reduced form. The syrup is good with pears, apples and most citrus fruit, and can also be added to a dressing for fish. Other wines can be substituted, such as Banyuls and fortified wines including port, Madeira and mead. One of our latest is pommeau, an apple aperitif from Normandy.

2 bottles of Maury wine
1 bottle of red wine, such as a Rhône
a small handful of golden raisins
25g demerara sugar

Place all the ingredients in a thick-bottomed pan and bring to the boil. Simmer slowly until reduced to 275ml, then strain through a fine sieve and leave to cool. Keep in a small squeezy bottle, ready for use.

white port and verjus syrup

This is just as simple as the Maury Syrup opposite. Verjus is sour grape juice, although it was once made with crab apples. In its bottled state you can use it as a seasoning or in dressings, or add sugar to it to make a glaze for finishing off roast quail.

We use this syrup for many things in the kitchen, from a seasoning on top of a piece of roasted wild bass or line-caught cod to the base of a sauce with some baby carrots and golden raisins to serve with John Dory.

2 bottles of white port
1 litre verjus
25g demerara sugar

Place all the ingredients in a thick-bottomed pan and bring to the boil. Simmer slowly until reduced to 300ml, then strain through a fine sieve and leave to cool. Keep in a small squeezy bottle, ready for use.

pickled apples

We have served these pickled apples with langoustines and several other fish dishes at the restaurant. They provide a freshness, especially with fatty fish such as mackerel. They go well with game, too. A good thing about this recipe is that you can save the pickling juices to use again next time. Besides apples, it also works well with pears, peaches, cherries and damsons.

800g demerara sugar
800ml red wine vinegar
800ml red wine
2 teaspoons mustard seeds
zest of 1 lemon
5 allspice berries
5 cloves
6cm piece of cinnamon stick
30g fresh ginger root
10 coriander seeds
10 Granny Smith apples

Put all the ingredients except the apples in a large pan and bring to the boil, stirring to dissolve the sugar. Reduce the heat and simmer for 20 minutes.

Peel and core the apples and cut them in half. Add them to the pickling juices and poach gently for 5–10 minutes, until they are tender but still holding their shape. Remove from the pan with a slotted spoon and leave to cool. Simmer the pickling juices until reduced by half, then leave to cool.

Pack the apples into a Kilner jar and pour the pickling juices over. Seal and store in the fridge. They can be used straight away but will take on a deeper, richer flavour if kept for at least a month.

spiced bread

A very useful addition to the storecupboard, this bread is suitable for savoury and sweet dishes alike: made into breadcrumbs and fried to add a crunchy finish to soups or cooked asparagus; toasted and served with a terrine, or as croûtons in a liver or sweetbread salad; or dissolved in a custard for a brûlée, ice cream or parfait. The spicing means it will go equally well with citrus fruit as with more substantial fruits such as figs, pears and apples. The bread is better after it has matured for at least a couple of days, the flavours developing into a deep, haunting mixture of honey and spices.

100ml milk
200g chestnut honey
150g rye flour
150g plain white flour
75g demerara sugar
25g baking powder
75g unsalted butter, diced
2 eggs
grated zest of 1 orange
grated zest of 1/2 lemon
50g candied orange peel, finely diced
  (optional)
50g candied angelica, finely diced
  (optional)
5g ground ginger
5g ground green aniseed
3g ground cinnamon
2g ground nutmeg
1g ground cloves

Warm the milk and dissolve the honey in it, then leave to cool.

Place both the flours, the demerara sugar, baking powder and diced butter in the bowl of an electric mixer. Mix on a low speed until the texture resembles breadcrumbs, then add the eggs and the honey mixture and beat until smooth. Add all the remaining ingredients and mix well. Pour into a greased lined loaf tin, about 20 x 7.5 x 7.5cm. Bake in an oven preheated to 160°C/Gas Mark 3 for 45–50 minutes, until deep golden and firm to the touch. Leave to cool in the tin for 20 minutes, then turn out on to a wire rack to cool completely.

marinated prunes in armagnac

Once these have been left to macerate for a month or two, they are ideal as a topping for vanilla ice cream, an accompaniment to rice pudding, or in a simple prune and frangipane tart or a toasted almond panna cotta (simply substitute toasted almonds for acorns in the Acorn Panna Cotta on page 166). Don't feel that you have to stick to the flavourings below: bergamot can be substituted, as can liquorice root, burdock root and warm spices such as star anise or green aniseed. Even a change of tea can bring a totally different and surprising taste – try Lapsang Souchong for a slightly smoky flavour, great with bitter chocolate or foie gras.

1 orange
1 lemon
750ml water
200g caster sugar
1 vanilla pod
1 cinnamon stick
1kg Agen prunes
3 English Breakfast tea bags
250ml Armagnac

Peel the zest off the orange and lemon in long strips, then squeeze out the juice. Place the zest and juice, water, sugar, vanilla and cinnamon in a pan large enough to hold the prunes and bring to the boil, stirring to dissolve the sugar.

Simmer for 5 minutes, then add the prunes and place the tea bags on top. Remove from the heat and leave to macerate overnight.

The next day, remove the tea bags from the mixture and pour in the Armagnac. Mix carefully to distribute the Armagnac evenly. Store in a Kilner jar for 1 month before use – if you can wait!

foundations

Good cooking depends on good foundation recipes – for stocks, pasta dough, pastry and so on. Master these and you have a sound basis for a whole repertoire of different dishes.

Making stock is quite a personal thing, with as many different recipes as there are chefs. Chefs with a subtle touch go for a lighter stock, often preferring to use chicken stock rather than veal or beef, while chefs such as myself prefer a purer, more meaty flavour, with few vegetables, if any, added. It's always worth taking care when making stock. If you have a weak stock, lacking in flavour, how will you ever achieve a great sauce?

Although I encourage you throughout this book to use my recipes as a guideline, pastry recipes are the one exception to the rule. Quantities matter, so do follow them to the letter. Having said that, it's perfectly okay to vary the flavourings, as long as the proportions stay the same.

white chicken stock

This is a good, light stock that can be made stronger by either halving the amount of water or substituting chicken stock for the water, thus giving a double-concentrated stock.

Makes 2 litres

30ml olive oil
1 large onion, finely sliced
1 large celery stick, sliced
2kg chicken bones (a mixture of wings and carcasses)
100ml white wine
10 black peppercorns, crushed
1 bay leaf
$^1/_2$ sprig of thyme
3 litres water

Heat the oil in a large saucepan, add the onion and celery and cook without colouring for 2–3 minutes. Add the chicken bones and cook for 5 minutes without letting them colour. Pour in the white wine and simmer until reduced by half. Add the peppercorns, herbs and water and bring to the boil. Reduce the heat and simmer for 2–2$^1/_2$ hours, regularly skimming the froth from the top.

Remove from the heat and leave to stand for 15–20 minutes; this allows the particles to settle. Strain through a fine sieve and leave to cool.

brown chicken stock

Use the same ingredients as for White Chicken Stock (page 23), but replace the white wine with red. Put the bones in a large roasting tin and roast in an oven preheated to 200°C/Gas Mark 6 until golden brown. Heat the olive oil in a large pan and add the vegetables. Cook until the vegetables are lightly coloured, then add 3 tablespoons of fresh tomato pulp, followed by the bones. Add the wine and continue as above.

lamb stock

You could make a stronger stock by substituting chicken or even veal stock for the water. You could also add 3–4 tablespoons of fresh tomato pulp, as long as the tomatoes are ripe.

Makes 2 litres

75ml olive oil
2kg lamb bones, chopped up into small pieces
1 large onion, finely sliced
3 garlic cloves, crushed
100ml Madeira
200ml red wine
10 black peppercorns, crushed
1 bay leaf
$^1/_2$ sprig of rosemary
3 litres water

Heat the oil in a large saucepan, add the lamb bones and cook for about 10 minutes, until they are a deep golden colour. Add the onion and garlic and cook for 2–3 minutes longer. Pour in the Madeira and simmer until evaporated. Pour in the red wine and simmer until reduced by half. Add the peppercorns, herbs and water and bring to the boil. Reduce the heat and simmer for 2–2$^1/_2$ hours, skimming regularly to remove excess fat from the surface.

Remove from the heat and leave to stand for 15–20 minutes; this allows the particles to settle. Strain through a fine sieve and leave to cool.

brown veal stock

Makes 2 litres

100ml olive oil
2kg veal knucklebones, chopped
1kg beef bones, chopped
1 veal trotter or 2 pig's trotters, chopped
200ml Madeira
200ml red wine
1 large onion, finely sliced
3 garlic cloves, crushed
1 bay leaf
a sprig of thyme
300g tomato pulp (optional)
4 litres water

Heat half the olive oil in a roasting tin, add all the bones and the trotter, then place in an oven preheated to 250°C/Gas Mark 9. Cook for about 30 minutes, until golden brown. Remove the bones from the tin and pour off the fat. Put the tin on the hob, add the Madeira and bring to the boil, stirring to scrape up all the sediment from the base of the tin. Repeat with the red wine.

Heat the remaining oil in a large, heavy-based saucepan, add the onion and cook until golden. Add the garlic, herbs and tomato pulp, if using, then add the bones, the juices from the roasting tin and the water. Bring to the boil and skim off any froth from the surface. Reduce the heat and simmer for 3–3$\frac{1}{2}$ hours.

Remove the bones and strain the stock through a fine sieve into another saucepan. Boil until reduced to 2 litres, skimming occasionally. Strain through a fine sieve again and leave to cool. If you chill it, any fat that sets on top can easily be removed.

brown beef stock

Follow the recipe for Brown Veal Stock, above, but replace the veal knucklebones with 2kg beef shinbones.

fish stock

Sometimes if I am making a meaty fish dish – with monkfish, bass or skate, for example – I use chicken stock (pages 23–24) as a base for the fish stock instead of water.

Makes 2 litres

1.5kg fish bones (from white fish such as
*   turbot, brill, sole and skate)*
50ml olive oil
1 onion, finely sliced
white of 1 leek, finely sliced
250ml white wine
10 black peppercorns
2.5 litres water

If you have any fish heads, remove the gills and eyes. Chop the bones roughly and rinse under cold running water for 2–3 minutes.

Heat the oil in a large saucepan, add the onion and leek and cook without colouring for 2–3 minutes. Add the fish bones and cook for 5 minutes, without letting them colour. Pour in the white wine and simmer until reduced by half. Add the peppercorns and water, bring to the boil, then reduce the heat and simmer for 20–30 minutes, skimming regularly.

Remove from the heat and leave to stand for 15–20 minutes; this allows the particles to settle. Strain the stock through a fine sieve and leave to cool.

pasta dough

This dough can be frozen. Simply wrap tightly in clingfilm and store in a polythene bag in the freezer for 1–2 weeks.

500g '00' pasta flour
3 eggs
2 egg yolks

Place the flour in a food processor, gradually add the eggs and yolks and pulse, stopping as soon as the mixture forms a loose ball; you may not need all the egg. Don't worry if you accidentally add too much egg; you can always add a little more flour to dry it out. Tip out on to a lightly floured work surface and knead for 3–5 minutes, until smooth. Divide in half, wrap in clingfilm and chill.

sweet pastry

This pastry is very quick and easy to make. Try changing the flavourings: you could substitute walnuts or pistachios for the almonds, or add some spices instead of the vanilla.

270g plain flour
150g cold unsalted butter
50g ground almonds
grated zest of 1 lemon or 1 orange
seeds from 1 vanilla pod
100g icing sugar
1 egg
1 egg yolk

Place all the ingredients except the egg and egg yolk in a food processor and pulse until the mixture resembles breadcrumbs. Add the egg and yolk and pulse until the mixture starts to form a ball. Turn out on to a floured surface and knead as lightly as possible, just until smooth. Form into a ball, flatten, then wrap in clingfilm and chill for at least 3 hours before use. This pastry is suitable for freezing; thaw for 24 hours in the fridge.

puff pastry

Making puff pastry is quite a long job but well worth it. Good puff pastry is a must in a classic mille feuille when the first British raspberries of the season appear. We put one on our menu as a special and that is all there is to it: a little pastry cream, lovely ripe raspberries and layers of feather-light puff pastry.

This recipe makes over 1kg of pastry so you could split it, wrap it in clingfilm and store in the freezer.

500g strong white flour
1/2 teaspoons salt
550g unsalted butter
1 teaspoon lemon juice or white wine vinegar
320ml ice-cold water

Sift the flour and salt into a bowl. Dice 100g of the butter, add to the flour and rub it in until the mixture resembles breadcrumbs. Add the lemon juice or vinegar to the water and gradually stir into the flour and butter until the mixture forms a smooth ball. Wrap in clingfilm and place in the fridge to relax for 30 minutes.

Soften the remaining butter by putting it between 2 sheets of clingfilm and hitting it with a rolling pin, being careful not to tear the clingfilm. Turn it over and repeat. Push the butter back into the centre of the clingfilm and repeat once more. Take the pastry out of the fridge and unwrap it. The pastry and butter should be the same temperature.

Roll the dough out to a 20 x 30cm rectangle. Roll out the butter, still wrapped in clingfilm, to 15 x 25cm. Unwrap the butter, place it on one half of the pastry and fold the other half over, pressing the edges together well to seal in the butter. Now think of your pastry as a book and turn the dough so you have the spine to the left and the pages to the right. Roll out to 3 times its original size. One of the keys to the success of a good puff pastry is that the corners and edges must be level and neat at all times, so if they are not, lightly stretch the pastry to shape and try to keep this perfect rectangle.

Fold the dough into 3, keeping the edges neat. Place in the fridge for 30 minutes to relax. Then roll out a second time, keeping the spine to the left and pages to the right. Fold into 3 again, making sure that the edges are in line and neat. Return to the fridge for 30 minutes. Remove from the fridge and repeat the rolling process for a third time. Wrap and place back in the fridge until needed.

white bread rolls

Bread is one of the most satisfying and also one of the most infuriating items in the kitchen. It's a living thing, and can therefore be a little unpredictable. But because of this unpredictability, when you get it right (and you will the more you practice) you will be well rewarded. The kneading, the cutting, the stretching and the rolling – you will learn to feel the right consistency of the dough at each stage. Of course, the rewards for baking your own bread are sublime – the most amazing smell throughout the house, the crisp crust cracking under the weight of your knife, and a great deal of satisfaction that you have conquered the technique.

Here is a simple recipe for plain white bread rolls. You can adapt it by replacing the butter with a stiff purée of tomato and cumin, or pumpkin or sweet potato. Flavoured breads like these have their place, although I prefer to keep to the plain varieties so the bread doesn't interfere with the flavours of a dish.

Makes 24

25g fresh yeast
25g caster sugar
450ml warm water
800g strong white flour
125g unsalted butter, at room temperature
25g salt
1 egg, beaten, to glaze
poppy seeds, for sprinkling

the starter
Crumble the yeast into a bowl, add the sugar and 100ml of the warm water and mix well. Whisk in 150g of the flour and mix until it forms a loose paste. Pour in the remaining water and lift the paste up so it is suspended in the water. Keep in a warm place for 10 minutes, until frothy.

the dough
Place the remaining flour in an electric mixer, add the butter and mix for 2–3 minutes to break the butter down. Add all the contents of the starter bowl and mix on a medium speed for 5–8 minutes, adding the salt half way through.

Turn out on to a floured surface. Pull, stretch and hit the dough on the table for about 5 minutes, until perfectly smooth, adding more flour if it's very sticky. Place the dough in a large bowl, cover with clingfilm and leave at fairly warm room temperature (about 26°C) for 50 minutes–1 hour, until it has doubled in size.

the rolls
Turn the dough out and knead just for a minute or so (called 'knocking back'). Divide it into 24 pieces and roll them into smooth balls on the work surface. Place on baking sheets lined with baking parchment, brush with the beaten egg and sprinkle with poppy seeds. Cover loosely with clingfilm and leave to prove at warm room temperature (26°C) for 20 minutes, until they have swollen slightly. Slash across the top to the desired shape; I nip each one 3 times with scissors.

Place a tray of hot water in an oven preheated to 220°C/Gas Mark 7, then place the rolls in the oven. Cook for 10–14 minutes, until golden brown and very crisp. Remove from the oven and tap the bottom of the rolls; they should give a deep thud sound. If they don't, return them to the oven for a few minutes.

brioche

This quick and easy recipe is the one we use at the restaurant. Instead of making 2 loaves, you could divide all or half the dough into small balls and cook them in lined rings.

Sometimes we add cooked diced bacon and shallots to the dough to make a savoury brioche. We also use it in pain perdu or serve it as an accompaniment to a terrine.

Makes 2 loaves

50ml warm water
20g fresh yeast
40g caster sugar
500g strong white flour
5 eggs, whisked and strained through a sieve
10g salt
300g unsalted butter, softened and diced
a little milk for brushing

Put the warm water in a small bowl and mix in the yeast and sugar until dissolved. Leave for 2–3 minutes, until frothy. Place the flour in an electric mixer and add the yeast mix. Slowly pour in the eggs and beat for 2 minutes on a low speed, adding the salt with the eggs. Add the butter bit by bit, waiting until each piece has been incorporated before adding the next.

Divide the mixture in half. Butter 2 loaf tins and line the bases with baking parchment. Put the dough in the tins, cover with a damp cloth and leave to prove at fairly warm room temperature (26°C) for 45–60 minutes, until doubled in size.

Lightly brush the top of the loaves with a little milk and place in an oven preheated to 180°C/Gas Mark 4. Bake for 45 minutes, until the brioche is golden and sounds hollow when tapped underneath. Leave to cool in the tins for 5 minutes, then turn out on to a wire rack and leave to cool completely. You could keep one loaf in the freezer if it is to be used for toast, as long as it is well wrapped.

starters

wood sorrel (oxalis acetosella)
used in
cannelloni of veal breast and burdock with celeriac cream,
horseradish froth and wood sorrel

gougères

We serve these tiny puffs of air as a nibble at the bar. They're intensely cheesy, and once you have had one you will want more. They are very convenient for dinner parties, as they can be piped earlier in the evening and stored in the fridge, then put in the oven just before your guests arrive. You can even keep them in the freezer and cook them from frozen. We use a mixture of Gruyère and aged Parmesan, but you could substitute a blue cheese or any favourite cheese. Feel free to add herbs such as thyme and rosemary, or even spices and chillies. A little extra finely grated cheese could be sprinkled over the gougères half way through baking.

Makes 36–40

100ml milk
50g unsalted butter, diced
100ml water
125g plain flour
3 eggs
85g Gruyère cheese, finely grated
85g aged Parmesan cheese, finely grated

Put the milk, butter and water in a heavy-based saucepan and bring to a rolling boil. Pull the pan to the side of the stove and tip in the flour, beating all the time with a wooden spoon. Place back on the stove over a medium heat and beat vigorously until the mixture is shiny and leaves the side of the pan. Continue to beat over a low heat for 1–2 minutes to dry out the mixture a little.

Transfer the mixture to a freestanding mixer and, using the K paddle, beat for 2 minutes to cool it down slightly.

Meanwhile, crack the eggs and whisk lightly to break them up. Add them to the dough a little at a time, fully incorporating them before the next lot is added. The mixture should be smooth, shiny and fairly firm; you might not need quite all the egg. Stir in the cheese and add some salt and pepper.

Transfer the mixture to a piping bag with a 1.5cm nozzle and pipe it in mounds of 3x3cm on a baking tray lined with baking parchment, allowing a 4cm gap between each one. Place in an oven preheated to 180°C/Gas Mark 4 and bake for 15–20 minutes, until well risen and a rich golden brown. Allow to cool slightly, then serve.

cheese sablés

This is another one of the appetisers we serve with our guests' aperitifs. Golden, incredibly short and wonderfully cheesy, they are a real winner. This recipe calls for a good goats' cheese, such as a Crottin de Chavignol, but you could use aged Parmesan, mature Cheddar, a mixture of both, or Mimolette.

Makes about 40

100g chalky goats' cheese, finely diced
75g aged Parmesan cheese, grated
100g unsalted butter
120g plain flour
1 teaspoon salt
1 teaspoon caster sugar
a pinch of cayenne pepper
a pinch of baking powder
3 egg yolks

Place all the ingredients except the egg yolks in a food processor and pulse until the mixture resembles fine breadcrumbs. Add the egg yolks and pulse again quickly until the mixture comes together into a ball. Shape into a long roll and wrap in clingfilm. Chill for at least 4 hours; overnight would be better.

On a lightly floured work surface, roll out the dough as thinly as you can – about 2mm. Cut with a 6cm round pastry cutter and place on a baking sheet lined with baking parchment. Bake in an oven preheated to 180°C/Gas Mark 4 for about 7 minutes, until golden brown. Cool a little before serving.

An alternative way of making the biscuits is to form the dough into a long roll about 3.5cm in diameter, wrap it in clingfilm and chill overnight, as before. Then remove the clingfilm and cut the dough into slices about 7mm thick. Place on a lined baking sheet, with a gap between each biscuit to allow for spreading, and bake for about 10 minutes, until golden and crisp.

crispy pig's ears

We use a lot of pork at the restaurant and truly live up to the French saying about using all of the pig except the oink. Blood for black pudding, trotters for stuffing with snails and bolete mushrooms, tails for a play on the French fromage de tête, etc. The ears make a very good nibble, but could also be served as an accompaniment to a split pea soup or added to a salad for texture.

We serve these with our version of tartare sauce, which has a good acid content to help with the richness and slight fattiness of the ears. There are many other options you could try, including aioli and Béarnaise sauce.

Serves 4

2 pig's ears
2 litres White Chicken Stock (page 23)
2 litres water
1/2 medium carrot, cut into 5
1 small onion, cut into quarters
4 garlic cloves, lightly crushed
1 celery stick, cut into 5
a sprig of thyme
2 bay leaves
vegetable or rapeseed oil for deep-frying

for coating
125g plain flour, seasoned with salt and pepper
2 eggs, beaten
150g fine dry breadcrumbs or coarse polenta, mixed with 1 teaspoon smoked paprika

for the tartare sauce
2 egg yolks
1 1/2 teaspoons white wine vinegar
2 teaspoons wholegrain mustard
200ml olive oil
30g gherkins, finely chopped
30g capers, finely chopped
30g shallots, finely chopped
1 teaspoon finely chopped parsley
1 teaspoon finely chopped tarragon
2 anchovy fillets, crushed to a paste with the flat of a knife

First clean the pig's ears: scrape them clean with the back of a knife and rinse in cold water. Singe off any hairs with a blowtorch. Put the ears, stock, water and aromatics into a large pan and bring to the boil. Reduce the heat and simmer for about 3 1/2 hours. The flesh of the ears should be very tender, but more importantly the cartilage should also be tender when pierced with the point of a knife. Remove the ears from the stock and place on a baking tray lined with clingfilm. Cover with another sheet of clingfilm, then another tray, and place a weight on top to press the ears flat. Keep in the refrigerator overnight.

The next day, trim the ears to a loose square and then cut into 8cm x 7mm strips. Coat the strips first in the seasoned flour, shaking off the excess, then in the beaten egg, again removing the excess, and finally in the breadcrumbs or polenta and smoked paprika.

Now the ears are ready to be used whenever you want. If you don't need them immediately, freeze them in a suitable container. You can fry them from frozen at a later date.

To make the sauce, whisk the egg yolks, vinegar and mustard together, then slowly add the oil in a steady drizzle, whisking continuously as if making mayonnaise. When all the oil has been added, season with salt and pepper and carefully mix in all the remaining ingredients.

To cook the ears, heat the oil to 180°C in a deep-fat fryer or a large, deep saucepan and fry in smallish batches until golden brown. Remove from the oil, drain on kitchen paper and season with a little salt and pepper. Serve with the sauce for dipping.

crispy pig's ears (top)
cheese sablés (middle)
gougères (bottom)

blanquette of coco beans

This is a little appetiser that we serve in autumn and winter. It's very warming and ideal for taking the chill out of your bones. Many things may be added; it really depends on your preferences. We drizzle the blanquette with truffle oil just before serving. Instead of the bacon you could use ham hock. The blanquette could be served as the main part of a fish dish, with a piece of roasted hake or monkfish.

If you can't get coco beans, substitute cannellini beans.

Serve 8 as a starter, 14–16 as an amuse-bouche

125g coco beans, soaked in cold water
  overnight
100g duck fat (or olive oil)
150g smoked bacon, diced
1 shallot, chopped
2 garlic cloves, chopped
a sprig of thyme
200g white cabbage, cut into 5mm dice
200ml good white wine
500ml chicken stock (pages 23–24)
500ml milk
100g cooked chestnuts, chopped
150ml double cream
100g Savoy cabbage (the greener the
  better), cut into 5mm dice
300g foie gras, cut into 1cm dice (optional)

Drain the beans, cover them with fresh water and bring to the boil. Drain, cover with fresh water again and bring to the boil. Simmer until tender, then remove from the heat and set aside.

Melt the duck fat in a thick-bottomed pan, add the smoked bacon and cook for 2 minutes, without letting it colour. Add the shallot, garlic, thyme and white cabbage and cook for 4 minutes, without colouring.

Add the white wine and simmer until reduced by half, then add the chicken stock and simmer until reduced by a third.

Add the milk, chestnuts and coco beans and bring to the boil. Pour in the double cream and return to the boil. Stir in the Savoy cabbage 3 minutes before serving, to keep the colour; it should be just cooked. Check the seasoning.

If you are using foie gras, heat a heavy-based frying pan until almost smoking, add the foie gras and cook very quickly, until just golden – a matter of seconds. Tip the contents of the pan into the bean pan. To serve, place the beans and cabbage in individual bowls and froth the liquor with a stick blender until light and airy. Pour the liquor over the beans.

velouté of pea and coconut with coconut froth

I just love this soup. We serve it in shot glasses at the restaurant, so you have to sip the velouté through the coconut froth. I first started to use coconut milk after a meal in Paris at a restaurant called L'Astrance, where I had a lettuce and coconut milk sauce. The bitterness of the lettuce was perfectly complemented by the coconut. This started me thinking about serving something a little more bitter with coconut, so I opted for asparagus – thus our asparagus velouté with coconut froth was born. This in turn has led us to use something just as fresh but with a sweet note – peas.

Serves 6 as a starter, 12–16 in shot glasses

100g unsalted butter
200g onions, chopped
75g celery, chopped
750ml chicken stock (pages 23–24)
200ml coconut milk
500g shelled fresh peas
150g green of leek, chopped

for the coconut froth
250ml coconut milk
150ml chicken stock (pages 23–24)
1g powdered lecithin

for the coconut froth
Bring the coconut milk and stock to the boil in a small saucepan, whisk in the lecithin and season with salt and pepper. Keep warm until needed.

for the soup
Melt the butter in a pan, add the onions and celery and cook for 5 minutes without letting them colour. Add the stock and coconut milk, bring to the boil and simmer for 15 minutes. Add the peas and green of leek and cook on a rolling boil for 5 minutes. Liquidise, pass through a fine sieve and season to taste.

to serve
Pour the soup into bowls or shot glasses. Froth up the coconut mixture with a stick blender – or, failing that, a liquidiser – and lay a good covering of froth on top of the soup.

vichysoisse of alexanders

This is one of the soups we serve in spring as a little appetiser. Lightly chilled, it tastes clean and refreshing. The secret lies in the rapid cooking of the alexanders at the end, retaining their freshness and vivid colour. If you have trouble finding alexanders, you could replace them with lovage or even celery leaves.

**Serves 4–6 as a starter,
12 in shot glasses**

125g unsalted butter
100g white of leek, chopped
1 celery stick, chopped
*500g potatoes, peeled and sliced (you will
  need 400g prepared weight)*
750ml chicken stock (pages 23–24)
500ml milk
200g green of leek, chopped
400g alexanders, chopped
100ml double cream

Melt the butter in a large, thick-bottomed pan, add the white of leek and the celery and cook gently until translucent. Add the potatoes, stock and milk, bring to the boil and simmer for 30 minutes. Add the green of leek and the alexanders and boil rapidly for 3–4 minutes. Purée in a blender until smooth, then pass through a fine sieve. Add the double cream, season with salt and pepper to taste and chill before serving.

royale of foie gras with sweetcorn cream

This is one of our standby appetisers at the restaurant. We would normally serve it with a shot glass of a contrasting flavour, such as Velouté of Pea and Coconut with Coconut Froth (see opposite). It always goes down very well, thanks in part to its presentation in a dramatic eggcup. I know of some establishments that have borrowed it for their menus already. It is both rich and light at the same time.

You could replace the sweetcorn with a parsley root cream or a chervil tuber cream.

Serves 6

125g raw duck foie gras
50ml milk
75ml double cream
1 egg

for the sweetcorn cream
200ml milk
300g sweetcorn kernels
50g unsalted butter

Preheat the oven to 95°C (or the lowest setting on a gas oven). Place the foie gras in a blender. Bring the milk and double cream to the boil and pour on to the foie gras. Blend until smooth, then add the egg and blend again. Push the mixture through a fine sieve and season with salt and pepper. Pour into 6 eggcups and place in the oven. Cook for about 15–18 minutes; the mixture should be slightly wobbly in the middle. Remove from the oven, cover with clingfilm and leave for 5 minutes. Remove the clingfilm and keep the royales warm.

to make the sweetcorn cream
Bring the milk to the boil in a thick-bottomed saucepan, add the sweetcorn and cook for about 5 minutes, until tender. Transfer to a blender and blend to a fine purée. Push through a fine sieve, getting as much of it through as you can. Place in a saucepan, reheat and beat in the butter. Pull to one side and season with salt and pepper to taste. Spoon a little of the warm sweetcorn cream on to the warm foie gras royale and serve.

clockwise from top:

velouté of pea and coconut
with coconut froth

vichysoisse of alexanders

blanquette of coco beans

royale of foie gras with
sweetcorn cream

veloute of saffron milk caps with garlic foam

Saffron milk caps (Lactarius deliciosus) are called deliciosus for a reason. One of my favourite mushrooms, they are available from early autumn. If you have problems finding them, try using blue limb (pieds bleus) instead. The effort to find the milk caps will be worth it. At the restaurant, we sometimes serve this soup in shot glasses filled with two thirds soup and one third froth. Very nice as a pre-starter.

Serves 6 as a starter, 12–16 as an appetiser

50g unsalted butter
200g shallots, chopped
2 garlic cloves, finely sliced
750g saffron milk caps, sliced
250g potatoes, peeled and sliced
a sprig of thyme
1 litre White Chicken Stock (page 23)
200ml milk

for the garlic foam
200ml milk
200ml White Chicken Stock (page 23)
1g powdered lecithin
50ml double cream
4 garlic cloves, finely sliced

Melt the butter in a thick-bottomed pan, add the shallots and garlic and sweat for 3–4 minutes without letting them colour. Add the sliced milk caps and cook for 5 minutes. Add the potatoes to the pan and cook for 2 minutes. Add the thyme, stock and milk and season lightly with salt and pepper. Bring to the boil, then reduce the heat and simmer for 30 minutes. Remove the thyme, then purée the soup in a blender and pass through a fine sieve into a clean pan. Season to taste.

for the garlic foam
Place all the ingredients in a pan, bring to the boil and simmer for 5 minutes. Remove the garlic with a slotted spoon and season the liquid to taste.

Just before serving, reheat the soup. Heat the foam to just below boiling point and froth it up with a stick blender until light and frothy. Serve the soup topped with the froth.

turnip velouté with vanilla and verjus

Turnips are a much underrated vegetable. They add a great deal of flavour to soups and stews. Their slight bitterness goes wonderfully well with the verjus, while the vanilla gives the soup a haunting perfume. You could replace the turnips with sweet potatoes; although sweet instead of bitter, they will also provide a good foil for the acidic verjus. I sometimes serve the turnip velouté heavily chilled, with just a little more verjus added for a refreshing soup.

Serves 8

125g unsalted butter
150g onions, chopped
100g white of leek, chopped
1kg turnips, peeled and sliced
200ml verjus
1 large potato, peeled and sliced (you will
need about 200g prepared weight)
1 litre White Chicken Stock (page 23)
2 vanilla pods
250ml milk
100ml double cream

Melt 75g of the butter in a large, thick-bottomed saucepan, add the onions, leek and turnips and sweat for 5 minutes without letting them colour. Pour in the verjus, add the potato and cook for about 3 minutes, then add the stock. Slit the vanilla pods open lengthways, scrape out the seeds and add the seeds and pods to the soup. Bring to the boil and cook on a rolling boil for 20 minutes. Add the milk and cook for 10 minutes, until the turnips and potatoes are soft. Purée in a blender and pass through a fine sieve into another pan. Bring to the boil, whisk in the cream and then whisk in the remaining butter a little at a time. Season to taste.

moroccan spiced split pea soup

This is wonderful comfort food, ideal for cold weather. I am a big fan of spices in general, but I think that Moroccan spices have to be my favourite. Ras el hanout is a spice mix that is used a lot in Morocco. The components vary from one home to another and there can be as many as 50 different ingredients in some recipes. If you have problems getting hold of the spices, try your nearest Indian or Middle Eastern shop.

The recipe here is my favourite mix, and makes a lovely, velvety soup. At the restaurant we sometimes serve it with a black lime froth, or a salted lemon cream to keep the Moroccan theme going.

Serves 6

150g unsalted butter
150g onions, chopped
1 carrot, chopped
1 white of leek, chopped
3 garlic cloves, chopped
400g yellow split peas
1 litre chicken stock (pages 23–24)

for the spice mix
15g cumin seeds
5g fennel seeds
10g coriander seeds
4cm piece of cinnamon stick
1 dried chilli
5g cardamom pods
5g ground ginger
20g ajowan seeds
7g medium curry powder
6 cloves
20 dried rosebuds

First make the spice mix. The quantities here will make more than you need but it will keep in a jar for about a month. Heat a sturdy frying pan and add all the spice mix ingredients except the rosebuds. Toast on a medium heat until the seeds begin popping and a wonderful smell starts to come forth. Place in a spice grinder, coffee mill or liquidiser, add the rosebuds and blitz to a fine powder.

Melt the butter in a large, heavy-based pan, add all the vegetables and cook without colouring for 5 minutes. Add the split peas and 15g of the spice mix and cook for 5 minutes, then pour in the stock and bring to the boil. Reduce the heat to a simmer and cook gently for 1–1^1/$_2$ hours, until the split peas are tender. Purée in a blender and pass through a fine sieve into another pan. Reheat and season to taste with salt and pepper.

chestnut soup

I very much look forward to autumn arriving. It is a lovely season with so much to offer: wild mushrooms, acorns, crab apples and, of course, chestnuts. All of which I can gather while walking with my wife, Helen, and our dogs, Twiglet and Truffle. The chestnuts are a great product when there is a shortage of mushrooms. When choosing chestnuts, try to pick the slightly larger ones.

The slow cooking in this recipe helps bring the sweetness of the chestnuts to the fore, held in check by the sherry vinegar. It's a hearty winter soup served drizzled with truffle oil, or can be made lighter with a little fish stock for a terrific background to shellfish or with a good game stock to go with quail or partridge.

After many years of peeling chestnuts, I have found the most successful method to be one of the simplest. Just heavily score the shell of each chestnut, digging into the skin a little. Then place them in a pan of boiling water for about 3 minutes. Leave in the water whilst peeling a few at a time. Simple.

Serves 6

50g duck fat
120g onions, chopped
100g white of leek, chopped
2 garlic cloves, peeled and smashed
30g smoked bacon, chopped
$^1/_2$ sprig of thyme
$^1/_2$ bay leaf
500g peeled chestnuts
15ml sherry vinegar
15ml Cognac
1.25 litres chicken stock (pages 23–24)
250ml milk
100g unsalted butter, diced

Melt the duck fat in a thick-bottomed saucepan and heat till good and hot. Add all the vegetables and the smoked bacon and cook, covered, until the vegetables are translucent. Add the herbs and chestnuts and cook for 3 minutes, then pour in the vinegar and cook, stirring, until evaporated. Repeat with the Cognac and then add the stock and milk. Bring to the boil and cook for 45 minutes on a slow simmer.

Purée the soup in a blender and pass through a fine sieve into a clean pan. Reheat gently, whisk in the butter a little at a time and season to taste.

jerusalem artichoke and almond soup

This is a very simple and satisfying soup. Jerusalem artichokes have a natural affinity with nuts. If you wanted to add another dimension, you could toast a few almonds, infuse them in some seasoned boiling milk, then strain the milk and froth them up for a topping on the soup. You could even use the soup as a base for seared scallops, tiger prawns or langoustines. Small Jerusalem artichokes can just be scrubbed but larger ones will need peeling.

Serves 4–6

600g Jerusalem artichokes
juice of 1/2 lemon
125g unsalted butter
100g onions, roughly chopped
1 celery stick, chopped
750g chicken stock (pages 23–24)
250ml milk
50g toasted almonds
100ml double cream

Peel the Jerusalem artichokes and put them in a bowl of cold water acidulated with the lemon juice (this will prevent them discolouring).

Melt 75g of the butter in a thick-bottomed saucepan, add the onions and celery and sweat for 5 minutes, until softened but not coloured. Drain and slice the artichokes, add them to the pan and cook for 2 minutes, then add the stock, milk and toasted almonds. Bring to the boil and simmer for 30 minutes, until the artichokes are soft. Purée in a blender and pour through a fine sieve into another pan. Bring to the boil, then whisk in the cream and the remaining butter a little at a time. Season to taste and serve.

pressed salmon, leek and potato terrine with oyster and nettle emulsion

This lovely terrine combines some of the ingredients that are available in spring and early summer. The salmon is only just cooked, so you get that wonderful deep pink set against the white of the Jersey Royals and the vibrant green of the watercress and leeks – colours redolent of the season. The oyster and nettle emulsion adds a delicious briny taste. In the past we have replaced the salmon with meaty skate wings and put a layer of shredded duck confit through the terrine. The little salad of peas, asparagus and broad beans completes the dish. If you can't find any hairy bittercress for the salad, you can replace it with baby watercress.

Serves 10

for the terrine
3kg wild salmon fillet, skinned and
*   pin-boned*
500g duck fat
2 green leeks
100g unsalted butter
200g watercress, chopped
10 medium Jersey Royal potatoes, peeled
*   and cut into slices 7mm thick*
Maldon salt

for the oyster and nettle emulsion
200g young nettles
3 oysters, shucked (reserve the juices)
1 egg yolk
150ml grapeseed oil

for the pea salad
10 asparagus spears, peeled and cooked
50g unsalted butter
100g shallots, finely chopped
150g peas, blanched in boiling water for
*   10–15 seconds*
150g shelled broad beans, blanched in
*   boiling water for about 45 seconds,*
*   then skinned*
100g hairy bittercress
virgin rapeseed oil

terrine
Cut the salmon into 3 fillets along its length, using a terrine mould 28 x 11cm and 8cm deep as your guide for width and length. Check to make sure there are no pin bones in them; if there are, remove them with tweezers.

Melt the duck fat in a high-sided roasting tin large enough to hold the salmon pieces. Heat it to 53–55°C, then slide in the salmon. Maintain the fat at this temperature on the stove over a very low heat; if necessary, use a heat diffusion mat. The salmon will take 25–30 minutes. Keep your eye on it; it should be just cooked but still very pink and moist. Remove the salmon from the fat in whole pieces.

While the salmon is cooking, remove the outer leaves from the leeks; you will need enough to line the terrine. Finely slice the remaining green of leek, discarding the white part. Blanch the outer leek leaves in boiling salted water for 30 seconds, then drain, refresh in cold water and drain again. Scrape the interior of the outer leaves with a sharp knife to make them thinner, then set aside.

Heat the butter in a pan, add the sliced leeks and cook gently until limp. Add the chopped watercress, season with salt and pepper and cook until wilted. Drain and set aside.

Poach the sliced potatoes in the duck fat for about 15 minutes, until they are very soft. Drain and set aside.

Line the terrine with a double layer of clingfilm, allowing a good overhang all around. Next line it with the leek leaves, overlapping them and allowing a good overhang again.

Slide one fillet of salmon into the terrine and season. Add some of the sliced watercress and leeks and season again, then add a layer of potato followed by another layer of leek. Repeat with the salmon, seasoning, leek, potato, leek and the final piece of salmon.

Fold the overhanging leek leaves over the terrine and then fold the clingfilm over – sides first, then the ends. Pierce the clingfilm around the edge of the terrine to release the juices when pressing.

Place a board that just fits inside the mould on top of the terrine and then place a weight on top. Press in the fridge on a tray overnight.

oyster and nettle emulsion
Cook the nettles in a large pan of boiling salted water for about 2 minutes, then drain and refresh in cold water. Drain again and squeeze out all the moisture. Mince or chop finely.

Place the oysters, nettles and egg yolk in a blender and blend to a smooth purée. Keep the motor running and pour in the oil in a slow, steady stream. The emulsion should be the consistency of thick custard. If it is too thick, add a little of the reserved oyster juice. Season to taste and keep in a sealed jar until needed.

pea salad
Cut the asparagus into 4cm tips and finely slice the rest of the stalk, then set aside. Heat the butter in a small pan, add the shallots and cook gently until soft and translucent. Remove from the heat and leave to cool. Put the peas, broad beans, shallots and their butter in a food processor and pulse to break the mixture down a little. Remove from the machine, stir in the sliced asparagus stalks and season to taste. Keep covered in the fridge until needed.

Unmould the terrine. Cut the ends off the terrine through the clingfilm and taste! Cut the terrine into 10 portions, again through the cling film, then carefully remove the clingfilm.

Place the slices of terrine on serving plates, then put a quenelle of pea salad to one side of the terrine. Place an asparagus spear on top. Dress the hairy bittercress with a little rapeseed oil and arrange on the salad.

Spoon a little of the oyster and nettle emulsion on to the plate. Brush the terrine with a little rapeseed oil and sprinkle with Maldon salt.

pressed terrine of guinea fowl with foie gras and smoked ham hock

Whenever we are visited by the press, the resulting reviews invariably shower praise on this dish. I think it is because, quite simply, it eats so well. The differing textures of the meats are a joy, and with the verjus syrup, golden raisin purée and the combination of sweet-sour beetroot and salty sea purslane, it has everything a top-class dish should have. Remember to cut the terrine a good 10 minutes before you need it. There is nothing worse than a slice of terrine that is fridge cold.

We use a metal cooking frame placed on a baking sheet to make this. You could use a terrine mould if necessary, but the layers may be slightly different.

Serves 10–12

for the terrine
1 ham hock
$^1/_2$ onion, chopped
$^1/_2$ carrot, chopped
1 celery stick, chopped
a sprig of thyme
2 bay leaves
chicken stock (pages 23–24) – enough to
    cover the ham hock
6 guinea fowl breasts
190g unsalted butter
3 large chicory heads
juice of $^1/_2$ lemon
100g caster sugar
125ml maple syrup
2 large leeks, green part only, finely sliced
1 lobe of foie gras, weighing about 700g,
    cut into 1.5cm slices
250ml reduced guinea fowl stock (follow
    the recipe for Brown Chicken Stock on
    page 24, using the guinea fowl carcasses,
    then reduce 1 litre to 250ml)
a little caster sugar

for the marinated beetroot
2 large beetroot
1 tablespoon honey
1 teaspoon soy sauce
1 teaspoon sesame oil
2 tablespoons red wine vinegar
juice of 3 limes
200ml olive oil

for the golden raisin purée
500ml verjus
250g golden raisins

to serve
5 sprigs of sea purslane
White Port and Verjus Syrup (see page 21),
    for drizzling
Maldon salt

terrine
Put the ham hock in a pan with the onion, carrot, celery, thyme and bay leaves and add enough chicken stock to cover. Bring to the boil, then reduce the heat and simmer very gently for about 3 hours, until the meat is very tender. Remove from the heat and set aside.

Place each guinea fowl breast in a sealable cooking bag with 15g of the butter and a little seasoning. Expel as much air as possible and seal the bags. Heat a large saucepan of water to 58°C. Place the bags in it and cook for 30–40 minutes, keeping the water at this temperature. (Alternatively you could leave the breasts on the crown of the birds, season and butter them and roast in an oven preheated to 140°C/Gas Mark 1 for 30 minutes. Keep the breasts on the crown until needed; this will ensure that they are moist.)

To cook the chicory, bring a large pan of water to the boil with the lemon juice and sugar, then add the chicory and simmer until tender. Remove from the pan and leave to cool. Gently squeeze any water out of the chicory and separate the leaves. Heat 25g of the remaining butter in a large frying pan until foaming. Add the chicory leaves and cook until coloured, adding the maple syrup half way through. Lay the leaves out on a baking tray.

Quickly cook the sliced leeks in the remaining 75g of butter, keeping their colour, then set aside.

Remove the meat from the ham hock while still warm, shredding it lightly as you go. Put to one side, keeping it warm.

Heat a large frying pan and dry fry the foie gras in it over a high heat for 1–1$^1/_2$ minutes in total, until golden on each side. Now the fun part, the building. Place a 36 x 11.5 x 4cm metal cooking frame on a tray, oil lightly and then line with 2 sheets of clingfilm, making the finish as smooth as possible and allowing a good overhang all around. Carefully line the frame with the caramelised chicory leaves, reserving a few for the top, then put the guinea fowl breasts in it in a single layer, followed by a little of the reduced stock. Remember to season each layer lightly as you go. Next make a layer of the leeks, followed by all the foie gras, more reduced stock, more leeks, and then the ham hock, then more reduced stock. Wrap around the overlapping chicory and place a few more leaves over the top. Finally bring the clingfilm over and seal tightly. Prick the sides of the clingfilm with a sharp knife to allow the juices to escape and give a flat finish. Place a board that just fits inside the mould on top of the terrine and then place a weight on top. Refrigerate overnight on a tray.

marinated beetroot
Peel the beetroot and then cut very thinly around each one to give you long, thin sheets. Cut these sheets into thin, spaghetti-like strips. Mix all the remaining ingredients together to make a marinade and season with salt and pepper. Place the beetroot strips in the marinade, cover and leave in the fridge overnight.

golden raisin purée

Bring the verjus to the boil in a heavy-based saucepan, add the raisins and simmer for about 10 minutes. Transfer to a blender and blend for a good 5 minutes to break down the raisins; the resulting purée should be fine and smooth. Keep, covered, in a container until needed.

serving

Strip the leaves from the sea purslane sprigs and put to one side.

Unmould the terrine. Cut the ends off the terrine through the clingfilm and taste! The juices that have come out of the terrine and set on the tray can be scraped off into a pan, brought to the boil and then kept for another use – excellent for when you want to give a sauce a lift.

Cut the terrine into 10–12 portions, again through the clingfilm, then carefully remove the clingfilm. Stand up the slices a little apart, top side up, sprinkle with a thin layer of caster sugar, as if making a brûlée, and heat with a blowtorch until a crisp, golden layer has formed on top of the slices.

Put a little golden raisin purée to one side of each plate and pull it across the plate with the spoon. Place the terrine at an angle across the purée. Wrap some of the beetroot around a fork, as if you were eating spaghetti. Stand the beetroot on the plate, arrange some sea purslane leaves on top of it, then scatter a few more leaves around. Drizzle the white port and verjus syrup around and sprinkle with Maldon salt.

jack-by-the-hedge panna cotta with pea cream, cleavers and crisp cumbrian ham

This dish just shouts spring, with the new season's peas and jack-by-the-hedge. Jack-by-the-hedge has a garlicky scent and flavour - indeed, you could substitute wild garlic. The peas are used in various ways to give different levels of texture and flavour to the dish: raw, cooked and puréed. The tiny tops of cleavers have an almost pea-like flavour, and are very easy to find.

Serves 6

for the panna cotta
100ml milk
400ml double cream
2g powdered agar-agar
200g jack-by-the-hedge, chopped

for the pea cream
250g fresh peas
a little milk

to garnish
12 asparagus spears, trimmed
200g fresh peas
3 slices of air-dried Cumbrian ham (or Parma ham)
100g pea shoots
18 cleaver tips (optional)

for the jack-by-the-hedge froth (optional)
75ml White Chicken Stock (page 23)
75ml milk
1g powdered lecithin
125g jack-by-the-hedge, chopped

for the dressing
50ml hazelnut oil
juice of 1/2 lemon
1/2 teaspoon sugar

panna cotta
Bring the milk and double cream to the boil, whisk in the agar-agar and add the chopped jack-by-the-hedge. Liquidise and pass through a fine sieve – you need to be quick to retain the colour. Season with salt and pepper to taste and pour into 6 ramekins. Chill until set.

pea cream
Blanch the peas in a pan of boiling salted water for 10–15 seconds. Drain and refresh in cold water, then drain again. Liquidise until smooth, adding a little milk to thin. Push through a fine sieve, season to taste and leave to cool.

garnish
Cook the asparagus spears in boiling salted water for 1 1/2 minutes, then drain. Refresh in cold water to keep the colour and drain again. Blanch 100g of the peas in the same way as for the pea cream, then drain and set aside (the remaining peas are left raw for a contrast of textures). Place the ham on a baking tray lined with baking parchment and cover with another sheet of baking parchment and another baking tray. Bake in an oven preheated to 180°C/Gas Mark 4 until crisp, checking from time to time. Remove from the oven and leave to cool.

jack-by-the-hedge froth
Bring the stock and milk to the boil, whisk in the lecithin and add the chopped jack-by-the-hedge. Simmer for 1–2 minutes. Remove from the heat and leave to infuse for 30 minutes. Strain the infused milk through a fine sieve and set aside.

dressing
Whisk all the ingredients for the dressing together. Place all the vegetables for the garnish in a bowl and toss with the dressing, then season to taste.

serving
Gently reheat the jack-by-the-hedge froth – do not let it boil. Place a little pea cream on each serving plate. Turn out the panna cotta and place on the plates, then arrange the raw peas, cooked peas, asparagus and pea shoots around them. Break the ham into pieces and arrange on the plates. Add the cleavers, if using. Whiz the froth with a stick blender and spoon just a little around the plate.

seared scallops with cauliflower purée, cumin velouté and ras el hanout caramel

I just love scallops and will not apologise at all for the frequent use of them in this book. They are quick to cook and have a wonderful natural sweetness.

The cauliflower works as a bitter foil to the scallops, while the acidity and sweetness of the apple garnish complement them. The ras el hanout caramel adds another texture to the dish altogether.

Serves 6

for the seared scallops
9 extra-large hand-dived scallops
50ml olive oil
50g unsalted butter

for the ras el hanout caramel
200g caster sugar
2 tablespoons water
3 pinches of ras el hanout (see page 41)

for the cauliflower purée
1 medium cauliflower
125g unsalted butter

for the cumin velouté
30g cumin seeds
250ml Fish Stock (page 25)
200ml milk
150ml double cream
2g powdered lecithin
a little lemon juice, if needed

to garnish
3 medium cauliflower florets, thinly sliced
1 Granny Smith apple, cut into matchsticks
1 punnet of pea shoots

preparing the scallops
Remove and discard the scallop 'skirt' and the orange roe, leaving only the pure white part of the scallop. If there is any grit, wipe it off with a damp cloth. Cut each scallop horizontally in half to give you 18 discs. Place on a damp cloth on a tray, cover and leave in the fridge. Remove 5 minutes before needed.

ras el hanout caramel
Put the sugar and water in a small, heavy-based saucepan and heat gently, stirring until the sugar has dissolved. Raise the temperature and boil, without stirring, until a golden caramel has been obtained; it should be the colour of teak. Have a baking tray lined with baking parchment, a rolling pin and another sheet of baking parchment ready. As soon as the caramel is the correct colour, pour it on to the lined tray and sprinkle immediately with the ras el hanout. Place the other sheet of paper on top and carefully roll out the caramel through the paper until very thin. Allow to set hard, then break into pieces; approximately the same size as the cauliflower slices for garnish.

cauliflower purée
Bring a large saucepan of water to the boil. Trim the cauliflower, discarding all the green and the major part of the stalk. Divide it into small florets, place in a sealable cooking bag, add the butter and some salt and pepper and seal, expelling as much air as possible. Place the bag in the water and cook for 30–40 minutes, until the cauliflower is very soft. Remove the bag and empty the contents into a blender. Blend until smooth, then check the seasoning.

Alternatively, if you do not have a cooking bag, place the cauliflower florets in a saucepan with 250ml milk, bring to the boil, then cover and simmer gently for 10–15 minutes, until the cauliflower is very tender. Drain, reserving the milk. Place in a blender, add 50g butter and blend until smooth, adding a little of the reserved milk if it is too thick.

In both cases, if the purée is too thick, add a little milk. If it is too thin, return it to a pan and cook gently until thick enough to hold its shape.

cumin velouté
Put the cumin seeds in a heavy-based saucepan and heat until they start popping and give off a pleasant scent. Add the fish stock and simmer until reduced by a third. Add the milk and cream and simmer for 3–4 minutes. Whisk in the lecithin and 2 tablespoons of the cauliflower purée. Season to taste, adding a little lemon juice if necessary, then pass through a fine sieve. Keep warm until needed.

cooking the scallops
Season the scallops with salt and pepper. Heat a large, heavy-based frying pan. When you feel the heat coming off it, put half the olive oil in it, then half the scallops. Cook for 30 seconds over a medium-high heat, then add half the butter. Cook for a further $1/2$–1 minute, until golden underneath. Turn and cook for about 1 minute. Transfer to a warm plate, wipe out the pan with kitchen paper and repeat with the remaining scallops. When all are cooked, season again.

serving
Place a little streak of cauliflower purée on either side of each serving plate. In the middle, arrange a piece of scallop, a slice of raw cauliflower and a piece of caramel. Repeat using 3 pieces of scallop for each portion. Carefully lay the apple matchsticks on top and then the pea shoots. Froth the cumin sauce with a stick blender and pour it over the scallops.

scallops and baby squid with squid ink and over farm pumpkin purée

This dish has been a favourite with our customers for many years. On our way back from a successful mushroom pick in Gloucestershire one day, we noticed Over Farm, which had a farm shop with an impressive display of pumpkins. We came away with 8 different varieties and set about quartering them, then steaming, roasting, frying and boiling each one for a pumpkin tasting. The best pumpkin for this dish was Crown Prince. It has a low water content, a good colour, very little starch and fibre, and the right amount of sweetness. Pumpkin marries so well with shellfish; it helps bring out the natural sweetness of the squid and scallops.

Serves 6

for the scallops and squid
6 extra-large hand-dived scallops
12 baby squid
100ml olive oil
100g unsalted butter

for the pumpkin purée
800g pumpkin
a little oil
200ml milk
200ml double cream
100g unsalted butter, diced

for the squid ink
250ml white wine
300ml Fish Stock (page 25) or White
  Chicken Stock (page 23)
200ml double cream
40ml fresh squid ink or 5 sachets of squid
  ink
a little lemon juice

preparing the scallops
Remove and discard the scallop 'skirt' and the orange roe, leaving only the pure white part of the scallop. If there is any grit, wipe it off with a damp cloth. Cut each scallop horizontally in half, or leave whole if you prefer. Place on a damp cloth on a tray, cover and leave in the fridge. Remove 5 minutes before needed.

preparing the squid
With one hand on the body and the other on the tentacles of each squid, pull gently so the tentacles and body separate from each other. Trim the head away from the tentacles by cutting just below the eyes; discard the head. Remove the 'beak' from the middle of the tentacles, if it's there. Inside the squid's body there is a transparent quill; pull it out and discard. Remove anything else in the body and rinse under cold running water. I like to leave the pink skin on small squid. You should now have 12 small, cleaned bodies with 12 small piles of tentacles. Place them on a damp cloth on a tray, cover and place in the fridge. Remove 5 minutes before needed.

pumpkin purée
Cut the pumpkin into quarters and remove the seeds. Place on a baking tray, drizzle with a little oil and cover with foil. Roast in an oven preheated to 200°C/Gas Mark 6 until the flesh is very tender. Remove from the oven and scrape the flesh off the skin. Place the flesh in a blender. Bring the milk and cream to the boil, pour into the blender and blend until smooth. Then add the butter little by little. The purée should be totally smooth – the hotter the ingredients the better. Season to taste and keep warm until needed.

squid ink
Pour the white wine into a heavy-based pan, bring to the boil and simmer until almost evaporated. Add the stock and simmer until reduced by two thirds. Add the double cream and simmer until the mixture is reduced by half. Whisk in the squid ink. Heat gently but do not let it boil again. Season to taste and add a few drops of lemon juice. Pass through a fine sieve and keep warm.

cooking the scallops and squid
Heat a large, heavy-bottomed frying pan over a medium-high heat. When you can feel the heat coming off it, add a quarter of the olive oil and then half the scallops. Season the scallops with salt and pepper, cook for 30 seconds, then add half the butter. Cook for a further $1/2$–1 minute, then turn and cook for 1 minute. Transfer to a warm plate. Wipe the pan clean and repeat with the other scallops. When all are cooked, re-season them.

Cook the squid in the same way, using the remaining oil – first the bodies and then the tentacles (the tentacles are nicer if a little crisper).

serving
Place a little pumpkin purée on each serving plate, then the squid ink sauce and finally the squid and scallops.

fillet of cod with risotto of spelt and ceps and chestnut velouté

Cod has to be my favourite fish. It can hold its own with meaty, powerful flavours and can be cooked simply without much fuss. Here I have combined it with spelt risotto. An ancient form of wheat, spelt has a nutty flavour and is able to keep its al dente texture for longer than rice. You could use pearly barley to similar effect. Chestnuts and ceps are a perfect match. They appear at the same time of year and, luckily for me, are both on our walking route.

Serves 6

for the cod
800g cod fillet (a thick top piece)
100ml olive oil
25g unsalted butter

for the risotto of spelt and ceps
400–500ml Brown Chicken Stock (page 24)
50g dried ceps
50ml olive oil
1 onion, finely chopped
2 garlic cloves, finely chopped
125g spelt
30g unsalted butter
150g fresh cep mushrooms, diced
50ml double cream
50g Mascarpone cheese

for the chestnut velouté
300g fresh chestnuts, peeled (page 42)
75g unsalted butter
400ml Brown Chicken Stock (page 24)
100ml double cream
350ml milk

to garnish
45g hairy bittercress
a little olive oil

preparing the cod
Remove any bones from the cod, then trim it to give you an even piece all the way round. Roll tightly in clingfilm to form a cylinder. Place in the fridge until firm, to set the shape, then cut straight through the clingfilm to give you 6 even pieces. Return to the fridge until needed.

risotto of spelt and ceps
Put the stock and dried ceps in a pan and bring to the boil. Remove from the heat and leave to infuse for 1–2 hours. Strain off and discard the dried ceps, then bring the stock back to the boil.

Heat the olive oil in a saucepan, add the onion and garlic and cook for about 4 minutes, until translucent but not coloured. Next add the spelt and cook for 3 minutes, until it gives off a nutty aroma. Add a quarter of the hot stock, stirring all the time, and simmer over a medium heat until the stock has almost disappeared. Repeat twice more. Heat the butter in a frying pan, add the fresh ceps and fry until golden. Add the remaining stock and the fried ceps to the spelt mixture. Bring to a low simmer and cook until the spelt is tender, with just a little bite; this can take up to an hour. Raise the temperature and cook quickly to evaporate any remaining liquid. Add the double cream and cook for 2 minutes, adding the Mascarpone just before serving. Season to taste and keep warm.

chestnut velouté
Roughly chop the chestnuts and cook gently in 50g of the butter for 3–4 minutes. Add the brown chicken stock, bring to the boil and cook on a slow simmer for about 30 minutes, until the chestnuts are soft. Add the double cream and milk, bring back to the boil and simmer for 3 minutes. Transfer to a blender and blend until smooth. Push the mixture through a fine sieve and whisk in the remaining butter. Season to taste and keep warm.

garnish
Season the hairy bittercress with salt and pepper and dress with a little olive oil.

cooking the cod
Heat the olive oil in a large frying pan, then add the butter. When it is foaming, add the cod, skin-side down, and season with salt and pepper. Cook over a medium-high heat until golden brown underneath, then turn the fish over, season again and cook until just done.

serving
Divide the risotto between 6 bowls. Place a piece of cod on top and scatter with the hairy bittercress. Froth the chestnut velouté with a stick blender and pour it around the cod.

eel tortelloni with watercress cream and bitter leaves

We first made this recipe many years ago and it has since become a firm favourite. It is clean and fresh, and the bitter, peppery taste of the watercress goes so well with the eel. To temper the eel's richness we have included baby capers and salted lemon, which add acidity to the dish.

If you can't get the salad leaves listed below, then substitute whatever is available. Do try to keep a mix of leaves, though, as they help with the freshness and texture of the dish.

Serves 6

for the eel tortelloni
1 tablespoon double cream
15g fresh breadcrumbs
150g conger eel flesh, finely chopped
100–125g spinach, cooked and finely chopped (you will need 50g cooked weight)
15g Salted Lemons (see page 18), finely chopped
30g watercress, chopped
a few drops of lemon juice
$^1/_2$ quantity of Pasta Dough (see page 26)
1 egg, beaten

for the watercress cream
50g unsalted butter
100g green of leek, finely chopped
100g watercress stalks, chopped
200ml Noilly Prat (or vermouth)
400ml Fish Stock (page 25)
250ml double cream
100g watercress leaves, chopped
lemon juice, if needed
white pepper

for the dressing
1 egg yolk
juice and grated zest of 1 lemon
125ml olive oil
30ml water
a pinch of sugar

for the salad
30ml olive oil
50g trompette noire (horn of plenty) mushrooms
25g watercress
25g hairy bittercress
25g buckler-leaf sorrel
25g red-veined sorrel

to finish
50g unsalted butter
25g watercress, chopped
50g trompette noire (horn of plenty) mushrooms
30ml olive oil
25g baby capers

eel tortelloni
Bring the cream to the boil in a small saucepan and pour it over the breadcrumbs. Add the eel, spinach, salted lemons, watercress and some salt and pepper and mix well. Add lemon juice to taste, then shape the mixture into 30 small balls. Place on a tray in the fridge to set their shape.

Roll out the pasta dough in a pasta machine to the finest setting and cut out 30 discs with a 7cm cutter. Place a ball of the eel mixture in the middle of each disc, brush the beaten egg around the ball, then fold over the top half of the dough and press the edges together to seal well, making sure no air is trapped or the tortelloni will burst on cooking. Curl the semi-circle around your finger and push the corners together well to form the traditional 'belly button' shape. Blanch in a large pan of boiling salted water for 1–1$^1/_2$ minutes, then drain, refresh in cold water and drain again. Place on a tray, cover with clingfilm and chill until needed.

watercress cream
Melt the butter in a saucepan, add the leeks and watercress stalks and sweat until softened but not coloured. Stir in the Noilly Prat and simmer until it has completely evaporated. Add the stock and simmer until reduced by a third, then add the double cream and boil for 3 minutes. Add the watercress leaves, bring back to the boil and cook for 1 minute. Purée the sauce in a blender and push it through a fine sieve. Divide it between 2 small saucepans. Set one aside; simmer the other one until reduced by half, to make a thick, vibrant-green cream. Season with salt and white pepper, add lemon juice if needed, then leave to cool.

dressing
Whisk the egg yolk in a small bowl, then whisk in the lemon juice and zest. Drizzle in the oil little by little, whisking constantly. Whisk in the water, add the sugar and season to taste.

salad
Heat the olive oil in a frying pan, sauté the mushrooms until limp, then drain and season. Toss the salad leaves with a little of the lemon dressing and mix with the mushrooms.

serving
Reheat the tortelloni for 1–1$^1/_2$ minutes in a large pan of boiling salted water with a little oil added. Drain and toss with the butter, then add the chopped watercress and season to taste.

Sauté the mushrooms in the olive oil. Drain and season to taste.

Heat the reduced watercress cream and the watercress sauce. Pour a little of the reduced watercress cream over each plate. Place some salad in the middle, arrange the tortelloni around, then scatter with the mushrooms and capers. Froth the watercress sauce with a handheld blender and pour it around the plate.

langoustines with cumbrian ham, pickled apple purée and brazil nuts

We get our langoustines from the Shetland Isles, from a wonderful supplier called Island Divers. They always arrive in peak condition.

Here I have pitched the golden langoustines against the acidity of the pickled apple purée and the faint saltiness of Cumbrian ham. This is a dish with differing tastes and textures: salt, sweet, acid, soft and crisp. You could use scallops instead of langoustines, hazelnuts instead of brazils, or pears instead of apples. It is a good light dish for spring or summer.

Serves 6

6 slices of air-dried Cumbrian ham
  (or Parma ham)
15 large shelled brazil nuts
6 Pickled Apple halves (see page 21),
  plus a dessertspoon of the pickling juices

for the red wine dressing
30g caster sugar
30ml water
30ml red wine vinegar
50ml port
200ml red wine
10ml balsamic vinegar
15ml olive oil

to garnish
1 tablespoon olive oil
150g land cress

for the langoustines
18 large raw langoustine tails, peeled
100ml olive oil
50g unsalted butter

cumbrian ham
Cut 3 slices of ham lengthways in half and place them on a baking tray lined with baking parchment, leaving a gap between each piece. Place another piece of parchment on top and then another baking tray. Place in an oven preheated to 180°C/Gas Mark 4 and cook for 20–30 minutes, until golden and crisp. Remove from the oven, take off the top tray and baking parchment and leave to cool. Cut the other 3 slices of ham into quarters and place on a plate in the fridge until needed.

brazil nuts
Remove the skins from the brazil nuts by blanching them in a pan of boiling water for 30 seconds. Drain and refresh in cold water, then drain again. Slice lengthways as finely as possible with a very sharp knife. Scatter over a baking tray and toast in an oven preheated to 150°C/Gas Mark 2 until crisp and golden.

red wine dressing
Put the sugar and water in a small, heavy-based saucepan and heat gently, stirring until the sugar has dissolved. Raise the temperature and boil, without stirring, until a golden caramel has been obtained; it should be the colour of teak. Add the red wine vinegar and boil until reduced by two thirds. Add the port and red wine and simmer until reduced and syrupy. Add the balsamic vinegar, then whisk in the olive oil.

pickled apple purée
Heat 4 of the pickled apple halves with the pickling juices, then purée in a blender until smooth. Season to taste and keep warm. Cut the remaining pickled apples into 4mm dice and set aside.

garnish
Heat the olive oil in a saucepan, add 100g of the land cress and stir until wilted.

langoustines
Season the langoustine tails with salt and pepper. Heat the olive oil in a large frying pan over a medium-high heat. When you can feel the heat coming off the pan, add the langoustine tails and sauté quickly for 30 seconds on one side. Add the butter, flip the tails over and cook on the other side until golden. Remove from the pan and drain on kitchen paper.

serving
Place a few streaks of pickled apple purée on each serving plate. Arrange the wilted land cress in the centre of the plate, then place 3 langoustines on top with a piece of uncooked ham between each. Scatter with toasted brazil nuts and diced apple. Arrange the raw land cress neatly on the plate and drizzle with the red wine dressing. Lay the crisp pieces of ham on top.

langoustines with cocks' kidneys, langoustine tortelloni and jus

This is one of those dishes that work on several levels, combining different textures and flavours. It's well worth trying to get hold of the cocks' kidneys. They have a creamy, mousse-like texture and a light chicken flavour. If you don't manage to obtain them, try using rabbit kidneys instead; you will need 4–5 per person.

We garnish this dish with pennywort, a juicy, umbrella-like plant. It could be replaced with purslane.

Serves 4

for the kidneys and langoustines
8 large cocks' kidneys
16 large langoustines
100ml olive oil

for the langoustine stock
100ml olive oil
the shells from the langoustines
2 garlic cloves, crushed
1 onion, chopped
1 celery stick, chopped
1 tablespoon tomato purée
50ml Cognac
250ml white wine
500ml Brown Chicken Stock (page 24)
750ml water

for the tortelloni
30g fresh white breadcrumbs
50ml double cream
a little lemon juice
1/2 quantity of Pasta Dough (see page 26)
1 egg, beaten

for the jus
75ml double cream
50ml milk
2g powdered lecithin
lemon juice, if needed

for the spinach
50g unsalted butter
400g spinach

16 small pennywort stems

preparing the kidneys and langoustines
Bring a large pan of water to the boil, add the cocks' kidneys and blanch for 1 1/2–2 minutes. Remove with a slotted spoon and set aside, then blanch the langoustines in the same water for about a minute. While they are still slightly warm, shell the tails, then use nutcrackers to remove the meat from the claws. Peel the skin off the kidneys. Place the kidneys, langoustine tails and langoustine meat in the fridge until needed.

langoustine stock
Heat the olive oil in a large, thick-bottomed saucepan until almost smoking. Add the langoustine shells and cook until golden. Add the garlic, onion and celery and cook for 5 minutes, until coloured, then add the tomato purée. Stir in the Cognac, scraping the base of the pan with a wooden spoon to deglaze it, then add the white wine and simmer until it has completely evaporated. Add the chicken stock and water, bring to the boil and simmer for about 1 hour. Strain through a fine sieve into another pan and boil until reduced to 400ml. Leave to cool, then chill until needed.

tortelloni
Finely chop 8 of the langoustine tails and all the claw meat and place in a bowl. Add the breadcrumbs and mix in the cream to bind. Season with salt and pepper and add the lemon juice. Shape into 8 small balls and chill until needed.

Roll out the pasta dough in a pasta machine to the finest setting, then cut out 8 discs with a 6cm cutter. Place a ball of filling on each disc, brush the edges with beaten egg and then fold over the top half of the dough. Press the edges together to seal well, making sure no air is trapped or the tortelloni will burst on cooking. Curl the semi-circle around your finger and push the corners together well to form the traditional 'belly button' shape. Blanch in a large pan of boiling salted water for 1–1 1/2 minutes. Drain well, refresh in cold water, then drain again. Place on a tray, cover with clingfilm and chill until needed.

jus
Bring the langoustine stock to the boil in a small saucepan. Add the double cream and milk and bring back to the boil, then whisk in the lecithin. Season to taste, adding a few drops of lemon juice to sharpen the flavour if necessary. Keep warm.

to cook the kidneys and langoustines
Heat the olive oil in a large frying pan over a medium-high heat. Add the peeled kidneys and the remaining langoustine tails and cook for about 1 1/2 minutes on each side, until golden. Season to taste and keep warm.

spinach
Heat the butter in a large pan, add the spinach and cook briefly until wilted. Season with salt and pepper.

serving
Reheat the tortelloni for 1–1 1/2 minutes in a large pan of boiling salted water with a little oil added. Drain well and season to taste.

Place a small mound of spinach in each of 4 serving bowls and add the tortelloni, langoustines and cocks' kidneys. Arrange the pennywort on top. Froth the jus with a stick blender until light and airy, then spoon it over and around.

seared red mullet with roasted buckwheat salad, oxalis and fresh almonds

I prefer to use British red mullet here rather than Mediterranean because the flavour is more delicate. It's a lovely quick dish, just right for a lazy summer's evening. The oxalis (wood sorrel) has a wonderful lemony zing and looks so pretty, rather like four-leaf clovers. You could replace it with baby sorrel leaves, if necessary. The natural nuttiness of the buckwheat is freshened up nicely by the juicy watermelon and the tomato confit. We finish this off with skinned fresh almonds to introduce another complementary texture; they have a milky consistency, nowhere near as dry as normal almonds. Available from the end of June to September, they are stocked by some good greengrocers.

Serves 6

for the roasted buckwheat salad
25g unsalted butter
25ml sunflower oil
1 garlic clove, finely chopped
1 large shallot, finely diced
150g roasted buckwheat (available from healthfood shops)
150ml White Chicken Stock (page 23)
125g watermelon, peeled, deseeded and cut into 5mm dice
50g Tomato Confit with Lemon (see page 17), diced
1 tablespoon chopped flat-leaf parsley
2 tablespoons finely chopped oxalis (wood sorrel)
lemon juice, if needed

for the seared red mullet
50ml olive oil
6 red mullet fillets

for the dressing
50ml extra virgin rapeseed oil
juice of 1 lemon
25ml oil from the Tomato Confit
$^1/_2$ teaspoon sugar

to garnish
50g red orache (available from good greengrocers; you could use pea shoots instead)
a little olive oil
72 fresh almonds, blanched and skinned
10g oxalis (wood sorrel)
Maldon salt

buckwheat salad
Heat the butter and oil in a thick-bottomed saucepan, add the garlic and shallot and sweat until translucent but not coloured. Stir in the buckwheat and cook for 1 minute. Add the stock, bring to the boil and simmer until the liquid had been absorbed and the buckwheat is cooked but still has a tiny bit of bite. Remove from the heat and leave to cool. Mix in the watermelon, tomato confit, parsley and oxalis. Season to taste with salt and pepper, adding a little lemon juice if needed.

red mullet
Heat the oil in a large frying pan over a medium-high heat, add the mullet, skin-side down, and flash-fry for 30 seconds. Immediately remove from the pan and transfer to an oiled baking tray, flesh-side down. Cook in an oven preheated to 180°C/Gas Mark 4 for 2–3 minutes, until just done.

dressing
Whisk all the dressing ingredients together.

serving
Arrange the buckwheat salad in the middle of each plate. Dress the orache with a little olive oil. Arrange the almonds, orache and oxalis down the sides of the plate. Place the mullet on top of the buckwheat. Sprinkle with Maldon salt and drizzle with the dressing.

roasted marinated red snapper with sardine rillettes

The creamy sardine rillettes go so well with the marinated vegetables and snapper. You could replace the sardines with mackerel or red mullet, if you prefer. Some crushed roasted hazelnuts could be scattered over the plate for a different texture.

Serves 4

for the marinade
30ml olive oil
150g baby carrots, sliced
250g red onions, sliced
3 garlic cloves, chopped
2 bay leaves
a sprig of thyme
15–20 coriander seeds
15–20 golden raisins
75ml extra virgin olive oil
150ml white wine
50ml red wine vinegar
75ml orange juice
juice of 1/2 lemon
a pinch of saffron

for the sardine rillettes
30ml olive oil
8 large, fresh sardines, cleaned
100ml mayonnaise, preferably home-made
50g unsalted butter, softened
20g grain mustard
8 spring onions, finely chopped
1 apple, cored and finely chopped
juice of 1/2 lemon

for the red snapper
2 x 200g red snapper fillets, cut in half
30ml olive oil

to garnish
silver leaf
baby tatsoi shoots

marinade
Heat the olive oil in a large pan, add the carrots, onions and garlic and cook for 3–4 minutes without colouring. Add all the remaining ingredients, bring to the boil and simmer for 10–15 minutes, until the vegetables are tender. Remove from the heat and set aside.

sardine rillettes
Heat the olive oil in a large, non-stick frying pan. Quickly fry the sardines over a medium-high heat for 1 minute on each side, then remove from the pan and leave to cool. Break the flesh into chunks, removing any bones as you go. Mix all the other ingredients together, adding 3 tablespoons of the marinade, then fold in the sardines. Season to taste and place in the fridge until needed.

red snapper
Roast the snapper, skin-side down, in the olive oil in a hot frying pan until golden. Flip over and cook for 1 minute. Remove from the pan and place in a shallow dish. Gently reheat the marinade and pour it over the snapper. Cover with clingfilm immediately and leave to cool. It should be served at room temperature.

serving
With 2 tablespoons, shape the sardine rillettes into 4 quenelles and place in the middle of each serving plate. Arrange a little of the marinade, vegetables and raisins around, followed by the silver leaf and baby tatsoi shoots. Place a piece of snapper on top and drizzle a little more marinade around.

brown trout with wild garlic quinoa and roasted garlic cream

This is a light starter that plays on the flavour of different kinds of garlic. Quinoa (pronounced keen-wa) is an Aztec grain from the spinach family that I started to use back in 1996. It has a natural nuttiness and can be served hot or cold.

We get our trout from Bibury, which is just a few miles from Cheltenham. At the restaurant we garnish this dish with pea shoots and blanched kohlrabi that has been filled with the quinoa and folded to look like semi-circular ravioli.

Serves 6

for the brown trout
2 x 450g brown trout fillets
50ml olive oil
25g unsalted butter

for the roasted garlic cream
2 heads of garlic
20ml olive oil
500ml Fish Stock (page 25)
50ml milk
200ml double cream

for the wild garlic quinoa
50ml olive oil, plus extra for drizzling
1/2 onion, finely chopped
2 garlic cloves, finely chopped
100g quinoa
300ml Fish Stock (page 25)
120g wild garlic leaves

preparing the trout
Make sure there aren't any bones left in the trout. Cut each fillet into 3 pieces and place in the fridge until needed.

roasted garlic cream
Remove the papery outer layers from the garlic. Moisten the heads with the olive oil and place on a baking tray. Roast in an oven preheated to 180°C/Gas Mark 4 for 20–30 minutes, until tender and golden. Pop the garlic cloves out of their skins and place in a saucepan with the fish stock. Bring to the boil and simmer until reduced by half. Add the milk and double cream, bring back to the boil and simmer for 2–3 minutes. Transfer to a blender and blend until smooth. Push through a fine sieve and season to taste.

wild garlic quinoa
Heat the olive oil in an ovenproof frying pan and add the onion, garlic and quinoa. Cook without colouring until you can smell the slight nuttiness of the quinoa. Immediately pour in the fish stock. Bring to the boil, stirring all the time, then reduce to a light simmer and cook until tender. When it is ready, the quinoa should have a white ring surrounding the centre of the grain. Taste; it should be tender with a little bite. Set aside 6–8 wild garlic leaves and blanch the remainder in a large pan of salted water for 30 seconds. Refresh the blanched wild garlic quickly in a bowl of iced water to set the colour. When it is cold, squeeze out excess water and place the garlic leaves in a food processor. Process to a purée, adding a little water if needed.

Finely chop the raw wild garlic leaves. Whilst the quinoa is still warm, fold them through it and then fold in the wild garlic purée. Season and drizzle with a little olive oil. Keep warm.

cooking the trout
Heat the olive oil in a large, heavy-based frying pan over a high heat. Season the trout fillets and add them to the pan, skin-side down. Add the butter and reduce the heat to medium. Cook for 3–4 minutes, until you see the trout change around the edges from translucent pink to a paler shade of pink. Turn the fish over, count to 10 and turn off the heat. Move the pan to a cooler part of the stove so the fish finishes cooking in the warmth of the pan. Drain and re-season the trout.

serving
Place a small mound of the quinoa in the middle of each serving plate and arrange the trout on top. Froth the sauce with a stick blender and pour it around the fish.

seared mackerel fillet with celeriac and pear remoulade and sardine dressing

For me there is something very British about mackerel. Maybe it is the memory of trips to the coast when I was a young lad – hours in a boat waiting and then all of a sudden lines and lines of mackerel.

Here the mackerel is cooked crisply and I have added pear to a classic celeriac remoulade to lend a sweetness to the slight acidity of the dish. Being a fatty fish, mackerel suits sweet and acidic combinations. I have included some cress to give a spicy bite and the sardine dressing just brings it all together.

If you want to make this dish a little more substantial, you could sauté a few sliced potatoes until golden and serve them under the mackerel.

Serves 6

for the sardine dressing
4 sardine fillets, weighing about 50g each
135ml virgin rapeseed oil
1 egg yolk
juice of ¹/₂ lemon

for the celeriac and pear remoulade
2 egg yolks
1 teaspoon white wine vinegar
30g wholegrain mustard
300ml groundnut oil
30g capers, finely chopped
30g gherkins, finely chopped
2 anchovy fillets, finely chopped
1 teaspoon chopped chervil
1 teaspoon chopped tarragon
1 teaspoon chopped parsley
1 medium celeriac
2 Williams pears

for the seared mackerel
6 mackerel fillets, weighing about 300g each
50ml olive oil, plus extra for drizzling

to garnish
100g land cress or small watercress
Maldon salt

sardine dressing

Trim the sardine fillets, removing any larger bones. Heat 10ml of the oil in a frying pan, add the sardines and fry, skin-side down, over a medium-high heat for 30 seconds. Turn and cook for another 30 seconds, then remove from the pan.

Place the egg yolk in a blender. Turn it on to slow and add half the remaining oil in a steady drizzle. When the mixture is thick, add the sardine fillets and blend until smooth. Blend in the remaining oil, then push the dressing through a fine sieve. Season to taste with salt and pepper and add lemon juice bit by bit until it has a nice acidity.

celeriac and pear remoulade

Whisk the egg yolks, vinegar and mustard together, then slowly add the oil in a steady drizzle, whisking continuously. When all the oil has been incorporated, season with salt and pepper and add the capers, gherkins, anchovies and herbs. Mix well. Peel the celeriac and pears and cut them into long, thin, matchstick-sized pieces. Mix them together and bind with the remoulade sauce – it should be quite creamy.

mackerel

Remove any pin bones with tweezers or pliers. Trim the fillets, maintaining their natural shape, then season them. Heat the olive oil in a large, cast-iron frying pan, add the mackerel and fry, skin-side down, over a medium-high heat for 2–3 minutes, until the edges take on a golden colour. Turn the fillets over and cook for 1 minute. Remove the pan from the heat and allow the mackerel to finish cooking in the residual heat.

serving

At the head of each plate arrange a long line of the remoulade. Top with a little cress. Lay a crisp mackerel fillet in front and place a line of sardine dressing in front of that. Drizzle with olive oil and sprinkle the mackerel with Maldon salt.

crab salad with jellied crab essence and lovage vichysoisse

When I used to take trips to the coast to go fishing, one of my treats was to have a boiled crab sprinkled with vinegar and olive oil and a good grinding of black pepper. I used to sit at the table and slowly pick away at the lovely sweet meat for what seemed like hours.

The whole essence of this dish is freshness, making it a great light starter for a summer dinner party. You only need the white meat from the crab. Save the brown meat for a risotto, or for sandwiches. The raw pea-like taste of the cleavers gives an added lift.

Serves 6

for the jellied crab essence
the shell and claw shells from the crab (see Crab Salad, below)
100ml olive oil
100g carrots, chopped
100g onions, chopped
3 garlic cloves, sliced
50g fennel, chopped
50g celery, chopped
50g tomato purée, or 300g ripe tomatoes, chopped
200ml white wine
2 litres Fish Stock (page 25) or chicken stock (pages 23–24)

for the clarification
50g carrots, chopped
50g celery, chopped
50g onion, chopped
1/2 chicken breast
3 egg whites
1 1/2 gelatine leaves

for the lovage vichyssoise
75g unsalted butter
50g white of leek, chopped
200g potatoes, peeled and sliced
500ml White Chicken Stock (page 23)
200ml milk
75g green of leek, chopped
200g lovage, chopped
50ml double cream

for the crab salad
350g white crabmeat from 1 large cooked cock crab (ask your fishmonger to remove the meat and give you the shells)
120ml mayonnaise, preferably home-made
1 small avocado, peeled, stoned and finely diced
1 small Granny Smith apple, cored and finely diced
12 rocket leaves, shredded
1/4 small iceberg lettuce, finely shredded
2 anchovy fillets, crushed
juice of 1/2 lemon

to garnish
25g chickweed
40g cleavers
a little olive oil

jellied crab essence
Put the crab shells in a pan and smash them with the end of a rolling pin until crushed. Heat the olive oil in a large saucepan until almost smoking, add the crab shells and cook until golden, stirring often to prevent them catching on the bottom of the pan. Add the chopped vegetables and cook for 5 minutes, stirring occasionally. Add the tomato purée or tomatoes and cook for 2–3 minutes. Pour in the white wine and boil until evaporated. Add the stock, bring to the boil and simmer for 1 1/2–2 hours. Strain the stock through a sieve but do not push it through – you do not want the little bits. Leave to cool.

clarification
Place all the vegetables, the chicken breast and egg whites in a food processor and process until well mixed. Add a little of the crab stock and pulse again. Transfer this mixture to a deep saucepan and stir in the crab stock. Place on a low heat and bring to just under the boil, stirring constantly. When you see that a crust is starting to appear, stop stirring and allow the crust to form. Make a small hole to one side of the crust. Simmer for 1–1 1/2 hours without ever letting it boil,

as this would break the crust and cloud the jelly. Then scoop out a ladleful of crust to make a larger hole and carefully ladle the stock out through it a little at a time, pouring it into a sieve lined with a piece of damp muslin and placed over a pan.

Simmer the stock until it has reduced to 300–350ml, then remove from the heat. Soften the gelatine leaves in a bowl of cold water for about 5 minutes, until limp and pliable. Squeeze out excess water and add the gelatine to the stock, stirring until dissolved. Pour the stock into a shallow oblong plastic container so it is about 3cm deep and chill until set: 3–4 hours, or overnight would be better.

lovage vichyssoise
Melt the butter in a thick-bottomed pan, add the white of leek and cook gently for 3–4 minutes, until translucent but not coloured. Add the potatoes, stock and milk, bring to the boil and simmer for 30 minutes. Add the green of leek and the lovage and cook for 2–3 minutes. Purée in a blender until smooth. Push through a fine sieve, then add the double cream. Season to taste and chill. If it is too thick, add a little more milk.

crab salad
Mix the crabmeat with the mayonnaise, avocado and apple. Fold in the shredded rocket and iceberg lettuce. Finally mix in the anchovies, season with salt and pepper and add enough lemon juice to help flavour but not overpower it. Cover and chill until needed.

serving
Place a ring, 5cm in diameter and 5cm deep, in the centre of each serving bowl and fill with the crab salad. Pour some vichyssoise around to a depth of 2cm, then remove the ring. Place 3–5 small spoonfuls of the jellied essence around the crab. Dress the chickweed and cleavers with a little olive oil and place on top of the crab. Drizzle with more olive oil.

crab ravioli with crushed parsnips and hazelnut velouté

I use breadcrumbs in the filling for the ravioli. This makes it far less fatty than the traditional fish mousse filling and allows the true flavour of the crab to shine through. Parsnips go so well with shellfish. Here I have flavoured them with woodruff, a plant that when heated smells a little like new-mown hay or tobacco.

Serves 8

for the crab ravioli
250g white crabmeat
100g fresh white breadcrumbs
25ml double cream
50g brown crabmeat
juice of ¹/₂ lemon
¹/₂ quantity of Pasta Dough (see page 26)
1 egg, lightly beaten
a little hazelnut oil for drizzling

for the crushed parsnips
150g unsalted butter
3 parsnips, peeled and roughly diced
150ml water
5g woodruff flowers or leaves

for the hazelnut velouté
100ml white port
100ml white wine
500ml fish stock
60g toasted hazelnuts, crushed
150ml double cream
100ml milk
30ml hazelnut oil

crab ravioli

Mix the white crabmeat with the breadcrumbs. Add the double cream and then the brown crabmeat. Season with salt and pepper, adding lemon juice to taste. Form into 8 balls and place in the fridge until needed.

Roll out the pasta dough in a pasta machine to the finest setting. Cut out 16 discs with a 10cm cutter. Lightly brush 8 of the discs with the beaten egg and place a ball of crab mix on each one. Next, place the remaining discs on top and pinch the edges of the pasta together, stretching them slightly to shape them around the filling. Make sure there are no air bubbles in the ravioli or they will burst during cooking. Cut with an 8cm cutter – plain or crimped – then pinch the edges together again gently just to make sure of the seal. Blanch in a large pan of boiling salted water for 1–1¹/₂ minutes. Drain well, refresh in cold water, then drain again. Place on a tray, cover with clingfilm and chill until needed.

crushed parsnips

Melt 75g of the butter in a pan, add the parsnips and cook for 5 minutes without colouring. Add the water, bring to the boil, then cover with a tight-fitting lid and simmer for 15–20 minutes, adding the woodruff half way through. Check the parsnips – they should be very tender and all the water should have disappeared. Using a fork, add the remaining butter and mix it in, lightly crushing the parsnips as you go. Season with salt and pepper and keep warm.

hazelnut velouté

Put the port and white wine in a saucepan, bring to the boil and simmer until reduced by three quarters. Immediately add the fish stock, then the crushed hazelnuts, and simmer until the stock is reduced by two thirds. Add the double cream, bring to the boil, then add the milk and bring back to the boil. Transfer to a blender and blend until smooth, adding the hazelnut oil half way through. Push through a fine sieve and season to taste. Keep warm.

serving

Bring a large pan of salted water to the boil, add the ravioli and cook for 3–4 minutes, until tender. Drain and drizzle with a little hazelnut oil, then season lightly.

Place a mound of crushed parsnip in the middle of each serving plate and a ravioli on top of that. Froth the sauce with a stick blender and pour it over the top.

pumpkin gnocchi with crisp pork belly, seared squid and peanut milk

The flavours and textures of this dish go so well together. As you can probably tell from this book, I am very fond of serving fish and meat together. The sweetness of the pumpkin gnocchi combines with the squid to create a match made in heaven. Once again, I like to use the Crown Prince variety of pumpkin because of its lack of water. If you can't get this, use half pumpkin and half baked potato. The peanut milk adds the final touch to bring forth their sweetness. The smaller the squid the better for this dish, as they are so tender.

Serves 6

for the crisp pork belly
1kg piece of boned belly pork
50g unsalted butter
1 carrot, chopped
1 onion, chopped
2 garlic cloves, chopped
1 celery stick, chopped
2 litres White Chicken Stock (page 23)
a sprig of thyme
$1/2$ bay leaf
50ml olive oil

for the pumpkin gnocchi
400g piece of pumpkin, preferably Crown Prince, seeds removed
a little olive oil
65g '00' pasta flour
$1/2$ beaten egg
25g Parmesan cheese, grated
50g unsalted butter

for the peanut milk
50g unsalted butter
$1/2$ onion, sliced
400ml milk
50g peanuts, toasted until golden

for the squid
18 baby squid, no bigger than your little finger in length, cleaned (ask your fishmonger to do this, or see page 52)
30ml olive oil
a few drops of lemon juice

crisp pork belly

Scorch any hairs off the belly pork with a blowtorch. Heat the butter in a casserole large enough to hold the belly, then add all the vegetables and sweat for 4–5 minutes, until softened but not coloured. Add the chicken stock and herbs and bring to the boil. Add the pork and cover with a tight-fitting lid. Place in an oven preheated to 150°C/Gas Mark 2 and cook for 4–5 hours, until the meat is tender enough to pierce easily with a knife. Carefully remove the pork from the stock and place on a tray lined with clingfilm. Cover with another sheet of clingfilm and place a heavy tray on top with a weight. Leave in the fridge overnight. The next day, trim the pork and cut it into strips 2cm thick along the length and then into 4cm pieces. You will need 3–4 pieces per person.

pumpkin gnocchi

Place the pumpkin on a baking tray, drizzle with a little oil and cover with foil. Roast in an oven preheated to 200°C/Gas Mark 6 until the flesh is very tender. Remove from the oven and scrape the flesh off the skin. Push the flesh through a fine sieve. Gently mix the pumpkin with the flour. Season with salt and pepper, then add the egg and Parmesan and stir until the mixture forms a loose ball. Sprinkle the worktop with flour and roll the gnocchi into 2 long sausages. Cut each sausage into 12–15 pieces and shape them into small balls. Lightly press each ball with the back of a fork to make the traditional line marks. Bring a large pan of salted water to the boil and drop in the gnocchi, cooking them in 3 batches. When they rise to the surface, scoop them out of the water into a bowl of cold water.

Drain well, place in a container and sprinkle with just enough olive oil to coat and prevent sticking. Turn the gnocchi over in the olive oil, then place in the fridge until needed.

peanut milk

Heat the butter in a pan, add the onion and sweat for 3–4 minutes. Add the milk, the roasted peanuts and 100ml liquid from cooking the pork belly and simmer slowly for about 30 minutes. Place in a blender and pulse – just to break up the peanuts. Leave to infuse for 1–2 hours, then pass through a sieve and season to taste.

squid

Heat a large, heavy-bottomed frying pan over a medium-high heat. When you can feel the heat coming off it, add half the olive oil and then half the squid. Season the squid with salt and pepper, cook for 1–$1^1/_2$ minutes, then turn. Cook for 1 minute and transfer to a warm plate. Wipe the pan clean and repeat with the remaining oil and squid. When all are cooked, re-season them, adding a few drops of lemon juice.

serving

To finish the belly pork, heat the olive oil in a large frying pan, add the pieces of pork and cook until golden on one side. Flip over and cook the other side until crisp and golden, then season with salt and pepper. Remove from the pan and place on a piece of kitchen paper to remove excess fat.

To finish the gnocchi, heat the butter in a large non-stick pan, add the gnocchi and cook until golden on both sides. Season to taste.

Divide the squid, pumpkin gnocchi and crisp pork belly between 6 bowls. Gently reheat the peanut milk, then froth it up with a stick blender and pour it over everything.

roast quail with marinated baby artichokes and cheltenham beetroot

This is just perfect for dinner parties in spring and summer. Try to use young, tender artichokes and beetroot. The quails are regular size but you could use jumbo quail for a bigger portion. They are roasted with yarrow, which grows everywhere in season. Its lovely bitter flavour plays off nicely against the sweetness of the beetroot. Cheltenham beetroot has a good flavour and an unusual elongated shape but you could, of course, use ordinary beetroot if necessary. If you can't get the candy-stripe beetroot, look for chioggia instead.

Serves 4

for the marinade
500ml water
150ml white wine
200ml olive oil
150ml white wine vinegar
50g honey
50g fresh horseradish root, peeled and
   sliced
1 bay leaf
a sprig of thyme
10 black peppercorns
10 coriander leaves

for the artichokes
8 baby artichokes
50ml olive oil
100ml orange juice

for the beetroot
2 young candy stripe beetroot
2 young Cheltenham beetroot

for the roast quail
4 quail
4 sprigs of yarrow
50ml olive oil

to garnish
20ml orange juice
50ml olive oil
plantain leaves
dandelion leaves

marinade
Put all the ingredients in a pan and bring to the boil. Reduce the heat and simmer for 20 minutes.

artichokes
Remove the outer leaves from the artichokes, leaving just the small, tender inner leaves. Trim the base, leaving about 6cm of stalk – the stalk is also good to eat. Peel the stalks. Slice 4 artichokes finely on a mandoline, place them in the marinade and bring to the boil. Cook for 2–3 minutes, until the artichokes are limp. Remove from the liquid, drain and leave to cool. Add the remaining artichokes to the pan and cook until tender. Remove with a slotted spoon, place in a blender with the olive oil and orange juice and blend to a purée. Season to taste.

Leave the cooking liquid to cool, then divide it in half. Return the sliced artichokes to one half of the liquid.

beetroot
Peel the candy stripe beetroot and slice them as finely as possible on a mandoline. Place in the other half of the stock. Keep both the artichokes and candy stripe beetroot in their stock for 3–4 hours.

Meanwhile, wrap the Cheltenham beetroot in foil with a little water and bake in an oven preheated to 160°C/Gas Mark 3 for 30–40 minutes, until tender, turning them over half way through. Peel them while still warm, then slice them lengthways. Put to one side.

quail
Season the quail with salt and pepper. Crush the yarrow between your fingers and sprinkle it over the quail. Heat the olive oil in an ovenproof frying pan over a medium-high heat. Lay the quail in on their sides, cook for 2 minutes, until golden, then turn on to the other side and cook for 2 minutes more. Place them on their backs with the breast up and transfer the pan to an oven preheated to 180°C/Gas Mark 4. Cook for 8 minutes, until tender. Remove from the oven and leave to rest for 5 minutes, then joint each bird into 2 legs and 2 breasts. Cut the breast in half and season again.

garnish
Whisk the orange juice with 2 tablespoons of the marinade and the olive oil, then season to taste. Toss the plantain and dandelion leaves with some of this dressing.

serving
Remove the beetroot and artichokes from their liquid and drain well. Place a streak of artichoke purée on each serving plate and arrange the quail, sliced beetroot, candy stripe beetroot and sliced artichokes neatly on the plates. Scatter the plantain and dandelion leaves over the plate and drizzle with a little more orange dressing.

cannelloni of veal breast and burdock with celeriac cream, horseradish froth and wood sorrel

Veal breast is one of those cuts of meat that don't get as much attention as they should. Here we have used it as a stuffing, but sometimes we stuff the veal breast itself – with snails, nettles and bay bolete mushrooms.

Burdock leaves are used here rather than the root. They have a bitterness that complements the dish. The cannelloni is not really pasta but finely sliced celeriac, which ties in with the celeriac cream. Oxalis (wood sorrel) adds a good lemony tang. You could use oxtail, ox shin or shoulder of lamb instead of veal, and the burdock could be replaced by spinach or rocket.

Serves 8

for the veal
1.5kg veal breast, on the bone
100ml olive oil
1 celery stick, coarsely chopped
1 carrot, coarsely chopped
1 onion, coarsely chopped
1 pig's trotter, split in half (you could ask your butcher to do this)
100ml red wine
1 litre Brown Veal or Brown Beef Stock (page 25)
1 bay leaf
a sprig of thyme

for the celeriac and celeriac cream
1 large celeriac
2 medium celeriac, peeled and chopped
200ml milk
200ml double cream
100g unsalted butter, diced

for the cannelloni filling
12 young burdock leaves
50ml olive oil
50g carrot, finely diced
50g onion, finely diced
25g celery, finely diced
3 garlic cloves, finely diced
100g girolle mushrooms, finely diced
100ml double cream

for the horseradish froth
250ml Brown Chicken Stock (page 24)
150ml double cream
15g fresh horseradish, grated
200ml milk
30g horseradish relish (bought is fine)
1 teaspoon white wine vinegar
2g powdered lecithin

to garnish
a little olive oil
100g small chanterelle mushrooms
20g oxalis (wood sorrel)

veal breast
Trim the veal breast, removing the bones and any silver skin. Heat the olive oil in a large frying pan until very hot, then add the veal breast and fry until golden brown all over. Transfer it to a casserole and add the vegetables, trotter and red wine. Place on the heat and bring to the boil. Add the stock and herbs, bring back to the boil, then cover and place in an oven preheated to 160°C/Gas Mark 3. Cook for 3½–4 hours, until the veal is very tender. Remove the meat and trotter from the casserole. Strain the cooking liquid into a clean pan and simmer until reduced by half.

Pull the meat apart into long shreds. Chop the trotter meat and add to the veal. Put to one side.

celeriac and celeriac cream
Peel the large celeriac and slice it on a mandoline to get 16 good thin slices. Keep the trimmings. Blanch the celeriac slices in a large pan of boiling salted water for about 1 minute, until translucent. Drain and refresh in cold water, then drain again and place on a cloth to dry a little.

Put the celeriac trimmings, chopped celeriac, milk and cream in a saucepan and bring to the boil. Simmer until the celeriac is tender, then transfer the mixture to a blender and blend to a smooth purée. Mix in the butter bit by bit. Season with salt and pepper and keep warm.

cannelloni filling
Blanch the burdock leaves in a large pan of boiling water for about 30 seconds, then drain, refresh in cold water and drain again. Mince or chop finely and set aside.

Heat the oil in a large sauté pan, add the vegetables and cook for 3–4 minutes. Add the garlic and mushrooms and cook until dry. Add the reserved veal breast and trotter meat, then add just enough of the reduced veal cooking liquid to moisten. Stir in the double cream and burdock, bring to the boil and season to taste. The mixture should be moist and sloppy, not dry. Remove from the heat and set aside.

horseradish froth
Put the stock, cream and grated fresh horseradish in a pan, bring to the boil and simmer until reduced by half. Add the milk and horseradish relish and bring back to the boil. Season to taste and add the vinegar. Mix in the lecithin with a stick blender, push the mixture through a fine sieve and keep warm.

Heat a little olive oil in a frying pan and toss the mushrooms in it until limp. Season and drain. Keep warm.

Lay the celeriac slices out on a work surface. Place a spoonful of veal mix in the centre of each one and roll up to form 16 small cannelloni. Trim the ends and place on a buttered baking tray. Season, then place in an oven preheated to 180°C/Gas Mark 4 for 3–4 minutes to heat through. Warm the celeriac cream and place a few streaks across each serving plate. Arrange the cannelloni on top, scatter with the chanterelles and wood sorrel, then pour over a little of the reduced veal cooking juices.

Froth the horseradish sauce with a stick blender and spoon it over the cannelloni.

croquette of pig's trotter with salt cod brandade

Here we have the creaminess of the salt cod against the richness of the pig's trotter, and a contrasting crispness from the breaded coating on the trotter. One of the delights of this dish is that when you first cut into the croquettes they release all the aromas of the trotter. If you don't fancy the brandade with them, they also go well with a purée of haricot beans or parsnips, or just good old plain mash.

Serves 8

for the brandade
300g very fresh cod fillet
30g sea salt
grated zest of $^1/_2$ lemon
3 garlic cloves, 1 finely chopped and 2 sliced
$^1/_2$ sprig of thyme
300ml milk
180g Desiree potatoes, peeled and finely sliced
50ml extra virgin olive oil

for the croquettes
4 pig's trotters
100ml olive oil
2 large onions, 1 finely chopped and 1 roughly chopped
2 carrots, roughly chopped
1 celery stick, roughly chopped
6 garlic cloves, chopped
1 bay leaf
3 sprigs of savory or thyme
2 litres Brown Veal or Brown Beef Stock (page 25)
200g spinach, blanched in boiling water for 1 minute, squeezed to remove excess water and minced or finely chopped
vegetable or rapeseed oil for deep-frying

for coating
50g plain flour, seasoned with salt and pepper
3 eggs, lightly whisked
200g fresh breadcrumbs

salting the cod
Pat the cod dry and sprinkle with the salt, lemon zest, finely chopped garlic and thyme. Cover and leave to marinate in the fridge overnight. The next day there will be a pool of juices from the cod. Discard these, rinse the cod and pat dry.

pig's trotters
Remove any dirt or nails from the trotters. Singe off any hairs with a blowtorch and rinse the trotters under cold water. Heat 50ml of the olive oil in a large casserole, add the roughly chopped onion, carrots and celery and cook until golden. Add half the garlic, plus the bay leaf and savory or thyme, then the stock and trotters. Bring to the boil, cover the casserole and transfer to an oven preheated to 150°C/Gas Mark 2. Cook for 3–4 hours, until the trotters are tender. Remove from the oven and leave the trotters to cool in the stock. When cool, remove the skin and meat from the trotters and cut them both into 5mm dice. Put to one side.

Strain the cooking liquid and skim off the fat. Pour half the liquid into a saucepan and simmer until reduced by half, to give a rich sauce. Season to taste and set aside.

In a large frying pan, heat the remaining olive oil, add the finely chopped onion and the remaining garlic and cook for 3–4 minutes. Add the diced pig's trotters and a ladleful of the unreduced cooking liquid. Cook, stirring constantly, until it starts to amalgamate and thicken. Mix in the spinach and season to taste. Place 8 rings, 8cm in diameter and 2cm deep, on a baking tray and divide the mixture between them. Leave overnight in the fridge to set.

coating
The next day, unmould the trotter mixture, running a knife round each one to loosen. You should have 8 nice discs. Put the flour in a bowl, the eggs in another and the breadcrumbs in a third. Coat the trotter cylinders in the flour, removing any excess. Then place them in the egg, coat evenly and remove the excess. Finally roll them in the breadcrumbs until evenly coated. Place in the fridge to firm up a little, then dip them in the egg again and then in the breadcrumbs. They must be totally covered or they will leak when fried, so check them over thoroughly. Return to the fridge until needed.

brandade
Bring the milk to the boil in a saucepan and add the sliced garlic plus the cod and potato. Simmer until the cod is cooked and the potatoes tender. Drain off the liquid and place the cod and potatoes in a food processor. Pulse a little until a coarse purée is obtained, adding a little oil and milk alternately to give a stiff consistency. Remove from the food processor and keep warm.

serving
Heat the oil for deep-frying to 165°C in a deep-fat fryer or a large, deep saucepan. Carefully place the croquettes in the oil and cook until golden. Remove from the oil, drain on kitchen paper and keep warm.

Heat the reduced trotter juices. Place a mound of brandade in the middle of each serving bowl and pour a little of the trotter juices over it. Place a croquette on top.

snail and wild garlic 'lasagne' with braised beef shin and roasted garlic froth

It isn't too much of a jump to put wild garlic with snails. I see plenty of them eating it when I go garlic picking. We get our snails from a friend called Tony, at L'Escargot Anglais in Hereford. He does all the laborious work for us and delivers them blanched and out of their shells. The lasagne isn't pasta but thin kohlrabi sheets, which allows us to construct the dish at the last minute – essential in a busy kitchen. The roasted garlic froth is a nice light way of finishing it all off.

Serves 6

for the braised beef shin
100ml olive oil
1 beef shin, weighing about 2kg
1 onion, sliced
4 garlic cloves, chopped
2 carrots, chopped
150ml red wine
500ml Brown Chicken Stock (page 24)
1 bay leaf
a sprig of thyme

for the snail and wild garlic lasagne
200g unsalted butter
1 onion, chopped
2 garlic cloves, chopped
30 prepared snails (see My Suppliers, *page 182)*
1 stick of liquorice root
1/2 star anise
200ml red wine
500ml Brown Chicken Stock (page 24)
200g wild garlic, blanched for 30 seconds and finely chopped
2 large kohlrabi

for the roasted garlic froth
2 heads of garlic
a little olive oil
100ml double cream
200ml milk

braised beef shin
Heat the olive oil in a large casserole until you can feel the heat coming off it. Add the beef shin and cook for 3–4 minutes, until golden all over. Remove from the pan and drain off the oil. Add the onion, garlic and carrots to the pan and cook until golden. Place the beef shin on top and pour in the red wine. Cook for 2 minutes, then add the chicken stock, bay leaf and thyme and bring to the boil. Cover with a tight-fitting lid and transfer to an oven preheated to 160°C/Gas Mark 3. Cook for 3½–4 hours, until the beef has no resistance when prodded with a roasting fork or skewer. Remove the shin from the casserole. Strain off the juices into a saucepan, bring to the boil and simmer until reduced by half. Remove the meat from the shin in muscle groups and pull it apart a little into shreds. Add enough of the cooking juices to moisten, then season with salt and pepper and keep warm.

snails
Heat 100g of the butter in a saucepan, add the onion and garlic and cook for 3–4 minutes, until soft and translucent. Add the snails, liquorice stick and star anise and cook for 5 minutes, without colouring. Add the red wine and simmer slowly until reduced by half. Finally add the chicken stock, bring to the boil and simmer for 1–1½ hours, until the snails are tender. Drain the snails.

Heat 50g of the remaining butter in a separate pan, add the snails and cook for 1 minute. Add the blanched wild garlic, then remove from the heat and set aside.

kohlrabi
Peel the kohlrabi and cut it into 18 discs about 2mm thick, using a mandoline or a very sharp knife. Blanch in a pan of boiling salted water for about 30 seconds, then drain and refresh in cold water. Drain again and set aside.

roasted garlic froth
Remove as much of the excess papery white skin from the garlic as you can, leaving the heads intact. Coat the garlic in a little olive oil, sprinkle with sea salt and wrap in foil. Place on a baking tray and roast in an oven preheated to 160°C/Gas Mark 3 for 30–35 minutes, until tender, turning over half way through.

Remove the foil packages from the oven and pop the garlic cloves out of their skins into a saucepan. Add 100ml of the reduced cooking juices from the beef shin, plus the double cream, and cook for 10–15 minutes on a slow simmer. Add the milk, bring to the boil, then immediately blend until smooth. Push through a fine sieve into a clean pan. Season to taste and keep warm.

serving
Reheat the snails and the beef shin. Add a few spoonfuls of the reduced beef cooking juices to the snails.

Heat up the kohlrabi slices in the remaining 50g of butter and 2 teaspoons of water in a frying pan, then season to taste. Bring the reduced beef cooking juices to the boil. Froth up the garlic sauce with a stick blender.

Put one disc of kohlrabi in each serving dish and place a good spoonful of beef shin on top, leaving a little gap around the edges. Pour a spoonful of beef juices over the meat. Top with another slice of kohlrabi, then arrange 5 snails with the wild garlic on top. Pour another small spoonful of beef juices over. Top with the remaining sheet of kohlrabi, making it look as if it has been draped. Add a few turns of the peppermill and spoon over the roasted garlic froth.

cabbage stuffed with duck confit, with confit of duck gizzards and bone marrow

Stuffed cabbage has frequently appeared on my menus. Whether stuffed with duck confit, quail or venison, it adds an extra element to a main course, as well as being able to stand alone in its own right.

Here it is served with a confit of duck gizzards and some poached bone marrow. For the photo we garnished it with diced cabbage and girolles but it is up to you. Try something earthy to go with it, or even a blanquette of beans.

Serves 8

16 Confit Duck Gizzards (see page 17)
200g middle veal bone marrow, removed
    from the bone (ask your butcher to do
    this for you) and soaked in salted water
    overnight
Maldon salt

for the stuffed cabbage
1 green cabbage (we use Primo)
200g duck leg meat
100g lean pork
75g pork fat
40g bread, soaked in a little milk
200g Duck Confit meat (see page 16),
    chopped into smallish pieces
25g garlic, finely chopped
50g shallots, finely chopped
a pinch of grated nutmeg
a pinch of ground cumin
50g unsalted butter
30ml Cognac

for braising the stuffed cabbage
50ml olive oil
200g mixed root vegetables, such as carrot,
    swede and celeriac, diced
600ml Brown Chicken Stock (page 24)

for the sauce
250ml Brown Veal Stock (page 25)
    or Brown Beef Stock (page 25)
50g unsalted butter

for the girolles
150g girolle mushrooms
50ml olive oil
25g unsalted butter

stuffed cabbage
Remove the leaves from the cabbage and pick the best 12 – they should be unblemished and have a vibrant colour. Blanch in a large pan of boiling salted water for 30–45 seconds, until supple, then drain and refresh immediately in cold water. Drain again and cut out the centre stem from 4 of the leaves.

In a mincer, coarsely mince the duck leg meat, pork, pork fat and the 4 cabbage leaves. Mix well together. Squeeze out the bread and beat it into the mixture. Stir in the remaining ingredients, plus some salt and pepper, then fry a small spoonful of the mixture in a pan and taste to check the seasoning. Adjust if necessary.

Divide the mixture into 8 balls. Take the 8 remaining cabbage leaves and cut the bottom of the stem away in a V shape. Put a ball of the stuffing in the middle of each leaf and wrap it up into a rough ball, then wrap tightly in clingfilm to get a perfectly round shape. Chill for 2 hours to set the shape.

braising
Heat the oil in a casserole, add the root vegetables and cook until lightly browned. Add the chicken stock and bring to the boil. Remove the clingfilm from the cabbage balls and carefully place them on the root vegetables – make sure they fit snugly as this will help them hold their shape. Place the lid on, transfer to an oven preheated to 180°C/Gas Mark 4 and cook for 20 minutes. Remove the lid and cook for a further 20 minutes, spooning the sauce over the cabbage balls every 5 minutes. Remove them from the braising liquor and re-shape them into perfect balls with clingfilm. Keep warm.

sauce
Strain off the braising juices from the casserole into a clean pan and add the veal stock. Bring to the boil and simmer until reduced to about 200ml. Whisk in the butter a little at a time. Season to taste and keep warm.

gizzards
Heat a little of the fat from the gizzards in a frying pan, cut the gizzards in half and sauté until golden. Remove from the heat.

girolles
Wash the girolles quickly to remove excess dirt, then trim the ends neatly. Heat the oil and butter in a large frying pan until the butter is foaming. Add the girolles and cook for 1–2 minutes, until tender. Season to taste and drain.

bone marrow
Drain and rinse the soaked bone marrow and cut it into 16 slices about 4mm thick – do more if you have more marrow. In a large frying pan, heat 2cm salted water to just under simmering point. Remove from the heat, add the bone marrow and let it heat through for about 2 minutes. Take the marrow out when it is opaque and soft. If you leave it in too long, it will melt.

serving
Place a stuffed cabbage ball in the middle of each serving plate. Arrange the marrow, duck gizzards and girolles round the cabbage, leaving a piece of marrow for the top. Pour over the sauce, put the remaining marrow on top and sprinkle the top of the cabbage with a little Maldon salt.

seared duck foie gras with lambs' tongues, quince and maury syrup

We use duck foie gras for this recipe as opposed to goose, which we prefer to use for a foie gras terrine (see page 46). The accompanying garnish includes the sweetness of quince, the slight bitterness of walnuts, and the crispness of fried tongue. You could replace the quince with Pickled Apples, the tongue with Duck Gizzard Confit and the Maury Syrup with White Port and Verjus Syrup, all of which can be found in the Storecupboard section, pp16–22. The foie gras is sprinkled with Maldon salt to give a burst of salty crispness.

Serves 6

1 lobe of duck foie gras, weighing 650–700g

for the quince
2 quince
300ml red wine
150ml port
30ml red wine vinegar
100g granulated sugar
4cm piece of cinnamon stick
¹/₂ bay leaf

for the lambs' tongues
1.5 litres water
¹/₂ carrot, chopped
¹/₂ onion, chopped
¹/₂ celery stick, chopped
2 garlic cloves, chopped
1 bay leaf
3 lambs' tongues
75ml olive oil

to garnish
24 walnut halves
100g rocket
25ml olive oil
Maury Syrup (see page 20), for drizzling
Maldon salt

quince
Peel the quince and cut them into quarters, removing the core. Place all the other ingredients in a saucepan and bring to the boil. Add the quince quarters and simmer gently for 40 minutes–1 hour, until tender. Leave to cool in the cooking liquid (they can be kept like this in a sealed jar in the fridge for 2–3 weeks). Drain and cut into 18 slices.

lambs' tongues
Place the water, vegetables and bay leaf in a pan, bring to the boil and simmer for 20 minutes. Add the lambs' tongues and simmer for 45 minutes–1 hour, until tender. Leave them in the stock until just cool enough to handle, then peel off the tough skin from each tongue. Return the tongues to the pan and leave until completely cold. Drain, dry and cut each one lengthways into 4 slices, maintaining the shape.

foie gras
Allow the foie gras to soften to room temperature for 1 hour. Pull apart carefully along the seams. Pull away the thick blood vessel, then carefully remove the larger tubes and vessels; don't worry about the smaller ones.

Cut the foie gras into 6 thick portions and place in the fridge until needed. To cook, heat a heavy frying pan and, when you can feel the heat, place the foie gras in the pan – with no oil. Cook over a very high heat for 1–1¹/₂ minutes, until golden, then turn over and cook for a further minute. Cooking for too long will mean that it loses more fat and becomes a greasy mess. Remove from the pan and keep warm.

serving
To finish the lambs' tongues, heat the olive oil in a large frying pan until it is almost smoking, then add the lambs' tongues and cook until golden and crisp underneath. Flip them over and cook the other side until golden. Season to taste, remove from the pan and drain well. Repeat this with the quince slices and in the last 10 seconds throw in the walnuts and turn the quince carefully.

Dress the rocket with the olive oil and some Maury Syrup, then season to taste. Arrange the rocket in the middle of each serving plate with the tongue, quince and walnuts. Drizzle with Maury Syrup and place the foie gras on top. Drizzle with a little more Maury Syrup, sprinkle with Maldon salt and serve.

poached duck eggs with chorizo purée, tomato confit, serrano ham and white onion soup

Eggs don't get used much these days in top restaurants – such a shame, as they are terrific when cooked correctly. I have chosen duck's eggs rather than hen's because of their richer flavour. The chorizo purée is not spicy, although you could substitute a spicier chorizo if you prefer.

This is almost breakfast in a bowl – egg, sausage, bacon and tomato. As always, you don't have to use these ingredients. How about black pudding with slow-cooked onion, poached egg and potato soup? Get thinking!

Serves 6

3 slices of Serrano ham
12 Tomato Confit halves (see page 17)

for the white onion soup
100g unsalted butter
500g white onions, sliced
700ml chicken stock (pages 23–24)
200ml milk

for the chorizo purée
200ml double cream
100ml milk
300g medium chorizo, finely minced

for the duck eggs
2 tablespoons white wine vinegar
6 large duck eggs

white onion soup

Melt the butter in a large saucepan and add the onions. Cover and cook for 5 minutes, stirring occasionally, until softened but not coloured. Add the chicken stock, bring to the boil and cook for 30 minutes. Add the milk and simmer gently for 10 minutes. Transfer to a blender and blend until smooth. Push through a fine sieve into another saucepan and season to taste. If the soup is too thick, add a touch more milk; if it is too thin, simmer until reduced to the desired consistency.

serrano ham

Cut each slice of ham in half, place on a baking sheet lined with baking parchment and cover with another sheet of parchment and another tray. Bake in an oven preheated to 180°C/Gas Mark 4 until crisp, checking from time to time. Remove from the oven and leave to cool.

chorizo purée

Bring the cream and milk to the boil in a saucepan and whisk in the minced chorizo. Boil for 30 seconds, then transfer to a blender and blend until smooth.

duck eggs

Add a good pinch of salt and the vinegar to a small, deep saucepan of water and bring to the boil. Turn down the heat to a simmer. Break each egg into a ramekin and slide them gently into the water (breaking them into a ramekin first means that if the yolk breaks, you haven't messed up the water). It's best to cook 6 eggs in 2 batches. Cook for 2–3 minutes, until the whites have set but the yolks are still runny. Remove with a slotted spoon and place in a bowl of iced water (this means you can poach the eggs well in advance of serving). Once they have cooled down, trim the egg white with a knife to give a neat shape. Return to fresh water until needed.

tomato confit

Cut the tomato confit halves into small rounds with a 3cm cutter. Chop the trimmings and warm gently in a pan.

serving

Reheat the poached eggs by putting them in a saucepan of boiling salted water for 30 seconds–1 minute. Remove from the pan and place on a tray lined with a cloth to drain.

Draw a line of chorizo purée across each of 6 wide serving bowls. Place a spoonful of the chopped tomato trimmings to the left and place an egg on top. Place 2 discs of tomato in the bowl. Rest a piece of ham up against the egg and grind a little pepper on top of the egg. At the table, pour a ladleful of soup over each bowlful and serve.

main courses

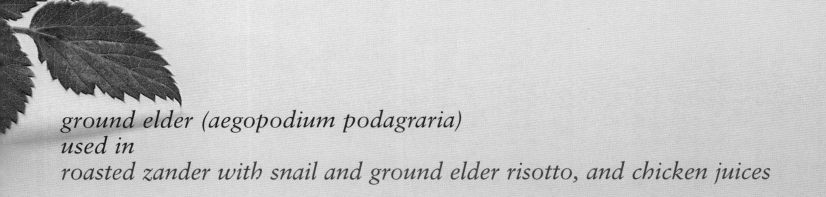

ground elder (aegopodium podagraria)
used in
roasted zander with snail and ground elder risotto, and chicken juices

roasted zander with snail and ground elder risotto, and chicken juices

Zander is a ferocious hunter that devours practically any other fish. It is one of the very few meaty freshwater fish. Here it is served with chicken juices made from chicken wings (which are themselves made into a confit), plus a snail and ground elder risotto. If you ask any gardener, they will tell you that ground elder is a real pest. Once you have it, it is very difficult to get rid of, so why not eat it? Make sure you use the young spring leaves. They can even be served simply wilted and buttered. In the photo, this dish is accompanied by asparagus and sautéed pied de mouton mushrooms.

Serves 6

for the chicken wings and juices
18 chicken wings
25g sea salt
2 garlic cloves, finely chopped
200g duck fat
50ml olive oil
100ml white wine
1 litre Brown Chicken Stock (page 24)
25g unsalted butter, diced

for the snail and ground elder risotto
150g young ground elder leaves
400ml chicken stock (pages 23–24)
50g unsalted butter
1 small onion, finely chopped
1 garlic clove, chopped
200g carnaroli risotto rice
125g prepared and cooked snails (see My Suppliers, page 182)
2 teaspoons Mascarpone cheese

for the roasted zander
6 x 175g zander fillets
50ml olive oil
25g unsalted butter
25ml hazelnut oil
Maldon salt

chicken wings
Joint the chicken wings by slicing through the ball and socket joint at either end – you need 12 of the middles for the confit and all the ends for the chicken juices. Chop both end bits of knuckle off the middle section and discard.

Sprinkle the 12 middle sections with the salt and garlic, cover and leave in the fridge for 6–8 hours, then rinse lightly and dry. Melt the duck fat in a casserole dish, add the chicken wings, then place in an oven preheated to 140°C/Gas Mark 1 and cook for 2 hours. The wings should be very tender. Remove them from the fat, allow to cool a little, then push out the 2 bones in each wing. The wings can be stored like this until needed.

chicken juices
Heat the olive oil in a saucepan, add the chicken winglet bones and cook until golden. Pour in the white wine to deglaze the pan, scraping the base of the pan with a wooden spoon to dislodge any sediment. Cook until the wine has evaporated, then add the chicken stock and simmer until reduced to 200ml. Strain the juices into a pan and keep warm.

snail and ground elder risotto
Blanch the ground elder in a large pan of boiling salted water for 30–45 seconds, then drain well. Mince or chop very finely and set aside. Bring the stock to simmering point in a small saucepan. Heat the butter in a separate pan, add the onion and garlic and cook for 5 minutes, until translucent. Add the rice and cook for 3–4 minutes, until translucent. Add the snails, then add 100ml of the stock, stirring continuously. When this has been absorbed, add another 100ml. Continue stirring and adding stock in this way until the rice is al dente – tender with a little bite. The rice should take 17–18 minutes altogether. About 5 minutes before it is done, stir in the ground elder; adding it at the end helps maintain its fresh colour. Mix in the Mascarpone cheese for a creamy texture and season to taste.

roasted zander
Trim the zander fillets and remove any small pin bones. Heat the olive oil in a large frying pan, add the butter, then add the zander fillets, skin-side down. Cook over a medium heat for 3–5 minutes, until the fish is golden underneath and changes from opaque to white at the sides. Remove the pan from the heat and turn the fish over. Leave for a minute to complete the cooking in the heat of the pan.

serving
Heat a little of the duck fat from the chicken wing confit and cook the wings on both sides until golden and crisp.

Reheat the chicken juices if necessary and whisk in the unsalted butter a little at a time.

Place a mound of snail risotto on each serving plate and arrange the chicken wings around it. Place the zander on top and spoon the chicken juices over. Drizzle with the hazelnut oil and sprinkle with Maldon salt.

brill fillet with salsify and artichokes, hazelnut emulsion, and red wine and tarragon jus

The brill is cooked on top of the stove to give it a pleasing textural contrast; you could, if you wish, poach it in the salsify bouillon instead. The nuttiness of the hazelnuts goes well with the salsify and artichokes, while the tarragon adds a light aniseed tang – liquorice would work very well too. Red wine is a good match for brill, as it is for any meaty fish – cod, monkfish, turbot or John Dory.

At the restaurant we serve this with buttered alexanders or wilted spinach and some creamed potatoes. We also serve it with Duck Gizzard Confit (see page 17).

Serves 4

for the salsify and artichokes
75ml olive oil
1/2 fennel bulb, sliced
1 carrot, sliced
1 onion, finely sliced
1 garlic clove, crushed
10 coriander seeds, crushed
5 black peppercorns, crushed
1 bay leaf
100ml white wine
200ml Fish Stock (page 25)
200ml water
50ml hazelnut oil
1/2 lemon
4 salsify stalks
6 poivrade (baby) artichokes
25g unsalted butter

for the hazelnut emulsion
1 egg yolk
50ml hazelnut oil

for the red wine and tarragon jus
125g unsalted butter
2 large shallots, finely diced
400ml red wine (Bandol or Cabernet)
400ml Fish Stock (page 25)
30ml double cream
2 sprigs of tarragon

for the brill
50ml olive oil
4 x 150g pieces of brill
30g unsalted butter

salsify and artichokes
Heat 50ml of the olive oil in a large saucepan, add the fennel, carrot, onion and garlic and cook for 4 minutes without colouring. Add all the other ingredients except the salsify, artichokes and butter, squeezing in the juice from the lemon and then adding the lemon half too. Bring to the boil, then reduce the heat and simmer for 20 minutes.

Peel the salsify quickly and rinse well, then cut into pieces about 6cm long. Place in the simmering stock and cook for 3–4 minutes.

Remove the small bottom leaves of the artichokes and then remove the large leaves. Snap off the stem, leaving about 2–3cm of it attached. Peel the stem and continue removing the leaves until only the tender inner leaves are left. Cut off the pointed top bit, then add the artichokes to the simmering stock and cook for 5–6 minutes, until both the salsify and artichokes are tender. They can be left in the stock to cool down until needed.

hazelnut emulsion
Place the egg yolk in a bowl and whisk lightly. Pour in 300ml of the warm salsify cooking stock drop by drop, whisking all the time. Then whisk in the hazelnut oil drop by drop. Season with salt and pepper and pour into a small pan. Keep warm but do not let it boil.

red wine and tarragon jus
Heat 25g of the butter in a saucepan, add the shallots and cook for 3 minutes without colouring. Add the red wine and simmer until reduced by half, then add the fish stock and reduce by half again. Add the cream and tarragon and bring back to the boil. Lower the heat and gently whisk in the remaining butter a little at a time. Season to taste and keep warm.

brill
Heat the olive oil in a large frying pan. Season the brill with salt and pepper and then put it in the pan, skin-side down. Add the butter and cook over a medium heat for 2–3 minutes, until golden brown underneath. Flip it over and cook for 1–2 minutes. The thickness of the fillet will determine the exact cooking time; it should be only just done. Remove from the pan and keep warm.

serving
Drain the salsify and artichokes and cut the artichokes into quarters. Heat the butter and the remaining 25ml of olive oil in a frying pan, add the salsify and artichokes and cook until a light golden brown. Drain and season.

Toss the salsify and artichokes in the hazelnut emulsion and arrange on each serving plate. Place the brill in the middle of the place and spoon the red wine and tarragon jus around.

brandade (poached cod, garlic purée and potato gnocchi)

Brandade is a rough salt cod pâté from the south of France. There is a difference of opinion over whether potato should be included in the original recipe. What I have done here is look at the ingredients and use them in a different way. When eaten together, they should resemble the original. You could replace the garlic purée with wilted wild garlic in the spring, and pan-fry the cod if you wish.

Serves 4

750g piece of cod fillet, cut from the top
   section
50g sea salt
400ml milk
1 bay leaf
a sprig of thyme
1/2 garlic clove, finely sliced
2g powdered lecithin
a few cracked black peppercorns
olive oil for drizzling

for the potato gnocchi
1kg Desiree potatoes
85g '00' pasta flour
1/2 beaten egg
olive oil for sprinkling
50g unsalted butter

for the garlic purée
3 heads of garlic
50ml olive oil
50ml milk
100ml double cream

preparing the cod
Make sure there are no bones left in the fillet and trim off any stray bits. Sprinkle with the sea salt, wrap in clingfilm and leave in the fridge for 6 hours.

potato gnocchi
Bake the potatoes in an oven preheated to 180–200°C/Gas Mark 4–6 for 1¼–1½ hours, until tender – if you insert a knife, it should come out clean. Immediately cut the potatoes in half to allow the steam to escape. Scoop out the flesh and push it through a fine sieve into a large bowl, trying to work the potato as little as possible. Allow to cool slightly, then cut in the flour and some salt and pepper with a knife. Finally add the beaten egg and mix until it forms a ball. Leave to rest for 5–10 minutes while you bring a large pan of salted water to the boil.

Sprinkle the worktop with flour and roll the potato mix into 2 long sausages. Cut each sausage into 12–15 pieces and shape them into small balls. Lightly press each ball with the back of a fork to make the traditional line marks on it. Cook the gnocchi in the boiling water in 3 batches – they are done when they rise to the surface. Scoop them out of the water and place in a bowl of cold water, then drain, place in a container and sprinkle with enough olive oil to coat. Turn the gnocchi over in the olive oil and place in the fridge until needed.

garlic purée
Remove the excess papery white skin from the garlic heads, then coat them in the olive oil and wrap in foil, including any remaining oil in the package. Place in an oven preheated to 180°C/Gas Mark 4 and cook for 30–40 minutes, turning occasionally, until tender. Pop the garlic cloves out of their skins, reserving the oil.

Place the garlic in a small saucepan with the milk and double cream and bring to the boil. Transfer to a blender and blend to a smooth purée, drizzling in the reserved oil little by little. Season to taste and keep warm.

cooking the cod
Remove the cod from the fridge and scrape off excess salt. Pour the milk into a saucepan big enough to hold the cod snugly. Add the bay leaf, thyme and garlic and heat to just under boiling point. Pull to one side and leave to infuse for 1 hour.

Reheat the milk, add the cod and poach gently for about 5 minutes, depending on thickness; it should be only just cooked. Remove the cod from the milk, drain well and keep warm. Strain the milk into another pan and, using a stick blender, mix in the lecithin. Season with salt and pepper and keep warm.

serving
To reheat the gnocchi, heat the butter in a large, non-stick frying pan, add the gnocchi and cook until golden on both sides. Season to taste with salt and pepper.

Place a circle of garlic purée on each serving plate, arrange the gnocchi on top and then the poached cod. Froth the sauce with a stick blender, and spoon it over the fish. Sprinkle the fish with a little cracked black pepper and drizzle a little olive oil around.

home-salted cod with roasted tomatoes, chickpeas and anchovy dressing

This is a very Mediterranean dish, just right for light eating. The secret lies in salting the cod yourself so you get a firm but moist piece of fish with a slightly salty taste. Roasting the tomatoes concentrates the flavour and brings out their sweetness. Serve with a rocket and grilled vegetable salad.

Serves 4

50g baby cavolo nero leaves

for the home-salted cod
1kg cod fillet (middle section would be best), scaled and pin-boned
30g sea salt
2 teaspoons sugar
zest of 1/2 lemon
zest of 1/2 orange
a sprig of thyme
50ml olive oil

for the chickpeas
200g chickpeas, rinsed, then soaked in cold water overnight
50ml olive oil
1 small onion, finely chopped
1/2 small fennel bulb, finely chopped
3 garlic cloves, chopped
bottled spring water, to cover
2 sprigs of savory
2 strips of orange zest
50ml orange juice
1 teaspoon cumin seeds, lightly toasted in a dry frying pan
15ml red wine vinegar

for the roasted tomatoes
8 small plum tomatoes
50ml olive oil
8–10 basil leaves, torn

for the roasted piquillo peppers
4 small, fresh piquillo peppers (or use canned ones from a good delicatessen)
4 basil leaves
50ml olive oil

for the anchovy dressing
1 garlic clove, finely chopped
20 anchovy fillets (preferably salt packed)
3 basil leaves
1 egg yolk
50ml olive oil

salting the cod
Sprinkle the cod fillet with the salt, sugar, zest and thyme, wrap tightly in clingfilm and chill for 4 hours. Remove the clingfilm and pour off the juices. Scrape excess salt off the fillet and cut it into 4 equal pieces.

chickpeas
Drain and rinse the soaked chickpeas. Heat the olive oil in a saucepan, add the onion, fennel and garlic and cook without colouring for 1–2 minutes. Add the chickpeas, cover with spring water, then add the savory and orange zest and bring to the boil. Simmer for 1–3 hours, until the chickpeas are very tender; the cooking time will depend on their age and how dry they were. Drain off half the liquid and stir in the orange juice, toasted cumin and red wine vinegar. Leave to cool.

roasted tomatoes
Core the tomatoes and cut them in half. Place on a baking tray, drizzle with the olive oil and sprinkle with the basil and some salt and pepper. Place in an oven preheated to 180°C/Gas Mark 4 and roast for 20 minutes, until well done. Remove from the oven and keep warm.

roasted piquillo peppers
Remove the stalks from the peppers and carefully scoop out the seeds. Place a basil leaf in each pepper. Drizzle with the olive oil, season and place on a baking tray. Roast in an oven preheated to 180°C/Gas Mark 4 for 20 minutes, then remove from the oven, cut in half and keep warm. (If using canned peppers, just warm them through on top of the stove with the other ingredients.)

anchovy dressing
Place the garlic, anchovies, basil and egg yolk in a blender and blend to a fine purée. Slowly add the olive oil in a steady stream until well mixed, then set aside.

cooking the cod
Heat the olive oil in a large frying pan and place the fish in it, skin-side down. Cook over a medium-high heat for 4–5 minutes, then turn over and cook for about a minute longer, until just done – the exact cooking time will depend on the thickness of the fish.

serving
Arrange the roasted tomatoes and piquillo peppers on 4 serving plates and scatter with some chickpeas and baby cavolo nero leaves. Place the cod on top, scatter with a few more chickpeas and a little of the chickpea juice. Finally spoon the anchovy dressing over.

roasted john dory with asparagus, salted grapes and verjus sauce

John Dory, also known as St Peter's fish because of the 2 black thumbprints on its side, is highly regarded, with good firm flesh. As with most fish, it doesn't require much cooking. For the best results, try to keep it slightly underdone. I have put it with both white and green asparagus here. The white is slightly more bitter than the green, making it a perfect match for the salted grapes and the sweet-sour verjus sauce. If you can't find white asparagus, then use all green, but do try to get Evesham asparagus – the best in the country. It is a pity it has such a short season. Here it is served with a white asparagus soup made from the trimmings.

Serves 4

24–32 Salted Grapes (see page 18)

for the asparagus
8 green asparagus spears, preferably
    Evesham
12 white asparagus spears
50g unsalted butter

for the white asparagus velouté
50g unsalted butter
50g onion, chopped
25g white of leek, chopped
125g stalks and trimmings from the
    asparagus, above
75g potato, peeled and sliced
250ml milk
250ml chicken stock (pages 23–24)

for the verjus sauce
400ml white port
250ml verjus
300ml Fish Stock (page 25)
125g unsalted butter, chilled and diced

for the john dory
4 x 120–150g John Dory fillets, skinned
30ml olive oil
30g unsalted butter

asparagus
Carefully bend the asparagus spears; they will snap just at the right point for the tops to be tender. Slice off the tips so they are 4cm long. Keep 4 of the green asparagus middles. Keep the bottom parts of the white asparagus to use for the velouté. Peel the tips of both the green and the white asparagus to 2cm from the very top of the spear. Keep the white asparagus peelings for the velouté.

Add the asparagus tips and the 4 green middles to a large pan of boiling salted water and cook until tender when pierced with a knife through the thickest part of the stem. Remove from the water and lay on a tray to cool. Slice the asparagus middles at an angle.

white asparagus velouté
Melt the butter in a heavy-based saucepan, add the onion, leek and white asparagus trimmings and cook for 5 minutes without letting them colour. Add the potato, milk and stock and bring to the boil. Simmer for 20 minutes, then pour into a blender and blend to a smooth purée. Push through a fine sieve and season to taste.

verjus sauce
Put the white port and verjus in a saucepan and boil until reduced by half. Add the fish stock and boil until reduced to 125ml. Lower the temperature to a simmer and add 60ml of the asparagus velouté (or 60ml double cream). Bring back to a simmer and whisk in the cold butter bit by bit. Season to taste and keep warm.

john dory
Season the John Dory on both sides with salt and pepper. Heat the oil in a large, heavy-based frying pan until very hot. Add the butter and, when it starts to foam, add the fish. Cook over a medium-high heat for 2–3 minutes, then carefully turn over and cook for 1–2 minutes longer. The fish should be golden but only just cooked through. Remove from the pan and keep warm.

serving
Reheat the asparagus by heating the butter in a pan until frothy, then adding the asparagus. Roll it in the pan by moving the pan from side to side. Season, remove from the pan and keep warm.

Reheat the asparagus velouté and blend with a stick blender until light and frothy. Pour into 4 shot glasses.

Gently warm the salted grapes in a frying pan with a teaspoon of the oil in which they were kept and a teaspoon of water. Scatter them over each serving plate, add the asparagus, then lay the John Dory over the spears and pour the sauce around the plate.

gilthead sea bream with cep gnocchi and red wine and hibiscus emulsion

I have had this on the menu for a little while and it has met with great approval. The red wine and hibiscus emulsion gives the bream a fruitiness and a slight floral bite. It is thickened with a little carrot purée to give it more body and help it keep its shape on the plate. Other purées will work too, as long as you bear in mind the slight sweetness of the carrots.

Serves 4

for the cep gnocchi
1kg Desiree potatoes
15g dried cep mushrooms
85g '00' pasta flour
$^1/_2$ beaten egg
olive oil for sprinkling
50g unsalted butter

for the carrot purée
750g carrots, finely sliced
100ml milk
200ml double cream
50g unsalted butter, diced

for the red wine and hibiscus emulsion
750ml red wine
300ml port
25g dried hibiscus (available from healthfood shops)

for the gilthead sea bream
4 x 150–180g gilthead sea bream fillets
50ml olive oil, plus extra for drizzling

for the ceps
50ml olive oil
25g unsalted butter
200g fresh cep mushrooms, cleaned and sliced

to serve
200g mixed leaves, such as red-veined sorrel, land cress and baby cavolo nero
25ml lemon oil
Maldon salt

cep gnocchi
Bake the potatoes in an oven preheated to 180–200°C/Gas Mark 4–6 for $1^1/_4$–$1^1/_2$ hours, until tender – if you insert a knife, it should come out clean. Immediately cut the potatoes in half to allow the steam to escape. Scoop out the flesh and push it through a fine sieve into a large bowl, trying to work the potato as little as possible. Allow to cool slightly. Grind the dried ceps to a fine powder in a spice grinder and add to the potato. Cut in the flour and some salt and pepper with a knife, then add the beaten egg and shape the mixture into a ball. Leave to rest for 5–10 minutes while you bring a large pan of salted water to the boil.

Sprinkle the work surface with flour and roll the potato mixture into 2 long sausages. Cut each one into 12–15 pieces and shape them into small balls. Lightly press each ball with the back of a fork to make the traditional line marks on it. Drop the gnocchi into the boiling water, cooking them in 3 batches – they will rise to the surface when they are done. Scoop them out of the water and put into a large bowl of cold water. Drain, place in a container and sprinkle with enough olive oil to coat. Turn the gnocchi over in the oil and place in the fridge until needed.

carrot purée
Place the carrots in a saucepan with the milk and double cream. Bring to the boil and simmer gently until the carrots are very tender. Transfer to a blender and blend to a smooth purée, adding the butter a little at a time at the end. Season with salt and pepper and keep warm.

red wine and hibiscus emulsion
Place the red wine, port and hibiscus in a saucepan and boil until reduced by two thirds. Whisk in 75g of the carrot purée and then whiz the sauce in a blender. Pass through a fine sieve and season to taste. Keep warm.

gilthead sea bream
Trim the fillets and check for any small pin bones. Oil a non-stick baking tray large enough to hold the fish. Place the fillets on the tray skin-side up, brush with the olive oil and season with salt and pepper. Place in an oven preheated to 180°C/Gas Mark 4 and cook for 4–6 minutes, depending on the size of the bream; it should be springy to the touch and only just done. Finish under a hot grill to crisp the skin, if necessary.

ceps
Heat the oil and butter in a large frying pan, add the sliced ceps and cook for 1–2 minutes, until soft and golden. Season to taste, then drain and keep warm.

serving
To reheat the gnocchi, heat the butter in a large, non-stick frying pan, add the gnocchi and cook until golden on both sides. Season to taste.

Dress the salad leaves with the lemon oil and some salt and pepper. Place 3 streaks of carrot purée on each serving plate. Arrange the gnocchi and ceps on the plate. Drizzle the sauce over and then add the salad leaves. Finally put the sea bream on top. Drizzle a little olive oil over and around and sprinkle with Maldon salt.

turbot fillet with smoked milk, celeriac cream and buttered hogweed

The turbot in this recipe is poached in smoked milk, which is then used to make the sauce. The milk can be smoked in a variety of ways. We generally do it in a smoker but here I have used smoked eel instead – an easier option than getting hold of a smoker. Alternatively smoked bacon – or even hickory smoke powder, available from spice shops – would do the trick. The hogweed shoots need to be very young. They can be replaced by alexanders or young lovage shoots or, failing that, some spinach with a few celery leaves.

Serves 4

for the celeriac cream
1 large celeriac, peeled and chopped
175ml milk
200ml double cream
50g unsalted butter, diced

for the smoked milk and turbot
400g smoked eel fillets
25g unsalted butter
300ml milk
4 x 175g pieces of turbot fillet, skinned

for the buttered hogweed
250g young hogweed shoots
100g unsalted butter

celeriac cream
Put the celeriac, milk and double cream in a pan, bring to the boil, then reduce the heat and cook gently for 20–25 minutes, until the celeriac is very tender. Transfer to a blender and blend to a smooth purée, adding the butter at the end a little at a time. Season with salt and pepper and keep warm.

smoked milk and turbot
Trim the smoked eel, reserving all the trimmings, then turn it over, remove the skin and set it aside with the trimmings. Cut the eel into 8 pieces.

Melt the butter in a pan, add the eel pieces and trimmings and pour the milk over. Bring just to the boil and poach the eel pieces for 3 minutes. Lift them out with a fish slice and drain. Cook the trimmings for a further 5 minutes to give the milk a smoky flavour. Pour the milk through a fine sieve into a shallow pan and season to taste.

Add the turbot to the milk and poach gently for 4–6 minutes, depending on thickness; it should be just cooked. Remove from the milk and keep warm. Strain the milk again and keep warm.

buttered hogweed
Peel the bottom 3cm of the hogweed shoots, then add to a large pan of boiling salted water and cook for 2 minutes. Drain and refresh in cold water, then drain again. The hogweed should be vibrant green and tender.

Just before serving, heat the butter in a pan and add the hogweed shoots. Season and keep turning over until hot.

serving
Place a pile of hogweed to one side of each plate and put the smoked eel on top. Spoon some celeriac cream to the other side and place the turbot on top of that. Reheat the smoked milk if necessary, then froth with a stick blender and spoon it over the fish.

roasted monkfish with pumpkin purée and toasted barley sauce

Monkfish is a great fish for serving with meaty accompaniments, such as ox cheek and oxtail, and can withstand powerful flavours such as the toasted barley sauce here. Small monkfish tails have an almost sweet, shellfishy taste. It is very easy to fillet, as there is only the central bone to remove, and this makes it an ideal fish for beginners. Here it is served with a pumpkin purée, which has a natural sweetness and richness. The barley is coloured in the pan before making the sauce, giving it a savoury, slightly nutty taste. A few slices of fried cep to finish – what could be better?

Serves 4

for the pumpkin purée
800g pumpkin, preferably Crown Prince
a little olive oil
200ml milk
200ml double cream
100g unsalted butter, diced

for the toasted barley sauce
50ml olive oil
50g pearl barley
150ml white wine
1 litre Brown Chicken Stock (page 24)
   or Fish Stock (page 25)
50g unsalted butter
juice of ¼ lemon

for the ceps
30ml olive oil
25g fresh cep mushrooms, brushed clean
   and thinly sliced
10g unsalted butter, diced

for the roasted monkfish
4 x 200g monkfish tails, filleted and
   membrane removed
50ml olive oil
25g unsalted butter
50ml hazelnut oil

pumpkin purée
Cut the pumpkin into quarters and remove the seeds. Place on a baking tray, drizzle with a little olive oil and cover with foil. Roast in an oven preheated to 200°C/Gas Mark 6 until the flesh is very tender. Remove from the oven and scrape the flesh off the skin. Place the flesh in a blender. Bring the milk and cream to the boil, pour into the blender and blend until smooth. Then add the butter little by little. The purée should be totally smooth – the hotter the ingredients the better. Season to taste and keep warm until needed.

toasted barley sauce
Heat the olive oil in a heavy-bottomed saucepan, add the pearl barley and cook over a medium heat until golden brown, stirring continuously to prevent it catching. Add the white wine and simmer for about 3 minutes, until it has completely evaporated. Then add the chicken stock and simmer slowly until it has reduced by two thirds and the barley is just cooked. Strain the barley through a sieve, reserving the liquid, and keep warm.

ceps
Heat the olive oil in a frying pan and add the ceps. Cook until golden, adding the butter just before they are ready. Season with salt and pepper and remove from the pan with a slotted spoon. Keep warm.

monkfish
Season the monkfish tails with salt and pepper. Heat the olive oil in a large, heavy-bottomed frying pan, add the monkfish tails and cook over a medium heat until golden brown on one side. Flip over, add the butter and cook for 3–4 minutes, until golden underneath. The fish should be only just cooked; it should give a little and feel springy when you prod it. Remove from the pan, season again and leave to relax in a warm place for 5–10 minutes.

serving
Place the barley sauce back on the stove, reheat gently and whisk in the butter little by little. Season and add a few drops of lemon juice.

Place an oval of pumpkin purée on each serving plate and cross the monkfish tails on top. Sprinkle with a little of the cooked toasted barley. Place a neat mound of the ceps in front of the fish and pour a little sauce over the fish and around the plate. Drizzle with the hazelnut oil and serve.

red mullet with a cockscomb and girolle stew, red amaranth, and white port and verjus syrup

This dish evolved as I was writing this book and it has become a firm favourite with customers because of its differing tastes and textures. A good butcher should be able to source cockscombs for you. It may be prudent to double or treble the recipe for them and keep them covered in duck fat in a sealed jar for later use. If you have problems obtaining them, use braised pig's trotters instead (see page 72). They both have that gelatinous, wobbly texture. The red amaranth and red-veined sorrel give a lemony tang to the dish. Baby sorrel leaves could be substituted, if necessary.

Serves 6

for the cockscomb and girolle stew
12 cockscombs, soaked in salted water
*   overnight to extract the blood*
10g sea salt
1 garlic clove, chopped
200g duck fat
500ml Brown Veal or Brown Beef Stock
*   (page 25)*
2 shallots, finely chopped
120g girolle mushrooms, diced
100ml double cream

for the carrot purée
100g unsalted butter
500g carrots, finely sliced
100ml double cream
100ml milk

for the choy sum
8 stems of choy sum
50g unsalted butter

for the red mullet
6 x 120–150g red mullet fillets
50ml olive oil
Maldon salt

for the garnish
50g red amaranth
50g red-veined sorrel
50ml olive oil, plus extra for drizzling
White Port and Verjus Syrup (see page 21),
*   for drizzling*

cockscomb and girolle stew
Drain the cockscombs from the bloody water and rinse off. Place in a pan of boiling salted water and blanch for 2–3 minutes. Drain, refresh under cold water, then rub the skin off with a cloth. Pat dry, sprinkle with the sea salt and mix with the chopped garlic. Leave for 4 hours, then scrape off any excess salt. Melt the duck fat in a casserole and add the cockscombs – the fat should cover them. Place the lid on the casserole and cook in an oven preheated to 140–160°C/Gas Mark 1–3 for 2 hours. They should be very soft and gelatinous when done.

Pour the stock into a pan and boil until reduced by two thirds. Heat a little of the duck fat from the cockscombs in a separate pan, add the shallots and cook until golden. Add the diced girolles and cook slowly for 2–3 minutes. Cut the cockscombs up, following the points so you have lots of jagged pieces, and add to the girolles. Pour in the reduced stock and the double cream and simmer until the sauce is thick and lightly binds the girolles and cockscombs. Season to taste and keep warm.

carrot purée
Heat half the butter in a saucepan, add the carrots and cook without colouring for 5 minutes. Add the cream and milk and simmer gently for 15 minutes, until the carrots are very tender. Transfer to a blender and blend to a smooth purée, adding the remaining butter a little at a time while the purée is still hot. Season to taste and keep warm.

choy sum
Trim most of the leaves off the choy sum, leaving just 2cm attached. Cook in a large pan of boiling salted water for 2 minutes, then drain and immediately refresh in cold water. Drain again and set aside.

red mullet
Lightly oil a baking tray and preheat the grill to medium. Arrange the red mullet on the tray, skin-side up, brush with the olive oil and season with salt and pepper. Cook gently under the grill, trying not to let the skin blister. They will take 3–4 minutes and should be firmish but give just a little to the touch.

serving
Reheat the choy sum in the butter, turning occasionally, then season to taste.

Dress the amaranth and sorrel leaves with the olive oil and season to taste. Arrange 3 streaks of carrot purée across each serving plate. Place the choy sum to one side, then spoon the cockscomb and girolle stew across the choy sum. Scatter a few leaves around the plate. Place the remaining leaves on top of the stew. Arrange the mullet fillets on top and drizzle some white port and verjus syrup and olive oil around. Season the top of the mullet fillets with Maldon salt.

meunière of dover sole with parsnip purée, razor clams and sea purslane

In this recipe the Dover sole is cooked in brown butter and finished off with a little lemon juice and parsley. The parsnip purée works well with shellfish such as razor clams, which have a delicious salty taste and a slightly chewy texture. Many of the naturally sweet vegetable purées would work here – pumpkin, carrot and beetroot, for example. Sea purslane has a salty flavour and a crisp texture. If you can't get it, you could try sea beet or samphire.

Serves 4

for the dover sole
2 large Dover sole, skinned and heads
  removed
50ml olive oil
50g unsalted butter
2 teaspoons chopped parsley
juice of 1/2 lemon

for the parsnip purée
200g parsnips, peeled and sliced
150ml milk
125ml double cream
75g unsalted butter, diced

for the razor clams
100ml olive oil
1 shallot, chopped
a sprig of thyme
8 large razor clams
100ml white wine
100ml milk
100ml double cream
4 large trompette noire (horn of plenty)
  mushrooms
2 spring onions, finely sliced
3 sprigs of sea purslane

preparing the dover sole
Cut each fish in half down the central bone. Trim off the tail end, as it would cook too quickly.

parsnip purée
Put the parsnips in a pan with the milk and cream and cook on a low simmer until tender. Transfer to a blender and blend to a smooth, velvety purée, adding the butter a little at a time towards the end. Season with salt and pepper and keep warm.

razor clams
Heat a large saucepan and add 50ml of the olive oil, plus the shallot and thyme. Cook for 30 seconds, then add the razor clams and pour in the white wine. Immediately place a tight-fitting lid on the pan and cook for 1 minute over the highest possible heat, shaking the pan from side to side. This should open the clams. Remove them from the cooking liquid as quickly as possible and allow to cool a little. Pass the cooking liquid through a sieve lined with a piece of damp muslin to catch any grit, then put to one side. Shell the clams, reserving 4 halves of shell. Remove the frilly bit round the edge of each clam and the dark top, keeping just the long white muscle. Cut this into 5–6 slices on the diagonal and put to one side.

Boil the clam cooking liquid until reduced by half, then add the milk and cream. Bring to the boil and whisk in 2 tablespoons of the parsnip purée. Taste and adjust the seasoning.

Sauté the mushrooms in 20ml of the remaining olive oil for 30 seconds, until limp. Season to taste and drain, then break them down into thin strips. Sauté the spring onions in the remaining olive oil until they are limp but still have their colour. Season to taste. Pick the leaves from the sea purslane and put to one side.

Gently reheat the clam sauce, add the sliced clams, spring onions and mushrooms and warm through quickly – do not boil.

cooking the dover sole
Heat the olive oil in a large frying pan, then add the butter and the Dover sole. Cook for 3–4 minutes, until golden, then flip over and cook for about a minute longer, until golden underneath. The flesh should be firm but only just cooked. Sprinkle in the chopped parsley and add the lemon juice, spooning it over the fish when it froths.

serving
Place a line of parsnip purée towards the top of each serving plate. Place the sole on it and lay a clam shell in front. Arrange the clams, spring onions and mushrooms in the shell. Top with a few sea purslane leaves and sprinkle the remaining leaves around. Froth the sauce with a stick blender and spoon it over the clams and around the plate.

john dory with braised ox cheek, roasted girolles and icicle radishes

This is another fish/meat combination that works really well. The secret again is to use a fish that can hold its own against the meat. John Dory is a big fish with lots of flavour and is quite capable of doing this. We have also use monkfish on occasion.

Icicle radishes are long and white and look a little like baby mooli. You could always use baby mooli instead but make sure that you fry them for longer so the water is driven out and the flavour intensified.

Serve this dish with creamed potatoes.

Serves 6

for the braised ox cheek
750g ox cheek (in 2 pieces, if possible)
2 garlic cloves, chopped
a sprig of thyme
1 bay leaf
400ml red wine
150ml olive oil
1 celery stick, chopped
1 onion, chopped
1 carrot, chopped
500ml Brown Veal or Brown Beef Stock
  (page 25)

for the icicle radishes
12 icicle radishes, about 6–8cm long,
  peeled but with 2cm stalk left on
30g unsalted butter

for the roasted girolles
30ml olive oil
30g unsalted butter
250g girolle mushrooms, cleaned

for the john dory
6 x 150–170g fillets of John Dory
50ml olive oil
30g unsalted butter

braised ox cheek
Trim any sinew or fat from the ox cheeks and cut each piece into 3. Place in a bowl with the garlic, herbs and red wine, cover and leave to marinate overnight.

The next day, drain the meat and pat dry. Heat half the oil in a large frying pan, add the cheeks and fry on both sides until well coloured. Remove from the pan and place in a casserole dish. Add the celery, onion and carrot to the frying pan and cook until golden. Add to the casserole dish. Pour the red wine, garlic and herb marinade into the pan and bring to the boil, stirring to scrape the sediment from the base of the pan. Simmer until reduced by two thirds, then add to the casserole dish. Pour in the stock, bring to the boil, then cover and place in an oven preheated to 180°C/Gas Mark 4. Cook for 3–4 hours, until the meat is extremely tender.

Remove half the cooking liquid and strain into a pan. Boil until reduced by two thirds and then mix in the remaining olive oil using a stick blender. Keep the meat warm in the remaining cooking liquid.

icicle radishes
Add the radishes to a large pan of boiling salted water and simmer for 3–4 minutes, until soft. Drain and refresh in cold water, then drain again and cut in half lengthways. Heat the butter in a frying pan, add the radishes, cut-side down, and cook until golden. Turn and repeat. Remove from the pan, drain and season with salt and pepper to taste.

roasted girolles
Heat the olive oil and butter in an ovenproof frying pan. Add the girolles and sauté for 1 minute, then place the pan in an oven preheated to 160°C/Gas Mark 3 and roast for 3–4 minutes, turning the mushrooms occasionally. Remove from the oven, drain and season to taste. Keep warm.

john dory
Season the John Dory on both sides with salt and pepper. Heat the olive oil in a heavy-based frying pan until very hot, then add the butter. When it starts to fizz, add the John Dory, skin-side down. Cook over a medium-high heat for 2–3 minutes, until golden. Flip the fish over carefully and cook for 1–2 minutes longer. It should be golden but only just cooked.

serving
Place a little creamed potato on each serving plate, if using. Place the ox cheek on top of that. Scatter around the girolles and arrange the icicle radishes on top. Finally, lean the John Dory fillet up against this. Froth the sauce with a stick blender and spoon it over the fish and ox cheek.

halibut roasted on the bone with baby broad beans, morels and sweet cicely velouté

Certain fish are wonderful cooked on the bone, halibut being one and turbot another. I remember a Michel Guérard recipe for osso bucco of monkfish, which was cooked on the bone and looked like little veal shanks. Here the moist, white fish is accompanied by the first broad beans and morels of spring, plus a light sweet cicely velouté, which has a delicate aniseed flavour. Speed is of the essence when making this sauce, to keep the vibrant colour and freshness of the cicely. Serve with buttered Jersey Royals or crushed buttered celeriac.

Serves 4

for the sweet cicely velouté
200ml Fish Stock (page 25)
100ml milk
50ml double cream
50g green of leek, finely sliced
50g sweet cicely, roughly shredded
30g spinach, roughly shredded

for the morels
32 small fresh morel mushrooms
50g unsalted butter

for the broad beans
50g unsalted butter
220g shelled young broad beans, blanched in boiling water for about 45 seconds, then skinned
a little chopped sweet cicely

for the halibut
50ml olive oil
50g unsalted butter
4 x 275–300g halibut steaks, each cut across the bone to resemble an A
ground white pepper
Maldon salt

sweet cicely velouté
Boil the fish stock in a saucepan until reduced by half. Add the milk, cream and green of leek and simmer for 4–5 minutes, until the leek is soft but still green. Add the shredded cicely and spinach and cook for 1 minute more. Transfer to a blender and blend to a smooth, light green sauce. Strain through a fine sieve and season with salt and pepper to taste.

morels
Rinse the morels well under cold running water to remove any grit and sand. Pat dry with a cloth and leave to dry completely. Heat the butter in a large frying pan until foaming, then add the morels. Cook over a medium-high heat for 2–3 minutes, shaking the pan occasionally. Drain and season to taste. Keep warm.

broad beans
As the broad beans have already been blanched to remove their skins, you will only need to cook them briefly. Heat 50ml of water in a large frying pan and add the butter. Add the beans and sweet cicely and cook for 2–3 minutes, then drain and season to taste.

halibut
Heat a large cast iron frying pan, then add the oil, followed by the butter. Add the halibut, dark skin-side down, and brown quickly, then turn and brown the other side. Remove from the pan and transfer to a roasting tray. Season with salt and white pepper and place in an oven preheated to 200°C/Gas Mark 6. Cook for 8–12 minutes, turning the fish over half way through. It should be only just done. The time will vary depending on the thickness of the steak, so give it a light squeeze every now and again. Remove from the oven, season again and keep warm.

serving
Bring the velouté to just below boiling point and froth it with a stick blender. Scatter the broad beans and morels over each serving plate in a circle. Add some of the frothed sauce and sit the halibut on top. Spoon a little more of the sauce over and sprinkle with Maldon salt.

steamed sea bass with asparagus, leek and black truffle

I rarely have truffles on the menu but occasionally I throw caution to the winds and make a white truffle risotto with lovely Alba truffles or, in this case, get some black Périgord truffles. Because of their expense, it is worth knowing how to make the most of them. If you store them in a sealed container with some risotto rice, it helps to flavour it. You can also do this with eggs – as the shells are porous, they absorb the flavour of the truffles and you can make great scrambled eggs. Here the black truffle is served with the steamed sea bass and the truffle trimmings are used to flavour the sauce. There is really no substitute for fresh truffle but if you can't obtain one you could always simply whisk some truffle oil into the sauce. Serve with crushed new potatoes.

Serves 4

for the steamed sea bass
800g–1kg line-caught sea bass fillet
30ml olive oil
juice of ¹/₂ lemon
Maldon salt

for the truffle and sauce
50g fresh black truffle
a little olive oil
100ml vermouth
100ml white wine
500ml White Chicken Stock (page 23) or
  Fish Stock (page 25)
100ml double cream
50ml milk

for the asparagus and leek
8 fat asparagus spears, preferably Evesham
  asparagus
1 leek, cut lengthways in half, then cut into
  10 x 1cm strips
60g unsalted butter

preparing the sea bass
Trim the sea bass fillet, make sure there are no pin bones, and cut it into 4 portions. Brush with the olive oil, squeeze the lemon juice over and season with salt and pepper. Carefully wrap in clingfilm, keeping the fillet's shape, and put it in the fridge.

truffle and sauce
Carefully trim and peel the truffle. Keep all the trimmings. Cut the truffle into slices 0.5–1mm thick, then use a small cutter to cut the slices into discs. Brush them with a little olive oil and set aside. Chop all the trimmings finely.

Pour the vermouth and white wine into a pan and boil until reduced to a glaze. Add the stock and boil until reduced by two thirds. Add the double cream and milk, bring to the boil and stir in all the chopped truffle trimmings. Put to one side for 20 minutes to infuse, then strain into a clean pan.

asparagus
Carefully bend the asparagus stalks; they will snap at the right point. Discard the bottom part. Trim the tips to 10cm in length and lightly peel up to 5cm from the top. Use a mandoline to cut each spear into 1mm slices along its length. Bring a large pan of salted water to the boil, add the asparagus strips and blanch for 30 seconds, until limp. Drain and refresh in cold water, then drain again.

leek
Blanch the leek for 45 seconds–1 minute in boiling salted water, then drain, refresh in cold water and drain again.

cooking the sea bass
Steam the cling-filmed sea bass for 4–5 minutes. Remove from the steamer and leave to rest for 1 minute before taking off the clingfilm. Keep warm.

serving
To reheat the asparagus, put 30g of the butter in a large pan with 30ml of water and bring to the boil. Add the asparagus and heat through, then season to taste. Repeat with the leek in a separate pan, using the rest of the butter.

Place the bass to one side of each serving plate. Toss the leek and asparagus together and pile to one side. Arrange the truffle slices among the leek and asparagus. Reheat the sauce and froth with a stick blender. Pour the frothed sauce around the fish, then sprinkle a little Maldon salt on the sea bass.

roast lobster, braised pig's tail, tomato confit and wilted sea beet, served with a warm lobster jelly with parsley root

This is one of my newest dishes. I wanted something meaty to go with the lobster tails and to play on the rich man/poor man concept – hence the pig's tails. The tomato confit goes well with their gelatinous texture. If you can't get sea beet, you could substitute spinach or perhaps Cos lettuce.

I serve this with a warm lobster jelly to use the shells. It has a deep lobster flavour and as long as it is heated to no more than 75°C it will remain jellied. If you cannot get parsley root, put a parsnip purée in the bottom of the glass.

The agar-agar measurement has to be precise – unless you have a set of chemical scales, you will need to ask your chemist to weigh it out for you.

Serves 6

12 large Tomato Confit with Lemon halves (see page 17), cut in half again

for the braised pig's tails
100ml olive oil, plus extra for drizzling
1 onion, chopped
1 large carrot, chopped
2 celery sticks, chopped
4 garlic cloves, chopped
150ml red wine
6 pig's tails – good and plump and long
1 bay leaf
a sprig of thyme
1.5 litres Brown Chicken Stock (page 24)

for the roast lobster
6 small native lobsters, weighing 500–600g each
50ml olive oil, plus extra for drizzling
30g unsalted butter
juice of 1/2 lemon

for the lobster jelly
the shells from the lobsters
100ml olive oil
1 onion, chopped
1/2 carrot, chopped
1 celery stick, chopped
2 garlic cloves, crushed
100g fennel, chopped
6 tarragon leaves
50g tomato purée, or 200g skinned, deseeded and chopped ripe fresh tomatoes
50ml Cognac
200ml white wine
2 litres Brown Chicken Stock (page 24)
1 1/2 gelatine leaves
1.2g agar-agar

for clarification
50g carrots, chopped
50g celery, chopped
50g onion, chopped
1/2 chicken breast
3 egg whites

to finish the lobster cream
50ml double cream
100ml milk

for the parsley root purée
200g parsley root, peeled and chopped
150ml milk
125ml double cream
75g unsalted butter, diced

for the sea beet
50g unsalted butter
200g young sea beet

braised pig's tails
Heat the olive oil in a large casserole, add the vegetables and cook until golden. Add the red wine and boil until reduced by half. Add the pig's tails and herbs, followed by the stock, and bring to the boil. Cover, transfer to an oven preheated to 160°C/Gas Mark 3 and cook for 3 hours, until the tails are very tender. Carefully remove the tails from the stock and cut each one into quarters. Strain the stock off through a fine sieve into a clean pan and boil until reduced by half. Set aside.

preparing the lobsters
Bring a very large pan of salted water to the boil. Lay the lobsters on a board with the stomach down. On top of the head you will see a cross. Quickly push the tip of a large, very sharp chopping knife into it; this will kill the lobster instantly. Place the lobsters in the boiling water (you will need to cook them in 2 or 3 batches) and cook for 4 minutes, then scoop out and immediately put in iced water to stop the cooking. Drain well.

Pull the head away from the body of each lobster and put the tail to one side. Remove the claws and set aside. Split the head open and remove the stomach sac and intestine. Then remove the liver and the coral (you can make a flavoured butter for use in sauces with these). Remove the meat from the claws and knuckles and keep for another time; they will be undercooked. Keep all the shells. Remove the tail meat in one piece by snapping each side of the tail and pulling the meat out. Keep in the fridge until needed.

(continued on page 104)

(continued from page 102)

lobster jelly

Put all the lobster shells in a pan and smash them with the end of a rolling pin until crushed. Heat the olive oil in a large saucepan until very hot, add the shells and cook until golden. Remove from the pan, add the vegetables and tarragon and cook until golden. Place the shells back in the pan, stir in the tomato purée or chopped tomatoes and cook for 2 minutes. Pour in the Cognac and bring to the boil, stirring well to deglaze the pan. Boil until the alcohol has evaporated, then add the white wine and boil until reduced by half. Add the stock, bring back to the boil and simmer for about 2 hours. Strain the stock through a sieve – do not push it through – then leave to cool.

clarification

Place the vegetables, chicken breast and egg whites in a food processor and process until well mixed. Add a little of the cold lobster stock and pulse again. Transfer this mixture to a tall saucepan and stir in the remaining lobster stock. Place on a low heat and bring to just under the boil, stirring constantly. When you see a crust starting to appear, stop stirring to allow the crust to form. Make a small hole to one side of the crust. Simmer for 1–1^1/$_2$ hours without ever letting it boil, as this would break the crust and cloud the jelly. Then scoop out a ladleful of crust to make a larger hole and carefully ladle the stock out through it, pouring it into a sieve lined with a piece of damp muslin and placed over a pan. Simmer the stock until reduced to about 800ml, then remove from the heat.

finishing the lobster jelly

Soak the gelatine in cold water for about 5 minutes, until limp. Heat 320ml of the clarified lobster stock to boiling point in a small saucepan and whisk in the agar-agar. Bring back to the boil and cook for 1 minute. Squeeze excess water from the gelatine and add to the stock. Stir in until dissolved and remove from the heat. Keep warm.

lobster cream

Boil the remaining 480ml of lobster stock until reduced to 300ml, then stir in the double cream and milk and return to the boil. Simmer for 3–4 minutes, then remove from the heat. Season with salt and pepper and set aside.

parsley root purée

Put the parsley root in a pan with the milk and cream and simmer gently until tender. Transfer to a blender and blend to a smooth, velvety purée, adding the butter a little at a time towards the end. Season with salt and pepper and leave to cool. Place a spoonful of the purée in the bottom of 6 thick glasses. Keep in the fridge. Place a spoonful of the warm, still-liquid lobster jelly on top of the parsley root purée, then return to the fridge. Once it has set, divide the rest of the warm lobster jelly between the glasses, filling them two thirds full. Return to the fridge to set.

tomato confit

Cut each tomato quarter into small discs and chop the trimmings finely.

sea beet

Heat the butter in a frying pan with 2 tablespoons of water, add the sea beet and cook over a medium heat until limp. Season with salt and pepper and keep warm.

lobster tails

Heat the oil and butter in a large, cast iron frying pan and add the lobster tails. Cook for about 6–8 minutes, until golden on both sides. Keep turning the tails over to make sure they do not burn. Season with salt and pepper and the lemon juice.

serving

Cover the lobster jellies with clingfilm and reheat for 10–15 minutes in a steamer, watching carefully to make sure the jelly doesn't melt too much. The outside should become liquid, while the middle should be very warm but still jellied. Reheat the lobster cream, froth it with a stick blender and place half on top of the hot jellies. Add 2 tablespoons of the reduced stock from the pig's tails to the other half of the lobster cream and keep warm (you won't need the rest of the stock).

Place a pile of buttered sea beet to one side of each serving plate and put a lobster tail on top. Put the tomato discs to the other side and place 4 little bits of the trimmings next to them. Arrange the pig's tails on the tomato trimmings and pour over the lobster cream, then drizzle with olive oil. Serve with the warm lobster jelly to one side.

spiced pollock with lentil and smoked bacon salsa and roasted red pepper sauce

This is a light and clean summer dish, just right for when the sun is beating down. The combination of the hot fish and cool salsa works very well. This is the sort of thing I would eat on my day off with a warm potato salad, or just some boiled new potatoes crushed with a little olive oil, sea salt and basil. The salsa can, of course, be made without the bacon but it is great with it.

Serves 6

for the lentil and smoked bacon salsa
100g Puy lentils
mineral water (enough to cover the lentils)
50ml olive oil
50g red pepper, finely diced
50g green pepper, finely diced
50g red onion, finely diced
3 spring onions, finely sliced
1 red chilli, deseeded and finely chopped
1 garlic clove, finely chopped
3 ripe plum tomatoes, peeled, deseeded and diced
120ml tomato juice
25ml red wine vinegar
1/2 bunch of coriander, chopped
100g smoked streaky bacon, diced

for the roasted red pepper sauce
200ml Fish Stock (page 25)
a pinch of saffron
10ml red wine vinegar
2 red peppers, roasted and peeled
100g ripe plum tomato flesh, no skin or pips
30ml extra virgin olive oil
5 basil leaves
a pinch of sugar
20ml double cream

for the spiced pollock
1 teaspoon cumin seeds
1 teaspoon coriander seeds
8 juniper berries
1 star anise
4 green cardamom pods

3 strips of orange zest
10g plain flour
6 x 180g pieces of pollock fillet
50ml olive oil
30g unsalted butter

to garnish
100g rocket
20ml olive oil, plus extra for drizzling
a little sea salt

lentil and smoked bacon salsa
The salsa can be made the day before but it's important to add the bacon at the last minute before serving. Put the lentils in a pan, add enough mineral water to cover and bring to the boil. Simmer until tender, then drain. Mix with 30ml of the olive oil and all the remaining ingredients except the bacon, then chill.

roasted red pepper sauce
Put the fish stock and saffron in a pan and simmer until reduced by two thirds. Add the vinegar and put to one side. Remove the seeds and any pith from the red peppers and place them in a blender. Add the reduced stock, tomato flesh, oil, basil and sugar and blend until smooth. Push through a fine sieve into a pan, reheat for 1 minute and add the double cream. Check the seasoning and froth up with a stick blender.

spiced pollock
Heat a large frying pan, then add all the spices and dry-roast on top of the stove until they release their fragrance and the seeds start popping. Remove from the heat and leave to cool. In a spice grinder, grind the spices, orange zest and flour to a fine powder. Season the pollock with salt and then sprinkle both sides with the spice mix. Any you don't use can be kept in a sealed jar.

Heat the olive oil in a large frying pan, add the butter and then the pollock, skin-side down. Cook over a medium heat for 3–4 minutes, until golden, then turn the heat down and flip the fish over. Cook for a minute longer. The pollock should be just done. Remove from the pan and keep warm.

serving
To finish the salsa, heat the remaining olive oil in a pan, add the smoked bacon and cook until crisp and golden. Remove the salsa from the fridge and add the bacon and all the fat from the pan. Check the seasoning.

Dress the rocket with the olive oil and a little sea salt. Place some salsa in the middle of each serving plate and arrange the rocket on top. Drizzle a little of the sauce on the plate. Place the pollock on top of the rocket, skin-side up. Drizzle with a little more sauce and a little olive oil.

monkfish cheeks with duck confit, crispy duck skin and ground elder shoots

Monkfish cheeks are lovely, meaty bits of fish that sear very well. If you can't get them, try cod cheeks or, failing that, monkfish tails or scallops. Here they are served with duck confit, shredded with a little vinegar and the crisp confit skin for a tasty contrast. Ground elder shoots contribute a light earthiness, while a foie gras vinaigrette adds depth.

Serves 6

for the duck confit
4 Duck Confit legs (see page 16)
50g duck fat
a few drops of sherry vinegar

for the lentils
50ml olive oil
1 celery stick, cut into 6
1 onion, cut into quarters
1 carrot, sliced
500ml Brown Chicken Stock (page 24)
200g Puy lentils

for the ground elder shoots
20g unsalted butter
100g ground elder shoots

for the foie gras vinaigrette
50g foie gras
2 teaspoons aged sherry vinegar
1 egg yolk
125ml virgin rapeseed oil

for the monkfish cheeks
6 x 120–140g monkfish cheeks
50g duck fat

duck confit
Heat the duck fat in an ovenproof frying pan, add the confit duck legs, skin-side down, and transfer to an oven preheated to 180°C/Gas Mark 4. Cook for 5 minutes, then remove from the oven and drain the duck legs. Remove the duck skin, place it between 2 small baking sheets lined with baking parchment (the bottom one should have a lip) and press flat. Place in the oven, still between the baking sheets, and cook for 15–20 minutes, until the skin is golden and crisp. Place the skin on paper to absorb excess fat, then snap it into large pieces and set aside.

lentils
Heat the olive oil in a saucepan, add the vegetables and cook until lightly browned. Add the chicken stock and then the lentils. Bring to the boil and simmer for about 45 minutes. The lentils should be very tender and there should still be some stock left; if they are too dry, add a little water. Strain the lentils, reserving the liquid. Remove the vegetables and blend half of them to a purée with the stock. Push the purée through a fine sieve and season with salt and pepper to taste. Season the lentils and keep warm.

ground elder shoots
Melt the butter in a large pan, add the elder and cook gently for 1–2 minutes, until wilted. Season to taste and drain.

foie gras vinaigrette
Cook the foie gras in a very hot, dry frying pan for about 30 seconds on each side. Put it in a blender with the sherry vinegar and egg yolk and blend to a purée, adding the rapeseed oil in a steady stream. Season with salt and pepper to taste.

monkfish cheeks
Trim the monkfish cheeks of any skin and season them with salt and pepper. Either leave them whole or cut them in half. Heat the duck fat in a large frying pan, add the monkfish cheeks and sear over a high heat until golden on both sides. Reduce the heat to medium and cook, turning occasionally, for about $1^1/_2$ minutes per side, until tender; the exact cooking time will depend on size. Remove from the pan and season again.

serving
Flake the duck leg meat and warm it in a little of the duck fat. Season with a little pepper and a few drops of sherry vinegar.

Place a mound of duck meat on each serving plate and put a monkfish cheek on top. Place a streak of lentil purée to one side, then some foie gras vinaigrette. Scatter a few lentils around and top with a piece of duck skin.

saddle of rabbit with rabbit leg bolognaise and carrot purée

We are very lucky that so much game is available in the Cotswolds. Here the saddle fillet is cooked very quickly to keep it moist and pink, while the legs are minced and made into a bolognaise sauce. I like to sauté the rabbit offal with it but if you can't get it you can just leave it out. Carrot goes very well with this dish – well, rabbits do love carrots, don't they! You could also serve it with one of their other favourites, lettuce, perhaps braised. We also serve a split pea or fresh pea soup with the rabbit offal as a garnish.

Serves 6

for the saddle of rabbit
3 rabbits, with their offal (kidneys, livers, hearts)
75ml olive oil
35g unsalted butter

for the rabbit leg bolognaise
50ml olive oil
6 hind legs from the rabbits, boned and minced
1 onion, finely chopped
4 garlic cloves, finely chopped
30g tomato purée
100ml port
200ml red wine
1 bay leaf
a sprig of thyme
500ml Brown Chicken Stock (page 24)

for the carrot purée
100g unsalted butter
500g carrots, finely sliced
100ml double cream
100ml milk

for the caramelised baby carrots
12 baby carrots, with tops
50g unsalted butter
2 teaspoons caster sugar

preparing the rabbit
Remove the rabbit meat from either side of the backbone (the bones can be used for a soup another day). Trim off any silver skin and you should be left with 6 nice rabbit fillets. Remove the skin from the kidneys and trim the livers and hearts.

rabbit leg bolognaise
Heat the olive oil in a pan until very hot, then add the minced rabbit and brown it quickly. Add the onion and garlic and cook for 2 minutes. Add the tomato purée and cook for 2 minutes longer. Add the port, stirring to deglaze the pan, and cook until completely evaporated. Add the red wine and simmer until reduced by half. Add the bay leaf, thyme and chicken stock. Bring to the boil and simmer slowly for 1^1/$_2$ hours, until the bolognaise has reduced and thickened and the meat is tender. Season with salt and pepper to taste.

carrot purée
Heat half the butter in a saucepan, add the carrots and cook for 5 minutes without colouring. Add the cream and milk and cook for 15 minutes, until the carrots are very tender. Transfer to a blender and blend to a smooth purée, adding the remaining butter a little at a time towards the end. Season to taste and keep warm.

caramelised baby carrots
Peel the carrots carefully and trim the stalks to 1.5cm. Cook in boiling salted water for 1^1/$_2$ minutes, then drain, refresh in cold water and drain again. Heat the butter and sugar in a frying pan. Cut the carrots in half lengthways and put them in the pan cut-side down. Cook for 1–2 minutes over a medium-high heat, until golden, then flip over and cook until the other side is golden. Remove from the pan and season to taste.

cooking the rabbit
Heat 50ml of the olive oil and 25g of the butter in a large frying pan. When sizzling, add the rabbit fillets and season with salt and pepper. Brown them quickly on all sides over a medium-high heat, then lower the heat and cook for about 3–4 minutes, until just done. Remove from the pan and keep warm. Heat the remaining butter and oil in another frying pan, add the kidneys, livers and hearts and cook over a medium-high heat for 1 minute, until golden, turning half way through. They should still be pink inside.

serving
Slice each saddle fillet into 3–4 pieces lengthways. Slice the offal in half. Arrange the carrots and saddle meat at the head of each serving plate. Place a streak of carrot purée to the front. Spoon on some of the bolognaise at an angle. Finally, arrange the offal on the plate.

stuffed saddle of rabbit with 'ravioli' of its offal and quinoa of angelica

This is an adaptation of a dish I cooked when I won the National Chef of the Year competition in 1996. Back then, I served a stuffed cabbage leaf with the rabbit but more recently I have been serving it with a ravioli of rabbit offal made with sheets of turnip. Quinoa, an ancient Inca grain, isn't used very much in professional kitchens but it has a wonderful texture and deserves to be better known. The angelica gives it a celery flavour. You could use lovage, alexanders or celery leaf instead.

Serves 4

for the saddle of rabbit
50ml olive oil
50g shallots, chopped
1 garlic clove, chopped
100g wild mushrooms, such as girolles, sliced
100g spinach, blanched in boiling water for
    1 minute, then drained and chopped
6 slices of air-dried Cumbrian or Bayonne ham
1 saddle of rabbit, weighing about 400g
    (ask your butcher to bone it for you,
    keeping it in one piece)

for the ravioli
2 large turnips
50g unsalted butter
4 rabbit livers, minced
8 rabbit kidneys, minced
3 rabbit hearts, minced
6 rabbit lungs, minced
1 hind leg of rabbit, boned and minced
100g belly pork, minced
25g carrot, minced
25g celery, minced
25g onion, minced
15g garlic, minced
100ml double cream

for the quinoa
150g fresh angelica leaves and stalks
50ml olive oil
100g onions, chopped
2 garlic cloves, chopped
100g quinoa
400ml chicken stock (pages 23–24)

for the sauce
50ml olive oil
the bones from the rabbit, finely chopped
    (ask your butcher to do this)
3 shallots, chopped
1 garlic clove, chopped
100g button mushrooms, sliced
100ml Madeira
200ml red wine
1 litre Brown Chicken Stock (page 24)

saddle of rabbit
Heat the olive oil in a frying pan, add the shallots, garlic and mushrooms and cook for 5 minutes without colouring. Add the spinach, stirring to bind, then remove the mixture from the pan and leave to cool. Season with salt and pepper to taste. Place a large sheet of foil on the work surface, fold it in half and grease with a little butter. Lay the slices of ham on it, overlapping them. Then put the saddle of rabbit on top, skin-side down, and open it out. Place the mushroom and spinach mixture in the middle and roll up the saddle into a cylinder wrapped in the ham. Then tightly wrap in foil, twist the ends to form a long sausage and chill.

ravioli of offal
Peel the turnips and slice them finely into large discs about 2mm thick. A mandoline or slicing machine is ideal for this; you will need 16 discs. Blanch in a large pan of boiling salted water for about 1 minute, until limp and slightly translucent, then drain, refresh in cold water and drain again. Keep to one side.

Heat the butter in a saucepan, add the offal, rabbit leg and belly pork and cook for about 5 minutes, until golden. Add the vegetables and cook for 3–4 minutes. Stir in the double cream and simmer for 10–15 minutes, until all the ingredients are tender. Season and leave to cool. Place small mounds of the mixture on 8 turnip discs and cover with 8 more discs, pressing down the edges lightly with your fingers. Place on a buttered baking tray and season.

quinoa of angelica
Blanch the angelica in a large pan of boiling salted water for 30–45 seconds, then drain, refresh in cold water and drain again. Mince or chop finely and set aside. Heat the olive oil in a casserole, add the onions and garlic and cook for 2–3 minutes without colouring. Add the quinoa and cook until the nutty aroma comes through. Add the chicken stock, bring to the boil and cover the casserole. Transfer to an oven preheated to 200°C/Gas Mark 6 and cook for 20 minutes. When the quinoa is done, there will be a white ring around the middle of each grain and the stock will have been absorbed. Stir in the angelica, place the casserole on the hob and heat through. Season to taste and keep warm.

sauce
Heat the olive oil in a large saucepan, add the chopped rabbit bones and cook until golden. Add the shallots, garlic and mushrooms and cook for 2–3 minutes. Add the Madeira and cook until reduced to a glaze, then add the red wine and boil until reduced by half. Finally, add the stock, bring to the boil and simmer for 1 hour. Strain through a fine sieve into a clean pan and simmer until reduced to 250ml. Season to taste and keep warm.

finishing the saddle of rabbit
Place the foil parcel in an oven preheated to 200°C/Gas Mark 6 and cook for 12 minutes. Remove from the oven and allow to rest for 10 minutes.

serving
Reheat the ravioli in an oven preheated to 160°C/Gas Mark 3 for 2–4 minutes.

Cut the ends off the foil package, carefully unwrap the rabbit and cut it into 4 neat cylinders. Stand them up on one side of the plate on a small mound of quinoa. Place 2 ravioli to one side and spoon the sauce around.

roast grey-legged partridge with chicory caramelised in maple syrup, and elderberry gastric

I'm happier using British grey-legged partridge than the French red-legged variety. It's local and the flavour is better. It is served quite simply here: roasted until pink and accompanied by caramelised chicory. To finish, it is served with an elderberry gastric – a sort of sweet and sour elderberry reduction. We have an abundance of elder trees near us. You should be able to find some near you – they grow in towns as well as in the countryside.

Serve with mashed potato with chopped pecans or walnuts running through it, and some buttered Savoy cabbage.

Serves 4

for the elderberry gastric
50g caster sugar
45ml red wine vinegar
150g elderberries
100ml water

for the caramelised chicory
4 small or 2 medium heads of chicory
juice of 1 lemon
50g caster sugar
50g unsalted butter
25ml olive oil
100ml maple syrup

for the roast partridge
4 juniper or sloe berries
4 sprigs of thyme
4 grey-legged partridge
50ml olive oil
25g unsalted butter

elderberry gastric
Put the sugar and vinegar in a small, heavy-based pan and heat gently, stirring to dissolve the sugar. Raise the heat and boil without stirring until it turns into a blond caramel. Add the elderberries and water and simmer for 5 minutes. Push the mixture through a fine sieve, getting as much of the juices through as possible. Place back on the stove and simmer until reduced to a syrup.

caramelised chicory
Bring to the boil a pan of water just large enough to hold the chicory. Add the lemon juice, sugar and a little salt and return to the boil. Remove the central core from each chicory head. Place the chicory in the boiling water and poach for 5 minutes for small chicory, 8–9 minutes for larger ones. Drain and leave until cool enough to handle, then squeeze out excess moisture. If using medium chicory, cut them in half lengthways. Heat the butter and oil in a frying pan and add the chicory (cut-side down, if using the medium ones). Cook over a medium heat until starting to colour, then add the maple syrup and cook for about 2 minutes longer, until caramelised underneath. Turn the chicory over and cook until golden brown. Remove from the pan, drain and season to taste. Keep warm.

roast partridge
Place a juniper or sloe berry and a sprig of thyme in the cavity of each bird and season the birds. Heat the oil and butter in a cast iron frying pan until sizzling, then add the partridges, on one leg side first. Cook for 1 minute, until golden, then turn on to the other leg and cook for 1 minute longer. Finally cook breast-side down for 1 minute, until golden. Place breast-side up in an oven preheated to 220°C/Gas Mark 7 and cook for 7–8 minutes for a nice pink bird. Remove from the oven, transfer to a warm plate, then cover with foil and leave to rest in a warm place for 5 minutes. Remove the legs and trim the ends. Remove the breasts and keep warm. Pour the juices that have escaped from the birds during resting into the roasting tin and place it on the hob. Stir over the heat with a wooden spoon for a few minutes, scraping up the sediment from the base of the pan, then add a little water and bring to the boil. Simmer for 2 minutes, season to taste and pass through a fine sieve.

serving
Arrange the partridge to one side of each plate. Place the chicory on the other side and spoon a little of the partridge juices around the plate, then the elderberry gastric.

chump of lamb with pea purée, wilted lettuce and eucalyptus foam

Lamb is such a popular meat that it has had to be on our menu from the beginning. I always prefer to use chump, which is the muscle at the top of the leg – if it were beef it would be the rump. Our butcher, Adrian, hangs the meat for us for an extra couple of weeks to give it a stronger flavour. Lamb, peas and mint go together so well. I have replaced the mint with eucalyptus here – they both have that cooling taste. Dried eucalyptus leaves are available from good spice shops and some herbalists.

Serves 4

for the eucalyptus foam
200ml chicken stock (pages 23–24)
20 fresh or 10 dried eucalyptus leaves
200ml milk
2g powdered lecithin

for the pea purée
500g petits pois (frozen will do)
the outer leaves of the Cos lettuce (below)
100g unsalted butter
100g onions, chopped

for the lamb
50ml olive oil
30g unsalted butter
4 x 225–250g chumps of lamb, boned

for the lamb juices
60ml Madeira
100ml white wine
2 dried eucalyptus leaves
800ml Lamb Stock (page 24)
30g unsalted butter, diced

for the wilted lettuce
1 Cos lettuce
25g unsalted butter

to garnish
100g peas
25g unsalted butter

eucalyptus foam
Put the chicken stock and eucalyptus leaves in a pan and boil until the stock has almost completely evaporated. Add the milk, bring to the boil and whisk in the powdered lecithin. Season to taste with salt and pepper. Remove from the heat and leave to infuse for 1 hour, then pour through a fine sieve.

pea purée
Cook the peas in a large pan of boiling salted water for 2 minutes, then drain, refresh in cold water and drain again. Blanch the lettuce leaves in a large pan of boiling water for 30 seconds, then drain, refresh and drain well. Heat the butter in a saucepan, add the onions and cook gently until tender. Place in a blender, add the peas and lettuce and blend to a smooth purée. Push through a fine sieve and season to taste. Keep warm.

lamb
Heat the olive oil and butter in a heavy cast iron frying pan. Season the lamb chumps and cook them on the fatty side until golden. Flip over and cook the other side for 1 minute. Place back on the skin side and transfer the pan to an oven preheated to 220°C/Gas Mark 7. Cook for about 12 minutes; this will give pink meat. Remove from the oven, season and leave to rest in a warm place for 4–8 minutes.

lamb juices
Pour the Madeira into a small saucepan and boil until it has completely evaporated. Add the white wine and eucalyptus and boil until reduced by two thirds. Add the stock, bring to the boil and simmer until reduced by about two thirds. Whisk in the butter a little at a time and check the seasoning. Remove the leaves before serving.

wilted lettuce
Cut the Cos leaves into 5cm squares along the vein of the lettuce so you have half the white vein running down one side of each piece of lettuce. Heat the butter in a frying pan over a medium heat, add the lettuce and some seasoning and turn the lettuce around a little until it wilts in the heat of the pan. Remove from the heat and drain.

garnish
Bring a saucepan of salted water to the boil. Cook the peas for 2–3 minutes, then drain, refresh in cold water and drain again.

serving
Reheat the peas in the butter with a dessertspoon of water and season to taste. Place some pea purée on each serving plate, arrange the wilted lettuce to one side and scatter with the peas. Carve each lamb chump into 5 slices and arrange on the plate. Coat with a little of the lamb juices. Reheat the eucalyptus foam, froth with a stick blender and pour it over the peas and lamb.

grouse breasts with walnut-infused jus, soured cabbage, morteau sausage and roast beetroot

Grouse is a lovely game bird with a powerful flavour. It comes into season on the 'Glorious 12th' of August. We, however, use them a little later in the year, when they are more easily available and a lot cheaper! The morteau is a smoked, heavily garlicky sausage. It could be omitted but it does add a good flavour. The soured cabbage is lightly acidulated so it goes well with any game, furred or feathered. Roast beetroot makes a good earthy, slightly sweet accompaniment.

Serves 6

1 morteau sausage
1/2 quantity of Soured Cabbage (see page 20)

for the roast beetroot
24 baby beetroot
50ml olive oil
5 coriander seeds
5g fresh horseradish, grated
25g unsalted butter

for the grouse breasts
6 juniper berries
6 small heather twigs
6 oven-ready grouse
50ml olive oil
25g unsalted butter

for the walnut-infused jus
50ml olive oil
100g shallots, sliced
100g button mushrooms, sliced
25ml sherry vinegar
50ml white port
100ml red wine
1 litre Brown Chicken Stock (page 24),
    boiled until reduced to 500ml
50ml walnut oil

morteau sausage
Bring a large pan of water to the boil, add the sausage and cook for about 45 minutes. Remove from the water, drain and slice – you will need 3–4 slices per person.

roast beetroot
Wash the beetroot and trim the tops, leaving 2–3cm of stalks attached. Toss them in the olive oil and season, adding the coriander seeds and horseradish. Put on a large sheet of foil and seal the edges to make a parcel. Place on a baking sheet and bake in an oven preheated to 180°C/Gas Mark 4 for about 15–20 minutes, until tender. Remove from the oven, leave until cool enough to handle, then peel the beetroot and cut in half.

grouse
Place a juniper berry and a heather twig in the cavity of each bird. Heat the oil and butter in a large frying pan, add the grouse, leg-side down, and cook over a high heat for 15–20 seconds to seal. Turn over and repeat. Finally turn on to the breasts and cook until coloured. Remove from the pan and place on a baking tray. Transfer to an oven preheated to 200°C/Gas Mark 6 and cook for 15–20 minutes, depending on the size of the grouse. Remove from the tray, cut the legs off and set aside. Allow the crowns to rest for 10–15 minutes, loosely covered in aluminium foil. Chop the legs up and keep for the sauce.

walnut-infused jus
Heat the olive oil in a large saucepan, add the chopped grouse legs and cook until a deep brown. Add the shallots and mushrooms and cook for 3 minutes. Pour in the sherry vinegar, stirring to deglaze the pan, and cook until evaporated. Add the white port and simmer until reduced by half. Add the red wine and reduce by half again, then add the chicken stock. Bring to the boil and boil until reduced by half. Skim off any fat from the surface and strain through a fine sieve into a clean pan. Simmer until reduced to 250ml, skim the surface again, then blend in the walnut oil with a stick blender. Season to taste and keep warm.

serving
To finish the beetroot, heat the butter in a pan, add the beetroot and cook until lightly coloured. Season to taste.

Gently reheat the cabbage. Remove the grouse breasts from the crown. Froth the jus briefly with a stick blender. Place a mound of cabbage to one side of each plate and lay the morteau sausage slices on top. Rest the grouse breasts up against the cabbage. Arrange the roasted beetroot to one side and spoon the sauce around.

roast wood pigeon with date purée and goats' cheese emulsion

We have a friend called Ginger who has been shooting for us for many years and brings us any game we require: pigeon, rabbit, hare and widgeon. I prefer the local wood pigeon to pigeon from Bresse. It has a gamier flavour and can stand up to some strong accompaniments. Here I have teamed it with a date purée that has had a few acidic capers puréed with it to balance the sweetness. We would normally serve this dish with some wilted greens and roasted radishes (see page 128).

Serves 6

100g black Provençal olives, chopped

for the roast wood pigeon
6 plump wood pigeons
50ml olive oil
30g unsalted butter

for the sauce
50ml olive oil
1/2 onion, chopped
1 celery stick, chopped
2 garlic cloves, chopped
45ml sherry vinegar
100ml port
200ml red wine
1 litre Brown Chicken Stock (page 24)
500ml water
1/2 bay leaf
a sprig of thyme

for the date purée
200g pitted dates
25g capers, rinsed and drained
100ml port
100ml water

for the goats' cheese emulsion
100ml double cream
300g goats' cheese log (we use young Sainte Maure), crumbled
40ml extra virgin rapeseed oil

preparing the pigeon

Check the pigeons for quills and stray bits of feather. Remove the legs from each bird, then cut out the bottom part of the backbone and reserve for the sauce. Remove the skin from the breasts, leaving a nice crown of pigeon, then set aside.

sauce

Heat the oil in a large saucepan and fry the legs and backbone pieces in it until golden all over. Add the vegetables and cook until coloured. Pour in the vinegar and cook until completely evaporated, then add the port. When this, too, has evaporated, add the red wine and boil until reduced by half. Add the stock, water and herbs and bring to the boil. Reduce the heat and simmer for 1 hour. Strain the sauce through a fine sieve into a clean pan. Skim off any fat and simmer until reduced by two thirds. You should now have a wonderful rich sauce. If it is too thick, add a little water; if too thin, reduce a little more.

date purée

Place all the ingredients in a saucepan, bring to the boil and simmer for 15 minutes. Transfer to a blender and blend to a smooth purée. Keep warm.

cooking the pigeon

Heat the oil in a heavy roasting tin and add the butter. When it foams, add the pigeons and colour on each side for 1 minute, then for a further 30 seconds on the breasts. Season and transfer to an oven preheated to 220°C/Gas Mark 7. Roast for 5–8 minutes. Check to see if the birds are cooked by pressing with your fingers. The flesh should give way when pinched. Remove from the tin and leave to rest in a warm place for 10 minutes.

goats' cheese emulsion

Heat the double cream in a saucepan. Add the crumbled goats' cheese and cook for 2 minutes, stirring all the time. Transfer to a blender and blend to a purée, gradually adding the rapeseed oil. Check the seasoning and keep warm.

serving

Remove the pigeon breasts from the carcasses. Season the underneath of the breasts a little. Place a streak of date purée on each plate, then a little of the goats' cheese emulsion. Scatter the chopped olives over, arrange the breasts on the plate and pour over the sauce.

roast wood pigeon with cockscombs, parsley root purée and swiss chard

Being a lean meat, pigeon can sometimes do with a little help in the fat department. Here I have served it with cockscombs, whose fatty, gelatinous texture goes well with pigeon. You could use a pig's trotter as a substitute, or even braised pig's head.

The parsley root purée comes from Hamburg parsley, which is grown just for the root and resembles parsnips. Parsnips could be substituted if you cannot source parsley root. Swiss chard is an underrated vegetable, which I like to use. The crisp white stalks and vivid, slightly bitter leaves add to the overall balance of the dish.

Serves 6

for the roast wood pigeon
6 plump wood pigeons
50ml olive oil
30g unsalted butter

for the pigeon sauce
30ml olive oil
1 shallot, finely sliced
1 garlic clove, crushed
100ml port
200ml red wine
1 litre Brown Veal or Brown Beef Stock
  (page 25)
500ml water
3 juniper berries, crushed
1/2 bay leaf

for the cockscombs
12 cockscombs, soaked in salted water
  overnight to extract the blood
10g sea salt
1 garlic clove, chopped
300g duck fat

for the garlic confit
18 garlic cloves, peeled
200ml olive oil (or duck fat)
20g unsalted butter

for the parsley root purée
300g parsley root, peeled and sliced
225ml milk
200ml double cream
100g unsalted butter

for the swiss chard
400g Swiss chard
50g duck fat
75g raisins
100g pine kernels, toasted until golden

preparing the pigeon
Check the pigeons for quills and stray bits of feather. Remove the legs from each bird, then cut out the bottom part of the backbone and reserve for the sauce.

pigeon sauce
Heat the oil in a large saucepan and fry the legs and backbone pieces in it until golden all over. Add the shallot and garlic and cook until coloured. Add the port and cook until evaporated, then pour in the red wine and boil until reduced by half. Add all the remaining ingredients and bring to the boil. Skim off any froth from the surface and simmer for 1 hour. Strain the sauce through a fine sieve into a clean pan. Skim off any fat, then simmer the sauce until reduced to 250–300ml. If it is too thick, add a little water; if too thin, reduce a little more.

cockscombs
Drain the cockscombs from the water, rinse well, then blanch in a pan of boiling salted water for 2-3 minutes. Drain, refresh under cold water, then rub the skin off with a cloth. Pat dry, sprinkle with the salt and garlic, then put to one side for 4 hours. Remove any excess salt. Melt the duck fat in a casserole and add the cockscombs; the fat should cover them. Cover with a lid, transfer to an oven preheated to 180°C/Gas Mark 4 and cook for 2 hours, until the cockscombs are very soft and gelatinous.

Drain off the fat and reheat the cockscombs in the pigeon sauce.

garlic confit
Place the peeled garlic cloves in a small saucepan, add the olive oil and cook for 20 minutes on a slow simmer. Allow to cool in the oil. The garlic can be kept like this in a jar, covered with the oil, for 2–3 weeks.

parsley root purée
Place the sliced parsley root, milk and double cream in a saucepan and cook over a low heat until the parsley root is tender. Transfer to a blender and blend to a smooth, velvety purée, adding the butter towards the end. Season and keep warm.

swiss chard
Cut the chard leaves off the stalks and cut them into squares. Peel the stalks and cut them into squares, too. Cook the leaves and stalks separately in a little salted water until tender, then drain, refresh in cold water and drain again. Heat the duck fat in a pan, add the raisins and cook for 2–3 minutes. Add the pine kernels, then the chard and warm through. Season to taste and keep warm.

cooking the pigeons
Heat the oil in a heavy roasting tin and add the butter, then the pigeons. Colour on each side for about a minute, then give them a further 30 seconds on the breasts. Season and place in an oven preheated to 220°C/Gas Mark 7. Roast for 5–8 minutes. Check to see if they are cooked by pressing with your fingers; they should give a little. Remove from the tin and leave to rest in a warm place for 10 minutes.

To reheat the garlic confit, heat a little of the garlic oil in a pan, add the garlic and butter and cook until golden. Drain, season to taste and keep warm.

Place a mound of Swiss chard on each plate. Remove the breasts from the pigeon and stand them up against the chard. Place a streak of the parsley purée on the plate. Trim the cockscombs and stand them up in the purée. Arrange the garlic confit around and spoon the sauce over.

roasted middle neck fillet of lamb with wild garlic purée, blond morels and wilted wild garlic

Middle neck fillet is not used enough, in my opinion. It has a lovely flavour and, when cooked correctly, can be wonderfully tender. Here it is served with wild garlic, which coincidentally arrives at the same time of year as the morels. I have searched for morels in the wild with Helen and the dogs but as yet haven't found any – shame for us, but great for Twiglet and Truffle. I have heard of them growing in shopping-centre car parks where they have wood chip in their planting areas. If you can't get blond morels, use ordinary ones.

Serves 4

for the lamb
4 x 250–300g middle neck fillets of lamb
50ml olive oil
25g unsalted butter

for the lamb sauce
50ml olive oil
trimmings from the lamb
2 shallots, sliced
8 button mushrooms, sliced
2 garlic cloves, chopped
100ml Madeira
100ml red wine
1 litre Lamb Stock (page 24)

for the wild garlic purée
200g wild garlic leaves
25ml double cream
50ml water
50g unsalted butter

for the wilted wild garlic
40g unsalted butter
150g wild garlic leaves
12 wild garlic buds

for the morels
20–24 blond morel mushrooms
25ml olive oil
15g unsalted butter

preparing the lamb
Trim off any bits of fat and the long sinew running down the side of the lamb fillets. Score the top of the fat in a crisscross pattern.

wild garlic purée
Blanch the wild garlic in a large pan of boiling salted water for 30–45 seconds, then drain and refresh in cold water. Drain again, squeeze out the excess moisture and chop finely. Bring the cream, water and butter to the boil in a pan. Place the garlic in a blender, add the boiling liquid and blend to a very smooth purée. Season with salt and pepper to taste.

lamb sauce
Heat the oil in a saucepan and add the lamb trimmings, shallots, button mushrooms and garlic. Cook until golden, then pour in the Madeira and boil until reduced to a glaze. Add the red wine and reduce to a glaze again. Add the lamb stock, simmer for 30 minutes, then pass through a fine sieve into a pan. Boil until reduced to 200ml. Season to taste and keep warm.

cooking the lamb
Season the lamb fillets with salt and pepper. Heat the oil in a cast iron frying pan and add the butter. When it is sizzling, add the lamb, skin-side up. Colour quickly to seal, then flip it over on to the skin side. Cook quickly until golden, then transfer to an oven preheated to 200°C/Gas Mark 6. Cook for 6–8 minutes, until medium rare. Remove from the pan, and leave to rest in a warm place for 5 minutes.

wilted wild garlic
Heat the butter in a frying pan, then add the garlic leaves and buds and a few tablespoons of water. Keep turning the garlic over in the pan over a medium heat until the leaves are tender. Drain and season to taste. Keep warm.

morels
Rinse the morels under cold running water to remove any grit, then pat dry with a cloth and allow to dry completely. Heat the oil and butter in a large frying pan until foaming. Add the morels and cook over a medium heat for 2–3 minutes, shaking the pan occasionally. Drain and season to taste.

serving
Reheat the wild garlic purée quickly to retain its colour, then place a streak on each serving plate. Arrange the wilted wild garlic leaves across the purée. Carve each lamb fillet into 4–5 slices and arrange at an angle over the purée, then arrange the morels on the plate. Spoon a little sauce over and around.

pork dusted with cep powder, with stuffed cabbage

This is one of my signature dishes. It has been on the menu many times and is always popular with our customers. Cep powder is available from some delis, or you can use a spice grinder to grind your own from dried ceps. It gives the pork a lovely savoury taste. I serve it with bay bolete mushrooms because they have a good flavour and belong to the same family as the ceps used to dust the pork; you could use fresh ceps instead.

Crosnes, also known as Japanese artichokes, are funny-looking things, almost like witchetty grubs, that taste of salsify and artichokes. If you can't get them, substitute salsify.

We usually serve this dish with green beans, mashed potatoes and a piece of home-made black pudding.

Serves 6

for the sauce
50ml olive oil
250g pork ribs, chopped small
4 shallots, finely sliced
2 garlic cloves, crushed
30ml red wine vinegar
100ml port
200ml red wine
a sprig of thyme
1 star anise
1 litre Brown Chicken Stock (page 24)
50g unsalted butter, diced

for the stuffed cabbage
200g lean pork
100g belly pork
50g pork back fat
50g bread, soaked in milk
3 shallots, finely chopped
1 garlic clove, finely chopped
25ml olive oil
6 large green cabbage leaves

for the pork
3 x 400g pork fillets, trimmed of sinew and fat
30g powdered ceps
75ml olive oil
25g unsalted butter

to garnish
180g crosnes, trimmed
100ml olive oil
50g unsalted butter
6 bay bolete mushrooms (or ceps), sliced

sauce
Heat the olive oil in a large saucepan, add the pork ribs and cook until they are a good deep brown colour. Add the shallots and garlic and cook for 2–3 minutes. Stir in the vinegar, scraping the base of the pan with a wooden spoon to deglaze, and simmer until completely evaporated. Add the port and simmer until that has evaporated too. Add the red wine and simmer until reduced by half. Stir in the thyme and star anise, followed by the chicken stock. Bring to the boil, then reduce the heat and simmer for 30–45 minutes.

stuffed cabbage
Mince the pork, pork belly and back fat. Place in a bowl and beat well. Squeeze the excess milk out of the bread and beat the bread into the pork mixture. Gently cook the shallots and garlic in the olive oil until translucent and soft, then add to the mince, together with some salt and pepper. Fry a little of the mixture, then taste to see if you have the seasoning right; adjust if necessary.

Blanch the cabbage leaves in boiling salted water for 1–1$^{1}/_{2}$ minutes, then drain, refresh in cold water and drain again. Cut the leaves in half along the stem and remove the stem. Trim the pieces so they are all the same size, chopping the trimmings finely and adding them to the mince mixture. Divide the mince into 12 small balls, wrap in the cabbage and then in clingfilm to get a perfect ball shape. Chill for about an hour.

pork
Cut the pork fillets in half, rub them with the powdered ceps and season with salt and pepper. Heat a large, cast iron frying pan and add the olive oil and butter. When foaming, add the pork and colour all over for about 2 minutes. Transfer to an oven preheated to 180°C/Gas Mark 4 and cook for about 5–7 minutes, until just done. Remove from the pan and leave to rest in a warm place for 5 minutes. Place the pan back on the hob, add a little water and bring to the boil, stirring and scraping the base of the pan with a wooden spoon to dislodge the sediment. Remove from the heat.

finishing the sauce
Add the juices from the pork fillet pan to the sauce and bring to the boil. Skim off any fat from the surface and pass the sauce through a fine sieve. Simmer until reduced to about 300ml, then whisk in the butter a little at a time and season to taste. Keep warm.

crosnes
Cook the crosnes in a large pan of boiling salted water for about 5 minutes, then drain, refresh in cold water and drain again. Heat half the olive oil and butter in a frying pan. When foaming, add the crosnes and cook for 1–2 minutes. Drain, season to taste and keep warm.

bay bolete mushrooms
Heat the remaining olive oil and butter in a frying pan until foaming. Add the mushrooms and cook until golden on both sides. Drain, season and keep warm.

serving
Put the cabbage balls in a steamer and steam for 7–9 minutes. Carve the pork into 6–7 slices each and place in the middle of each serving plate. Place a stuffed cabbage ball at either end and then scatter with the mushrooms and crosnes. Finally spoon the sauce over and around the pork.

roasted rib eye of black angus beef with braised lettuce and winkles

Winkles were always a treat when I visited the coast as a small child. If the crab wasn't very good, we always had a pint or two of winkles, which I ceremoniously picked with my own little winkle pin. Winkles and beef may seem like an odd combination but I can assure you it works well. In France it is quite traditional to serve snails with beef, so I have simply replaced them here with winkles, which I think work even better because of their saltiness. You could try using other shellfish, too. Serve with some thick-cut chips cooked in goose fat, or fondant potato and a crisp green salad – lettuce in a different form!

Serves 2

for the winkles
1 carrot, sliced
1 onion, sliced
1 celery stick, sliced
1 garlic clove, crushed
a sprig of thyme
$1/_2$ bay leaf
2 slices of lemon
1 tablespoon white wine vinegar
32 winkles, rinsed well
50g unsalted butter
$1/_2$ garlic clove, chopped

for the rib eye of beef
50g duck fat
about 1kg rib eye of beef, 6–7cm thick, trimmed and fat cut off so just the eye is left
10 black peppercorns, cracked
25g unsalted butter

for the braised lettuce
2 Little Gem lettuces
50ml olive oil
150ml White Chicken Stock (page 23)
25g unsalted butter
a good pinch of savory leaves

for the red wine sauce
250ml red wine
500ml Brown Veal or Brown Beef Stock (page 25)
25ml olive oil
4 shallots, finely chopped
6 black peppercorns, crushed
a sprig of savory
50g unsalted butter

winkles
Place the vegetables, thyme, bay leaf, lemon slices and vinegar in a medium saucepan. Top up with enough water to cover, bring to the boil and simmer for 30 minutes. Add a little salt and then the winkles, cover the pan and cook for 2–3 minutes over a medium heat. Remove from the heat and leave the winkles in the pan for 5 minutes, then remove with a slotted spoon and hook them out of their shells. Remove the black part at the end (this is the intestine) and place the winkles to one side to cool.

rib eye of beef
Heat the duck fat in a large frying pan. Season the beef with the cracked peppercorns and a little salt, then place in the frying pan and cook over a medium-high heat for about 6 minutes, until golden all over. Add the butter, lower the heat and continue cooking for about 25–30 minutes, turning over and basting the meat every 5 minutes. If the rib is particularly thick, you may need to cook it a little longer. Remove from the pan and leave to rest in a warm place for 10–15 minutes.

braised lettuce
Cut a little of the core out of each lettuce, keeping the lettuce whole. Wash in cold running water, then drain and pat dry. Heat the oil in a small casserole, add the lettuce and cook over a medium heat until limp on all sides and lightly caramelised. Add the chicken stock and butter and bring to the boil. Season, cover with baking parchment, then place in an oven preheated to 200°C/Gas Mark 6 and cook for 20 minutes, basting every 5 minutes and turning the lettuce over halfway through. Keep warm.

red wine sauce
Pour the wine into a pan and boil until reduced to 50ml. Add the stock and boil until reduced by half. In another saucepan, heat the oil, add the shallots and cook until golden. Add the peppercorns and savory, then pour in the reduced stock mixture. Simmer for 10–15 minutes to allow the flavours to develop, then remove the savory sprig. Whisk in the butter a little at a time and season to taste. Keep warm.

serving
To finish the winkles, heat the butter in a frying pan until foaming, add the garlic and cook for 10 seconds. Then add the winkles and heat them through briefly. Place the rib flat on a board and carve across into 8–10 slices. Place to one side of each plate. Drain each lettuce of its stock and place on the other side of the beef. Pour the red wine sauce over and around it. Scatter the winkles and their butter over the meat and lettuce.

braised blade of beef
with nettle risotto and spring onions

I was first introduced to blade of beef by one of my sous chefs, Robert Clive Dixon, who I'm sure is responsible for making it such a popular cut of meat and an addition to restaurant menus across the country. Well, here is my version, served with a nettle risotto. There are several species of nettle, including white and red dead nettles, but we use the common stinging nettle as it is so prolific. Choose young nettles, as they have a better flavour. The spring onions are simply blanched, which gives a refreshing burst of water to the palate – very welcome with a rich dish such as this one. Do not be put off by the big piece of gristle running through the centre of the blade of beef. This helps with the flavour and, when cooked, turns into a delicious jelly.

Serves 6–8

for the blade of beef
1.5–2kg blade of beef
125ml olive oil
50g unsalted butter
1 carrot, chopped
1 onion, chopped
1 leek, cut into 4
3 garlic cloves, chopped
1 small can of stout
2 sprigs of thyme
1 bay leaf
2 litres Brown Veal or Brown Beef Stock
  (page 25)

for the spring onions
30–40 spring onions, trimmed and outer
  skin removed
30g unsalted butter

for the nettle risotto
250g young nettles
600ml chicken stock (pages 23–24)
50g unsalted butter
4 shallots, finely chopped
250g carnaroli risotto rice
5 spring onions, finely chopped
1 tablespoon Mascarpone cheese

blade of beef
Remove any skin or fat surrounding the blade of beef. Heat 75ml of the olive oil in a large frying pan and add 25g of the butter, followed by the meat. Cook on all sides until golden brown, then transfer to a plate. Add the chopped vegetables to the pan and cook until golden. Pour in the stout, stirring to scrape up the sediment from the base of the pan. Add the herbs and stock and bring to the boil. Place in a casserole dish large enough to take the blade and then add the blade. Cover with a lid, transfer to an oven preheated to 140°C/Gas Mark 1 and cook for $4^1/_2$–5 hours, until the meat is very tender when pierced with a knife. Allow to cool a little, then remove the meat from the casserole while still warm. Drain and wrap tightly in clingfilm to form a cylinder. Place in the fridge overnight to set the shape. Strain the sauce through a fine sieve.

spring onions
Quickly blanch the spring onions in a large pan of boiling salted water until limp. Refresh immediately in cold water, then drain and set aside.

nettle risotto
Blanch the nettles in a large pan of boiling salted water for 30–45 seconds, then drain, refresh in cold water and drain again. Mince or finely chop the nettles and set aside, together with any liquid that comes out of them. Bring the stock to boiling point in a small saucepan. In another saucepan, heat the butter, add the shallots and cook gently for 3 minutes, until softened but not coloured. Add the rice and cook for 3–4 minutes, until translucent. Add the hot stock 100ml at a time, stirring constantly. When each addition has been absorbed by the rice, add another 100ml, until the last of the stock has been used up; it should take 17–18 minutes in total.

About 5 minutes before the end, add the nettles and their liquid, and the chopped spring onions. The risotto should be moist and al dente. Stir in the Mascarpone to give a creamy texture. If the risotto is too sloppy, cook for a little longer; if it is too thick, add a little more chicken stock. Season to taste.

finishing the beef
After the beef has been in the fridge overnight, cut it through the clingfilm into 6 or 8 pieces. Remove the clingfilm. Reheat the sauce. Fry the blades on each side in a the remaining 50ml oil and 25g butter until golden. Transfer to a baking tray, pour over enough sauce to come halfway up the meat and place in an oven preheated to 180°C/Gas Mark 4 to heat through and glaze the top, basting every 5 minutes. The top should be shiny.

Meanwhile, simmer the remaining sauce until reduced to a coating consistency, then check the seasoning.

serving
To finish the spring onions, heat the butter in a frying pan with 2 tablespoons of water, add the spring onions and warm them through. Season to taste.

Place a mound of risotto to one side of each serving bowl and arrange the spring onions on the other side. Carefully lift out the braised blade and place on top of the risotto, then spoon the sauce around.

rack of veal with black mustard seeds, roasted garlic purée and white asparagus

This is quick and easy to cook and makes a lovely light dish for spring or summer. The black mustard seeds give the veal a little burst of flavour when you bite into it. The garlic purée makes a good accompaniment to roast meat but if you don't like garlic (unbelievable, I know, but there are a few people out there who don't), a purée of roasted onions would work well, or a parsnip or celeriac purée for a different flavour combination. White asparagus is nice and thick. Here it is rolled in the veal pan juices after cooking to give it a delicious savoury taste.

Serve with a crisp green salad and perhaps a gratin of potatoes and turnips.

Serves 6

for the garlic confit
30 garlic cloves, peeled
200ml olive oil or duck fat
20g unsalted butter

for the veal juices
50ml olive oil
the backbone and trimmings from the rack of veal
100ml Madeira
100ml red wine
1 litre Brown Veal Stock (page 25)
50g unsalted butter
5g black mustard seeds
a few drops of lemon juice

for the roasted garlic purée
4 heads of garlic
50ml olive oil
150ml double cream
50ml milk
40g unsalted butter

for the rack of veal
1 rack of veal with 6 bones, trimmed and chined (ask your butcher to remove the backbone, chop it and give it to you with the trimmings)
1 tablespoon black mustard seeds
75ml olive oil
50g unsalted butter

for the white asparagus
18–24 fat white asparagus spears
25g unsalted butter

garlic confit
Place the peeled garlic cloves in a small saucepan, add the olive oil or duck fat and cook for 30 minutes on a slow simmer – the cloves should be very tender. Leave to cool in the oil. The garlic can be kept like this in a jar, covered with the oil or fat, for 1–2 weeks. When needed, heat a little of the oil or fat in a pan, add the garlic and cook until golden. At the last minute, add the butter, season with salt and pepper, then drain well.

veal juices
Heat the olive oil in a saucepan, add the chopped veal bones and cook until golden all over. Add the Madeira and boil until reduced to a glaze. Add the red wine and reduce to a glaze again. Finally add the veal stock, bring to the boil and simmer for 30 minutes. Skim off any fat from the surface and pour the sauce through a fine sieve into a clean pan.

roasted garlic purée
Separate the garlic into individual cloves; don't worry about peeling them. Toss them in the olive oil and wrap loosely in foil. Seal the ends, place in an oven preheated to 180°C/Gas Mark 4 and cook for 20 minutes, until the garlic is soft. Squeeze the cloves out of their skins into a small saucepan. Add the double cream and milk, bring to the boil and transfer to a blender.

Blend to a smooth purée, adding the butter at the last minute. Season to taste and keep warm.

rack of veal
Season the veal rack with salt and pepper and press the mustard seeds into the fatty side. Heat an ovenproof frying pan and add the olive oil and butter. When they are hot, add the veal and seal it all over until nice and golden. Place, fatty-side down, in an oven preheated to 200°C/Gas Mark 6 and cook for 30–40 minutes. Turn the meat over so the fat is uppermost and cook for another 30–40 minutes, basting 2 or 3 times. The meat should be pink inside. Remove from the oven, transfer to a warm plate and cover loosely with foil. Leave to rest in a warm place for 20 minutes.

finishing the veal juices
In a small saucepan heat 10g of the butter, add the mustard seeds and cook until they start popping and are fragrant. Add the reduced sauce and any juices from the veal. Bring to the boil, then simmer until reduced to 250ml. Whisk in the remaining butter a little at a time. Season and add a few drops of lemon juice.

white asparagus
Trim the asparagus so the spears are just 10cm long and peel to within 2cm of the tips. Blanch in boiling salted water for 1–2 minutes, until tender, then drain, refresh in cold water and drain again. Dry and toss in a little of the veal cooking juices.

serving
Trim the ends of the rack of veal and carve into 6 cutlets. Place a smear of roasted garlic purée on each plate, then the veal. Arrange the asparagus and garlic confit on the plates and spoon the sauce around.

roasted calf's sweetbreads with grue de cocoa, purée of chervil tuber and liquorice root jus

Whenever I see calf's sweetbreads on a menu I just have to order them. Crisp on the outside and soft and creamy inside, they are one of my favourite things. Here chervil tubers, a root with a sweet aftertaste, provide a complementary flavour. The sweetbreads are cooked with grue de cocoa, the outer husk of the cocoa bean, which has a bitter and intoxicating taste. The liquorice root sauce adds depth to the whole dish and links all the flavours together.

You may be able to get grue de cocoa from a good chocolatier. Chervil tubers are a different species from the chervil herb. They used to be grown as a crop for cattle but are now being cultivated for human consumption. A good greengrocer should be able to obtain them for you. If you can't get chervil tubers, try serving this with a parsnip purée instead.

Serves 4

for the sweetbreads
4 veal sweetbreads, weighing 200–250g
* each (you need the pancreatic breads,*
* also known as heart breads)*
10g grue de cocoa
50ml olive oil
25g unsalted butter

for the liquorice root jus
50ml olive oil
2 shallots, chopped
15ml sherry vinegar
1 garlic clove, chopped
a sprig of thyme
2 sticks of liquorice root, crushed with the
* back of a knife*
100ml port
200ml red wine (such as Cahors)
1 litre Brown Veal Stock (page 25)

for the chervil tuber purée
225g chervil tubers, peeled and sliced
150ml milk
125ml double cream
75g unsalted butter

preparing the sweetbreads
Check the sweetbreads to make sure they are of pristine quality; they should be bright pink and fresh looking and shouldn't smell of anything. Soak them in cold water for 4 hours to remove the blood, then drain. Trim the fine outer membrane off the sweetbreads and any bits of gristle. Keep the trimmings for the sauce.

liquorice root jus
Heat the oil in a saucepan, add the shallots and sweetbread trimmings and cook until golden brown. Add the vinegar, stirring well with a wooden spoon to deglaze the pan. Add the garlic, thyme and crushed liquorice root and cook for 2 minutes. Now add the port and boil until reduced by half. Add the red wine and reduce that by half, too. Finally, add the veal stock, bring back to the boil and simmer for 1 hour. Pass through a fine sieve into a clean pan and boil until reduced to 200ml. Season with salt and pepper to taste and keep warm.

chervil tuber purée
Place the sliced chervil tubers in a saucepan with the milk and cream. Bring to the boil, then reduce the heat to low and simmer until tender. Transfer to a blender and blend to a smooth, velvety purée, adding the butter towards the end. Season to taste and keep warm.

cooking the sweetbreads
Grind the grue de cocoa down in either a spice mill or a pestle and mortar. It should be medium ground but not too coarse. Season the sweetbreads on all sides with salt and pepper, then coat them in the grue de cocoa, pressing it on well. Heat the olive oil in a large, cast iron pan, add the butter and then the sweetbreads. Cook over a medium heat until golden on one side. Flip over and cook until golden on the other side, then transfer the pan to an oven preheated to 220°C/Gas Mark 7. Cook for 7–8 minutes, turning the sweetbreads over 2–3 times. They should be crisp and golden on the outside and just done in the middle. Drain well, season and keep warm.

serving
Cut the sweetbreads in half at an angle. Arrange the chervil tuber purée in a circle on each plate and place the halved sweetbreads on top. Soon a little sauce over and around.

roast venison with lapsang souchong and orange, and jerusalem artichoke purée

I have included venison in this book because it is quick to cook and has such a good flavour. When I worked at La Tante Claire for Pierre Koffman, he served venison with a bitter chocolate sauce, which has since become a classic. Here I have coated the venison with Lapsang Souchong tea, which gives it a lovely smoky flavour, and a little grated orange zest. It is served with a light purée so as not to detract from the venison flavour.

We often accompany this dish with some buttered Savoy cabbage flavoured with a little crushed juniper. I have in the past reduced the portion size by half and served it with belly of pork braised with Chinese spices.

Serves 4

for the venison
1 x 700g venison steak, taken from the
   saddle
grated zest of 1 orange
1 tablespoon Lapsang Souchong tea
50ml olive oil
25g unsalted butter

for the venison sauce
75ml olive oil
1 onion, finely chopped
2 garlic cloves, chopped
5 juniper berries, crushed
3 sprigs of thyme
1 bay leaf
100ml port
300ml red wine
1 litre good Brown Veal or Brown Beef
   Stock (page 25)
50g unsalted butter, diced

for the onions
50g unsalted butter
20 small button onions, peeled
a pinch of sugar

for the jerusalem artichoke purée
500g Jerusalem artichokes
juice of 1/2 lemon
50g unsalted butter
100ml double cream
200ml milk

preparing the venison
Carefully remove the silver skin from the venison. Coat the meat in the grated orange zest and Lapsang Souchong. Wrap in clingfilm and leave for 30 minutes to allow the flavours to develop, then cut it into 4 equal portions. Season with salt and pepper.

venison sauce
Heat the olive oil in a large saucepan and add the onion, garlic, juniper, thyme and bay leaf. Cook until the onion is caramelised to a deep golden brown. Add the port and cook until it has completely evaporated, then add the red wine and boil until reduced by two thirds. Add the veal stock and boil until reduced by two thirds again. Strain through a fine sieve into a clean pan and reheat gently, then whisk in the butter a little at a time. The sauce should be thick enough to coat the back of a spoon. If it is too thin, reduce it a little more; if too thick, add a little more stock.

onions
Heat the butter in a pan large enough to hold the onions in a single layer, add the onions and cook over a medium heat until golden brown all over. Reduce the heat and sprinkle with the sugar. Add enough water to come about a quarter of the way up the onions and simmer until tender. Season to taste.

jerusalem artichoke purée
Peel the artichokes and slice them finely, dropping them in some water acidulated with the lemon juice as you go to prevent discoloration. Heat half the butter in a saucepan, drain the artichokes and add them to the pan. Cook for 3–4 minutes without letting them colour. Pour in the cream and milk and simmer for 20–25 minutes, until the artichokes are very tender. Transfer to a blender and blend to a smooth purée, adding the remaining butter towards the end. Season and keep warm.

cooking the venison
Heat the olive oil in a heavy, cast iron frying pan, then add the butter, followed by the venison. Brown quickly all over to seal, taking care not to burn the coating. Transfer to an oven preheated to 180°C/Gas Mark 4 and cook for 4–6 minutes, depending on the thickness. It should feel springy to the touch. Leave to rest in a warm place for 3–4 minutes.

serving
Place a little purée on each plate (and then some buttered cabbage, if using). Cut each venison portion into 4–5 thick slices and arrange neatly on the plate. Scatter the onions around the plate and spoon over the sauce.

fillet of roe deer crusted in sloes, with smoked ox tongue and creamed celeriac

I get whole roe deer at the restaurant and butcher them myself. It gives us many good cuts. You could even make this recipe with one of the leg muscles from the haunch. It won't be quite as tender but it will taste wonderful. I have coated the meat in crushed sloes and peppercorns here, which give it a slightly fruity, sour taste, and served it with smoked ox tongue – a must from your butcher if you don't have a smoker. Celeriac cream gives the dish its comfort appeal, while the roasted radishes add a bit of texture. I like to use Easter Egg radishes – a lovely multi-coloured variety that includes purples, reds and whites. They look spectacular on the plate.

Serves 6

for the smoked ox tongue
1 litre water
1 bay leaf
a sprig of thyme
3 juniper berries
1 garlic clove, crushed
2 strips of orange zest
1 smoked ox tongue, weighing 1–1.5kg

for the sauce
75ml olive oil
500g venison bones, chopped
1 onion, sliced
2 garlic cloves, sliced
50ml red wine vinegar
500ml red wine
a sprig of thyme
1 bay leaf
8–10 black peppercorns, crushed
6–8 sloes
1.5 litres Brown Chicken Stock (page 24)

for the creamed celeriac
300g celeriac, peeled and diced
125ml double cream
150ml milk
75g unsalted butter, diced

for the venison
6 x 150g venison steaks from the saddle
1 tablespoon black peppercorns, crushed
2 tablespoons sloe berries, crushed
50ml olive oil
25g unsalted butter

for the roasted radishes
50ml olive oil
25g unsalted butter
24 medium Easter egg radishes

ox tongue
Bring the water to the boil in a large saucepan with the herbs, garlic and orange zest. Add the tongue and simmer for 2–2$^{1}/_{2}$ hours, until very tender. Remove the tongue from the stock, drain and peel off the thick skin while it is still warm. Return the tongue to the stock until needed, keeping it warm.

sauce
Heat the olive oil in a large saucepan, add the bones and brown them all over. Add the onion and garlic and cook for 2 minutes. Add the red wine vinegar, stirring well to deglaze the pan, and cook until it has completely evaporated. Pour in the red wine and boil until reduced by half. Add the herbs, peppercorns, sloes and stock, bring to the boil and simmer for 1 hour. Strain the sauce through a fine sieve into a clean pan and return to the stove. Simmer until reduced to 300–350ml. Season with salt and pepper and keep warm.

creamed celeriac
Place the celeriac in a saucepan, add the cream and milk and bring to the boil. Cover and simmer gently for 15 minutes, until the celeriac is very soft. Transfer to a blender and blend to a smooth purée, adding the butter a little at a time towards the end. Season to taste and keep warm.

venison
Season the venison steaks with salt and pepper, then coat them in the crushed peppercorns and sloes. Heat the oil and butter in an ovenproof frying pan, add the meat and cook for 1–2 minutes, until sealed on all sides. Transfer to an oven preheated to 220°C/Gas Mark 7 and cook for 4–5 minutes. Remove from the oven and leave to rest in a warm place for 5 minutes.

roasted radishes
Heat an ovenproof frying pan and add the oil and butter. When hot, add the radishes, season and place in an oven preheated to 180°C/Gas Mark 4. Cook for 5–6 minutes, turning occasionally.

serving
Place a streak of creamed celeriac in the middle of each serving plate. Place a venison steak to the left of the plate. Finely slice the tongue and place to the right of the meat. Cut the radishes in half and arrange on the plate. Spoon the sauce around.

roast fillet of hare and casserole of its legs with juniper, pickled pears and glazed turnips

I occasionally put hare on the menu. It has a wonderful deep, rich flavour and the saddle fillet is the most tender thing you can imagine.

The legs and shoulders are cooked with juniper berries here, which give the sauce a real tang. The best thing to serve with this is some creamed potato or spätzel, a Swiss dumpling that is like a cross between gnocchi and pasta.

Serves 6

for the hare
100ml olive oil
90g unsalted butter
1 hare, divided into 2 saddles, 2 legs and
    2 shoulders (you could ask your butcher
    to do this)
1 celery stick, chopped
2 carrots, chopped
1 onion, chopped
4 garlic cloves, crushed
200ml port
6–8 juniper berries, crushed
500ml red wine
500ml Brown Veal or Brown Beef Stock
    (page 25)

for the glazed turnips
3 turnips, about 7cm diameter
50g unsalted butter
20ml honey
100ml port
1 teaspoon red wine vinegar
1/2 bay leaf

for the wilted cabbage
6 large green cabbage leaves
50g unsalted butter

for the pickled pears
3 pickled pears, made as for Pickled Apples
    (see page 21)
25g unsalted butter

hare
Heat half the oil and 30g of the butter in a casserole large enough to hold the legs. First of all, colour the shoulders on both sides. Remove them from the casserole, add the legs and cook until golden on both sides. Remove from the casserole. Add the vegetables to the pan and cook until golden. Stir in the port and juniper berries and cook until the port is reduced to a glaze, scraping up the sediment from the bottom of the casserole with a wooden spoon. Put the shoulders and legs back in the pan, add the red wine and simmer until reduced by two thirds. Add the stock and bring to the boil. Cover the casserole, transfer to an oven preheated to 150°C/Gas Mark 2 and cook for 1³/₄–2 hours or until the hare is very tender.

Remove the shoulders and legs, take off the meat in bite-sized pieces, then return it to the casserole. Take out three-quarters of the sauce and strain it through a fine sieve into a clean saucepan. Boil until reduced to 200ml. Whisk in 30g of the remaining butter a little at a time and season to taste. Keep the sauce and the hare warm until needed.

glazed turnips
Peel the turnips and cut them into cylinders 4cm in diameter. Cut these into slices 1.5cm thick; you need 12–18 in total. Heat 30g of the butter in a frying pan, add the turnips and cook until coloured on both sides. Add all the other ingredients, including the remaining butter, and bring to the boil. Lower the heat and simmer for 10–15 minutes, until the turnips are tender. Turn the heat up and make sure the juices are reduced, turning the turnips over and over until glazed and shiny. Season to taste and keep warm.

wilted cabbage
Blanch the cabbage leaves in boiling salted water for 1–2 minutes, then drain, refresh in cold water and drain again. Cut in half and discard the central core from each leaf, then set aside.

hare saddle
Heat the remaining butter and oil in a frying pan, add the hare saddle fillets and cook gently until golden on both sides and just done, but still very pink in the centre. This should take about 4–5 minutes, depending on the size of the hare. Remove from the pan and leave to rest for 5–10 minutes. Season with salt and pepper.

pickled pears
Dice the pickled pears and warm them in the butter. Season to taste and keep warm.

serving
Gently reheat the cabbage in the butter. Place a little hare casserole on each serving plate, then pile the cabbage on the plate, then a little more hare casserole. Cut each saddle fillet into 9 slices on the diagonal and place 3 slices on top of the casserole on each plate. Arrange the turnips and pickled pear on the plate and spoon the sauce over and around.

crisp belly of gloucester old spot pork with surf clams and pumpkin purée

We use pork from a traditional breed of pig for this dish, the Gloucester Old Spot, which used to be bred in the apple orchards of Gloucestershire – hence its other name of orchard pig, or cottager's pig.

Belly of pork is one of those ingredients that are at home in both bistros and fine dining restaurants. Here I have served it with surf clams, lovely sweet, tender clams from Salcombe. They go so well with the pumpkin and add a third texture to the dish, so you have crisp, soft and slightly chewy. Parsnip purée also works well, as does cauliflower purée. Why not roast the cauliflower first for a different flavour?

Serves 6

for the belly pork
1 medium onion, sliced
2 bay leaves
a sprig of thyme
1.5kg piece of belly pork, ribs removed and saved for the sauce
1 head of garlic, cut in half
1 litre White Chicken Stock (page 23)
50ml olive oil

for the pork sauce
50ml olive oil
200g ribs from the pork, chopped small
2 shallots, finely sliced
1 garlic clove, finely sliced
100ml Madeira
200ml red wine
a sprig of thyme
30g unsalted butter

for the pumpkin purée
800g pumpkin
a little oil
200ml milk
200ml double cream
100g unsalted butter, diced

for the surf clams
750g–1kg surf clams
50ml olive oil
1 large shallot, chopped
a sprig of thyme
200ml white wine
150ml water

for the choy sum
12 small choy sum
50g unsalted butter

for the mushrooms
6 large trompette noire (horn of plenty) mushrooms
50ml olive oil
120g girolle mushrooms

belly pork

Spread the onion, bay leaves and thyme out in a heavy baking tray, just large enough to hold the pork. Put the pork in it and then put the garlic in two of the corners. Pour in the stock, cover tightly with foil and place on the stove. Bring to the boil, then transfer to an oven preheated to 160°C/Gas Mark 3 and cook for $3^1/_2$–4 hours, until very tender.

Carefully remove the pork belly from the stock and place it on a tray lined with clingfilm. Cover with more clingfilm and place another tray on top. Place a couple of heavy weights on the tray to press the pork, then leave it overnight in the fridge. The next day, trim the meat to give a neat rectangle (you could keep the trimmings to fry with some potatoes for another occasion). Cut the pork into 6 pieces and set aside.

pork sauce

Heat the olive oil in a large saucepan, add the pork ribs and cook until deep brown. Add the shallots and garlic and cook for 2–3 minutes. Stir in the Madeira and simmer until completely evaporated, then pour in the red wine and simmer until reduced by half. Add the thyme and the braising juices from the pork and simmer for 45 minutes–1 hour, skimming off any fat that rises to the surface. Pass through a fine sieve into a clean pan and set aside.

pumpkin purée

Cut the pumpkin into quarters and remove the seeds. Place on a baking tray, drizzle with a little oil and cover with foil. Roast in an oven preheated to 200°C/Gas Mark 6 until the flesh is very tender. Remove from the oven and scrape the flesh off the skin. Place the flesh in a blender. Bring the milk and cream to the boil, pour into the blender and blend until smooth. Then add the butter little by little. The purée should be totally smooth – the hotter the ingredients the better. Season to taste and keep warm until needed.

surf clams

Wash the clams under cold running water to remove any grit. Heat the olive oil in a large saucepan, add the shallot and thyme and cook for 30 seconds. Add the clams, pour in the white wine and water, then immediately place the lid on the pan. Cook for 1 minute over a fairly high heat, shaking the pan from side to side. The clams should open. Remove from the cooking liquor as quickly as possible and allow to cool a little. Pass the liquid through a damp piece of muslin to catch any grit and put to one side. The clams can be kept in these juices until needed.

finishing the pork sauce

Add 200–250ml of the clam cooking juices to the sauce and simmer until the sauce has reduced to about 400ml. Whisk in the butter, season to taste and add the clams. Heat through gently but do not let it boil.

choy sum

Trim off most of the leaves of the choy sum, leaving just 2cm still attached. Cook in a large pan of boiling salted water for 2 minutes, then drain and refresh immediately in cold water. Drain again and set aside.

mushrooms

Sauté the trompettes noires in 20ml of the olive oil for 30 seconds, until limp. Season to taste and drain. Break the mushrooms into thin strips.

Heat the remaining oil in a frying pan and toss the girolles in it for 2–3 minutes, until tender. Season to taste and drain.

serving

To finish the pork, heat a large cast iron frying pan on the stove and add the olive oil. When it is very hot, place the pork in it, skin-side down, and turn the heat down to medium. Cook until the skin is crisp, then turn over and cook for a further 3–4 minutes, until the pork is heated right through.

Reheat the choy sum in the butter and season to taste.

Place 2 slashes of pumpkin purée on each plate at different angles. Lay the crisp pork belly on the plate, scatter with the surf clams and arrange the girolles, choy sum and trompettes noires in little mounds. Finally spoon some of the sauce around.

roast mallard with crab apple purée, chestnuts and salsify

This dish has the advantage of everything being in season at around the same time – give or take a couple of weeks depending to the weather. Mallard is less fatty than duck and a lot gamier. Helen and I gather crab apples and chestnuts with mushrooms in the autumn. Occasionally I serve spiced pickled crab apples with game, so you could substitute pickled apples from the store cupboard, just warmed through, for the crab apple purée (see the recipe for Pickled Apples on page 21).

Serves 6

for the sauce
50ml olive oil
250g duck bones (if you can't get them, use chicken wings – or a couple of duck legs)
3 shallots, sliced
2 garlic cloves, sliced
25ml sherry vinegar
50ml Cognac
100ml Madeira
500ml Brown Chicken Stock (page 24)
25g unsalted butter
the livers from the birds

for the roast mallard
3 mallards, with their livers
3 crab apples
3 juniper berries
3 sprigs of thyme
50ml olive oil
25g unsalted butter

for the crab apple purée
50g unsalted butter
400g crab apples, cored and quartered
50–70g caster sugar

for the salsify
12 small sticks of salsify, peeled and cut into even lengths (you will need 6 pieces per person)
250ml chicken stock (pages 23–24)
50g duck fat

for the chestnuts
75g unsalted butter
24 chestnuts, cooked and peeled (see page 42)
3 tablespoons chicken stock (pages 23–24)

for the cabbage
4 Savoy cabbage leaves
25g unsalted butter

sauce
Heat the olive oil in a large saucepan, add the duck bones and cook until browned all over. Add the shallots and garlic and cook until golden. Pour in the sherry vinegar, stirring well to deglaze the pan, and cook until it has completely evaporated. Add the Cognac and boil until that, too, has evaporated. Add the Madeira and boil until reduced by half. Add the chicken stock, bring to the boil and skim off any fat from the surface. Reduce the heat and simmer for 30–40 minutes. Strain through a fine sieve and set aside.

Heat the butter in a small frying pan. When foaming, add the mallard livers and cook over a high heat for 30 seconds on each side. Place the contents of the pan in a blender, add the sauce and blend until smooth. Pass through a fine sieve into a clean pan. Season with salt and pepper and set to one side.

roast mallard
Remove the legs from the birds and keep for another occasion (try a confit – see page 16 – or braise them with baby onions). Cut the crab apples in half and place 2 halves, a juniper berry and a thyme sprig in the cavity of each mallard. Heat the oil and butter in a large frying pan. Season the birds and seal on one side for about a minute, until golden. Flip over and seal the other side and finally place on the breast side and seal until golden. Transfer to a roasting tin and place in an oven preheated to 200°C/Gas Mark 6. Roast for 20 minutes; the birds should be rare to medium rare.

Cover loosely with foil and leave in a warm place for 15 minutes. Keep any juices that escape for the sauce.

crab apple purée
Heat the butter in a saucepan, add the apples and sugar and cover the pan. Cook for 5–10 minutes, shaking the pan occasionally, until the apples are tender. Transfer to a blender and blend to a smooth purée. Push through a fine sieve, then taste. If too sharp, add a little more sugar; if too sweet add a little lemon juice. Season and keep warm.

salsify
Place the salsify in a saucepan with the chicken stock and duck fat and bring to the boil. Cook over a medium-high heat until the stock has evaporated and the salsify is tender and light brown in colour. Season and keep warm.

chestnuts
Heat the butter in a frying pan until foaming, then add the chestnuts and chicken stock. Cook until light golden brown. Season to taste and keep warm.

savoy cabbage
Blanch the cabbage leaves in boiling salted water for 1–2 minutes, then drain, refresh in cold water and drain again. Cut the leaves into even pieces. Heat the butter in a frying pan, add the cabbage and warm through, then season to taste.

serving
Take the breasts off the birds. If they are too rare, put them back in a hot oven, skin-side down, for 2 minutes. Place a streak of crab apple purée to one side of each plate. Cut each duck breast into 5 or 6 slices and place on the purée. Arrange the salsify, cabbage and chestnuts on the other side of the plate. Add any juices from the mallard to the sauce, then spoon the sauce over the mallard and around the garnish.

warm salad of moroccan spiced duck confit, couscous with salted lemon and land cress

I like Moroccan spices a lot. They can be both subtle and powerful. Here I have used Moroccan spicing in the curing mixture for a confit. It gives the duck legs the most amazing flavour. The couscous has some salted lemon running through it to freshen it up and the land cress adds a lovely peppery bite. It could be replaced by watercress, if necessary. You could also try replacing the duck legs with a small boned shoulder of lamb, although it would have to be cooked a good hour longer.

Serves 6

200g land cress

for the spiced duck confit
1 teaspoon coriander seeds
1 teaspoon cardamom pods
2cm piece of cinnamon stick
1 teaspoon cumin seeds
2 strips of orange zest
3 garlic cloves, peeled
1/2 teaspoon fennel seeds
6 duck legs
50g sel gris (grey sea salt)
750g duck fat

for the sauce
a pinch of saffron threads
200ml olive oil
2 shallots, finely chopped
1 garlic clove, finely chopped
10 coriander seeds, crushed
1/2 teaspoon cumin seeds
juice of 1/2 lemon
2 tablespoons chopped coriander
*2 roasted piquillo peppers, chopped
(canned ones are fine)*

for the couscous
100ml olive oil
1 onion, finely chopped
2 garlic cloves, finely chopped
300g couscous
*the peel from 1 Salted Lemon (see page
18), finely chopped*
400ml White Chicken Stock (page 23)
juice of 1/2 lemon
50g land cress, chopped

spiced duck confit

First make the spice mix. Heat a sturdy frying pan, then add all the spices and toast until the seeds start popping and a wonderful smell comes forth. Place in a spice grinder with the orange zest and blend to a fine powder. Make the confit according to the recipe on page 16, replacing the herbs, juniper, coriander and peppercorns with the spice mix.

sauce

Put 2 tablespoons of hot water in a cup or small bowl, add the saffron and leave to stand for 10 minutes.

Heat about a third of the olive oil in a pan, add the shallots and garlic and cook for 2–3 minutes without colouring. Add the spices, including the saffron liquid, and the remaining olive oil and cook on the gentlest possible heat for 5 minutes to allow the spices to infuse the sauce. Add the lemon juice, coriander and piquillo peppers, bring to a simmer and cook for 1 minute. Remove from the heat and season to taste. Keep warm.

couscous

Heat the olive oil in a saucepan, add the onion and fry until it is a deep golden brown. Add the garlic and couscous, cook for 30 seconds, then add the salted lemon and chicken stock. Bring to the boil, remove from the heat and cover the pan. Leave in a warm place for 15–20 minutes. The couscous should swell up and all the stock should be absorbed. Fluff up the couscous with a fork, add the lemon juice and season to taste. Mix in the chopped land cress.

serving

Crisp up the duck legs in a frying pan, as described on page 16. Place a mound of couscous in the middle of each serving plate. Dress the land cress with a little of the sauce and place on top. Place the duck confit on top of this and spoon the remaining sauce around.

desserts

rose-scented geranium (pelargonium graveolens)
used in
rose geranium cream with lychee sorbet

rose geranium cream with lychee sorbet

A good friend of mine, Marion Jones, used to own the Croque-en-Bouche restaurant in Malvern with her husband, Robin. A talented chef, she held a Michelin star for 20 years and grew much of her own food. She introduced me to the scented geranium, and I still get the occasional surprise package of geranium from her as a very welcome present.

At the restaurant we serve this, or variations on it, as a pre-dessert – something to refresh the palate after the main course. As a bigger portion, it makes a lovely light dessert. We tend to keep the cream's lemon base and change the leaves, using ones that have a strong scent, such as lemon thyme, lemon verbena, Mabel Grey geranium or orange pekoe tea. The sorbet can change, too, but try to use something that complements the cream. The slight rose scent of the geranium goes extremely well with lychee, which has a scent all of its own. The cream can also be used as a custard layer in a trifle.

We serve this with popping candy to create a lightness and to show that cooking has its amusing side. When using, do not let it come into contact with water, as that will set it off.

Serves 8

for the lychee sorbet
200g caster sugar
25ml liquid glucose
250ml water
1kg fresh lychees, peeled and stoned
juice of ¹/₂ lemon

for the rose geranium cream
75ml lemon juice
grated zest of 1 lemon
15g rose geranium leaves, chopped
200ml double cream
1 egg
4 egg yolks
65g caster sugar

to glaze
caster sugar
icing sugar
popping candy (available in some sweet
  shops)

lychee sorbet
Put the sugar, glucose and water in a pan and bring to the boil, stirring to dissolve the sugar. Simmer for 2 minutes to make a syrup, then leave to cool.

Liquidise the lychees with the syrup and push through a fine sieve. Add the lemon juice little by little, checking the taste as you go. Freeze in an ice-cream machine according to the manufacturer's instructions.

rose geranium cream
Place the lemon juice, zest and chopped geranium leaves in a saucepan and bring to the boil. Remove from the heat and leave to infuse for 1 hour. Return to the heat, stir in the double cream and bring to the boil again.

Whisk the egg, egg yolks and sugar together until pale. Pour the cream mixture on to the eggs, whisking all the time, then pour back into the saucepan. Cook over a low heat, stirring constantly with a wooden spoon, until the mixture is thick enough to coat the back of the spoon (it should register about 84°C on a thermometer). Be careful not to let it boil or it will become scrambled. Remove from the heat and strain through a fine sieve, pushing on the leaves to extract as much flavour as possible. Pour into ramekins or other heatproof bowls and leave to cool, then chill.

serving
Sprinkle the creams with a thin layer of caster sugar and then glaze with a blowtorch. Leave to cool. Immediately before serving, sprinkle with a thin covering of popping candy and a dusting of icing sugar. Shape the sorbet into quenelles with 2 small dessertspoons and place on top of the geranium cream.

pineapple roasted with molasses sugar, with pineapple and angelica sorbet

Pineapple is one of my favourite things to eat for dessert. I love its sweet-sour taste and it has the added benefit of helping the digestion. In this recipe the pineapple is roasted in butter and molasses sugar to give it a very rich flavour. To balance this, the pineapple and angelica sorbet has a refreshing taste. If you have problems getting fresh angelica leaves, try your local nursery. Failing that, substitute lovage, basil or chamomile leaves; they all work well.

Serves 6–8

for the pineapple and angelica sorbet
1kg ripe pineapple
250g caster sugar
juice of $^1/_2$ lemon
50g fresh angelica leaves, shredded

for the roasted pineapple
1 large, ripe pineapple, peeled
200g unsalted butter
125g molasses sugar
30ml water

pineapple and angelica sorbet
Peel the pineapple and remove the 'eyes'. Cut the flesh into 3–4cm chunks and place in a bowl. Sprinkle with the caster sugar, lemon juice and shredded angelica, stir well, then cover and leave in the fridge overnight. The next day liquidise this mixture in a blender or food processor until fine and push through a fine sieve. Place in an ice-cream maker and freeze according to the manufacturer's instructions.

roasted pineapple
Using the tip of a small knife, gouge out the 'eyes' of the pineapple. Slice it into 6–8 wedges, depending on size. Cut out the core from each wedge to give you a flat side and then trim the ends; you should end up with something resembling a long rectangle.

Melt the butter in a large, ovenproof frying pan. When it is foaming but not coloured, add the pineapple, skin-side down, and cook over a medium heat until lightly coloured. Meanwhile, dissolve the molasses sugar in the water in a heavy-based saucepan and cook over a medium heat for 4 minutes. Pour into the frying pan, being careful as it will spit. Bring to the boil, remove from the heat and transfer to an oven preheated to 190°C/Gas Mark 5. Cook for about 20 minutes, basting with the cooking juices every 5 minutes; you should end up with very deeply coloured and rich pineapple. Remove from the oven and cool for 3–4 minutes before serving.

serving
Serve the slices whole or cut in half at an angle, with a little of the cooking juices and a scoop of sorbet.

spiced bread iced mousse with orange and liquorice sorbet

This recipe uses the Spiced Bread from the storecupboard (see page 22) but you could replace it with some ginger cake, if you prefer. The orange and liquorice sorbet reminds me of my Aunt Pat. When I used to visit her, she would give me a liquorice root to chew on instead of sweets. She also made a lovely drink out of orange juice and crushed liquorice root, with some Pernod added for the adults. It was wonderfully refreshing in the summer and became the inspiration for this pairing. The sorbet also works well with pineapple and star anise.

Serves 8

for the orange and liquorice sorbet
1 gelatine leaf
750ml fresh orange juice
125g caster sugar
50ml liquid glucose
grated zest of 2 oranges
35g dried liquorice root, sliced
juice of 1 lemon
20ml Pernod

for the spiced bread iced mousse
165g caster sugar
50ml water
4 egg yolks
200ml milk
150g Spiced Bread (page 22)
225ml double cream
4 egg whites

for the spiced breadcrumbs
4 slices of Spiced Bread, made into crumbs
50g icing sugar

orange and liquorice sorbet
Soak the gelatine in cold water for about 5 minutes, until soft and pliable. Put 250ml of the orange juice in a small saucepan with the sugar, glucose, orange zest and liquorice root. Bring to the boil, then reduce the heat and simmer for 5 minutes. Pull to one side of the stove, squeeze the excess water out of the gelatine and add to the pan, stirring until dissolved. Leave to cool, then stir in the remaining orange juice. Pour into a container, add the lemon juice and Pernod, then cover and leave in the fridge overnight.

The next day, strain the mixture and place in an ice-cream machine. Freeze according to the manufacturer's instructions.

spiced bread iced mousse
Place 125g of the caster sugar in a small saucepan with the water and heat gently, stirring to dissolve the sugar. Raise the heat and boil without stirring until the mixture reaches the soft-ball stage (115°C on a sugar thermometer).

Meanwhile, whisk the egg yolks in a freestanding electric mixer until very thick and almost white. When the sugar syrup is ready, drizzle it on to the yolks in a slow, steady stream with the mixer running on high. Carry on whisking until cool.

Heat the milk to boiling point in a pan and add the spiced bread. Pull to one side and leave for a few minutes, so the spiced bread absorbs a little of the milk, then transfer to a blender and blend until smooth. Fold this spiced bread purée into the egg yolk mixture. Whip the double cream and fold it into the mixture. In a separate bowl, whisk the egg whites until they form soft peaks, then sprinkle in the remaining sugar. Whisk until the mixture is shiny and peaks form, then fold into the spiced bread mixture.

Divide between 8 metal rings, 5cm in diameter and 5cm deep. Place in the freezer for at least 4 hours, until set.

spiced breadcrumbs
Mix the spiced breadcrumbs with the icing sugar and spread over a baking sheet lined with baking parchment. Place in an oven preheated to 160°C/Gas Mark 3 and bake for 4–5 minutes, watching to make sure they don't burn. They should be golden and dry. Leave to cool, then separate any that are stuck together. Store in a jar until needed.

serving
Unmould the iced mousse on to serving plates and sprinkle with the crisp spiced crumbs. Serve with a scoop of sorbet. You could also accompany it with a little of the Burnt Orange Syrup on page 152.

chocolate délice with salted caramel and malted barley ice cream

This recipe has been a work in progress for a long time, as we have been trying to get the texture just right and to stabilise the mixture. Well, I've finally done it. It started out as an olive oil and bitter chocolate mousse. My second chef at the time, Marcus McGuiness, suggested adding a salted caramel filling and set about working out the recipe. It quickly became apparent that this was a good idea but the mixture was very unstable, with a success rate of about 50 per cent. I then worked on a way of stabilising it, and discovered that the key was making a mayonnaise, which gave the olive oil something to hold on to. As a result, this is now one of our biggest sellers on the dessert menu. A great combination of tastes and textures, and a great collaboration between Marcus and myself.

Serves 8

for the malted barley ice cream
125g pearl barley
250ml double cream
500ml milk
1 vanilla pod, slit open lengthways
5 egg yolks
50g caster sugar
75g malt extract

for the sesame wafers
25g golden syrup
75g demerara sugar
25ml milk
75g unsalted butter
25g ground almonds
30g sesame seeds

for the salted caramel
250g granulated sugar
25ml water
150ml double cream
150g unsalted butter, diced
Maldon salt, to taste

for the chocolate délice
300g bitter chocolate (64–70 per cent cocoa solids), chopped, plus 125g bitter chocolate for the chocolate discs
25g unsalted butter
1/2 gelatine leaf
25ml hot water
2 egg yolks
5g bitter cocoa powder
200ml olive oil
5 egg whites (approximately 145g)

malted barley ice cream
Spread the pearl barley out on a baking tray and place in an oven preheated to 180°C/Gas Mark 4. Toast for about 5 minutes, until golden brown.

Put the cream, milk and split vanilla pod into a heavy-based pan, add the toasted barley and bring to the boil. Remove from the heat and leave to infuse for 30–40 minutes. Place back on the heat and bring back to the boil. Whisk the egg yolks, caster sugar and malt extract together in a bowl, then pour in half the hot milk mixture, whisking continuously. Return the mixture to the pan and cook on a low heat, stirring constantly with a wooden spoon, until the mixture thickens enough to coat the back of the spoon (it should register about 84°C on a thermometer). Do not let it boil or it will become scrambled. Immediately strain through a fine sieve into a bowl and leave to cool. Pour into an ice-cream machine and freeze according to the manufacturer's instructions. Place in the fridge to soften slightly about 10 minutes before serving.

sesame wafers
Put the golden syrup and demerara sugar in a small pan and heat gently until the sugar has dissolved. Add the milk and leave to cool a little. Mix in the butter, ground almonds and sesame seeds. Place in the fridge for 30 minutes.

Spread the mixture on to a baking sheet lined with baking parchment, keeping it away from the edges as it will expand during cooking. Bake in an oven preheated to 180°C/Gas Mark 4 for 4–5 minutes, until golden brown. Remove from the oven and leave to cool. Carefully break into the desired shape; we create random jagged pieces. Store in a sealed container until needed; the wafers can be made 3–4 days in advance.

salted caramel
Put the sugar and water in a heavy-based pan and heat gently, stirring, until the sugar has dissolved. Raise the heat and cook without stirring until a rich, deep golden caramel is obtained, being careful not to take it too far or it will be bitter. The moment you are happy with the colour, remove the pan from the heat and pour in the double cream little by little; take care, as it will spit. Whisk until the caramel has dissolved. Cool slightly, then whisk in the butter a little at a time. Add the salt to your taste; start off with a pinch and gradually increase it until you achieve a slight saltiness. Leave to cool completely.

chocolate délice
Put the 300g chocolate in a heatproof bowl set over a pan of gently simmering water, making sure the water doesn't touch the base of the bowl. Stir until melted, being careful to keep any water away from the chocolate or it will thicken and become grainy. (Alternatively you could melt the chopped chocolate in a microwave, giving it 20 seconds, then stirring, 20 seconds, then stirring, and so on until silky and melted.) Stir in the butter, then place the bowl to one side, keeping it warm.

Soak the gelatine in cold water for about 5 minutes, until soft and pliable. Put the hot water in a small bowl. Squeeze out excess water from the gelatine and add it to the hot water, stirring until dissolved. Set aside. Whisk the egg yolks together and

mix in the cocoa powder. Slowly drizzle in the olive oil a little at a time, whisking constantly, as if making mayonnaise.
Stir in the gelatine water and then carefully add the mixture to the chocolate. Whisk the egg whites briefly, just to break them down (they should not be white and frothy), then carefully fold them into the chocolate mixture. Pour the mixture into 8 metal rings, 5cm in diameter and 5cm high, filling them two thirds full. Chill for 2 hours, until set. Keep the remaining chocolate mixture at room temperature.

When the chocolate has set, push it up the sides of the moulds with your fingers so a well is formed in the centre. Pour in the salted caramel to just below the top of the mould. Place a chocolate disc on top and cover with the remaining chocolate mix. Return to the fridge until needed. They will keep for 3–4 days.

chocolate discs
Melt the extra 125g chocolate as described above. Spread it out on a sheet of cellophane (you can even use a black bin bag) and leave to set. Cut into eight 4cm discs with a metal cutter.

serving
Unmould the chocolate délice either by flashing a blowtorch quickly over the rings or by rolling them in the heat of your hands to release the mousse. Invert on to 8 serving plates. Place a scoop of ice cream on each plate and stud with a sesame wafer.

millas cake with liquorice bramble compote and lemon verbena ice cream

Millas is the Gascon name for a sort of cornmeal porridge, which can be sliced like bread and served as an accompaniment to beef stews. It's the French version of polenta, if you like. Here I have taken some of the main ingredients and turned them into a cake. Gascon cornmeal is quite fine and white, but you could use a medium polenta. The duck fat sounds strange but it does give the cake a wonderful richness. The lemon in the cake ties in with the lemon verbena ice cream, while the liquorice gives the brambles a dark, mysterious depth.

Serves 10–12

for the lemon verbena ice cream
600ml milk
300ml double cream
4 good sprigs of lemon verbena
8 egg yolks
175g caster sugar
20ml liquid glucose
50ml lemon juice

for the millas cake
3 eggs
200g demerara sugar
125g duck fat, melted
25g plain flour
75g cornmeal or polenta
200g ground almonds
1 teaspoon baking powder
juice and grated zest of 3 lemons

for the liquorice bramble compote
750g blackberries
100g caster sugar
1 stick of liquorice root
juice of 1 lemon
2 gelatine leaves

lemon verbena ice cream
Put the milk, cream and lemon verbena in a heavy-bottomed saucepan and gently bring to just below the boil. Remove from the heat and leave to infuse for 2 hours, or even overnight. Then gently bring to the boil again. Meanwhile, whisk the egg yolks, sugar and glucose together in a bowl until pale and creamy. Pour half the milk mix on to the eggs, whisking to incorporate, then pour this back into the saucepan. Cook over a gentle heat, stirring constantly with a wooden spoon, until the mixture thickens enough to coat the back of the spoon (it should reach about 84°C on a thermometer). Don't let it boil or it will become scrambled. Immediately strain through a fine sieve into a large bowl and stir in the lemon juice. Leave to cool, then pour into an ice-cream machine and freeze according to the manufacturer's instructions. Transfer to the fridge to soften slightly about 10 minutes before serving.

millas cake
Put the eggs and demerara sugar in a mixing bowl and whisk on high speed until pale and fluffy. Mix in the melted duck fat little by little on medium speed – like making mayonnaise. Mix the flour, cornmeal, ground almonds and baking powder together and fold them into the egg mixture. Add the lemon juice and zest and mix well.

Pour into a buttered, lined 22cm loose-bottomed tart tin and bake in an oven preheated to 160°C/Gas Mark 3 for 30–40 minutes, until the cake is a deep golden colour and the point of a knife comes out clean. Remove from the oven and leave to cool for 10–15 minutes, then turn out of the tin.

liquorice bramble compote
Put the blackberries, sugar, liquorice and lemon juice in a pan and heat gently until the juices run freely; do not overcook or the blackberries will become mushy. Meanwhile, cover the gelatine with cold water and leave to soften for about 5 minutes.

Drain the berries gently, being careful not to break them up, and remove the liquorice stick. Place the juice and 50g of the brambles in a blender and blend until smooth. Strain through a fine sieve, pushing as much of the fruit through as you can. Squeeze excess water out of the gelatine and dissolve it in the hot bramble juice. Put the liquorice stick back in the juice to impart more flavour. Cool a little, then add the brambles and place in the fridge.

serving
Cut the cake into 10–12 portions and serve with the bramble compote and a scoop of lemon verbena ice cream.

chocolate and coriander tart with lexia raisin ice cream

This is another one of our big sellers. It makes a good standby for a dinner party, as it is quite simple to prepare and the taste is sensational. The flavour of the tart is decidedly grown up, almost bordering on savoury, due to the use of a fine, bitter chocolate and no sugar whatsoever. You could substitute cardamom, lavender, thyme or even tea for the coriander, or add grated orange or lemon zest for a fresher taste. The ice cream goes so well with the tart, but again, play with variations, try using prunes, dates or dried cherries instead of the sultanas; it's entirely up to you. Lexia raisins are the truffles of the raisin world. They are two or three times the size of normal raisins and have an intensely caramelly, fruity taste.

Serves 10–12

for the lexia raisin ice cream
300g Lexia raisins
150ml water
100ml good dark rum
500ml milk
600ml double cream
12 egg yolks
175g caster sugar
50ml liquid glucose

for the chocolate and coriander tart
1 quantity of Sweet Pastry (see page 16)
375ml double cream
375ml milk
675g bitter chocolate (71 per cent cocoa solids), finely chopped
3 eggs, lightly beaten
10g coriander seeds, ground and sifted to make a powder

lexia raisin ice cream
Put the raisins, water and 50ml of the rum into a saucepan and bring to the boil. Remove from the heat and cover, so the raisins plump up.

Meanwhile, put the milk and cream in a thick-bottomed pan and bring to the boil. Whisk the egg yolks, caster sugar and glucose together in a bowl and pour half of the milk mixture on to them, whisking continuously. Pour back into the pan and cook over a low heat, stirring constantly with a wooden spoon, until the mixture thickens enough to coat the back of the spoon (it should register about 84°C on a sugar thermometer). Do not let it boil or it will become scrambled. Immediately strain through a fine sieve into a bowl. Leave to cool, then add the remaining rum and strain in the juices from the raisins. Pour into an ice-cream machine and freeze according to the manufacturer's instructions. When almost frozen, add the raisins, then finish freezing. Transfer to the fridge to soften slightly about 10 minutes before serving.

chocolate and coriander tart
Roll out the pastry on a lightly floured work surface and use to line a buttered loose-bottomed tart tin, 22cm in diameter and 3–3.5cm deep. Chill for 40–50 minutes, then prick the base with a fork. Line the pastry case with baking parchment and fill with rice or baking beans. Place on a baking sheet in an oven preheated to 180°C/Gas Mark 4 and bake blind for 10–15 minutes, until very lightly coloured. Remove the paper and beans and return to the oven for 1–2 minutes to dry out the base. Put the pastry case to one side while you make the filling.

Put the cream and milk into a thick-bottomed saucepan and slowly bring to the boil, then remove from the heat. Place the chopped chocolate in a bowl and slowly pour in the hot cream, stirring all the time. Mix in the eggs. Strain the mixture through a fine sieve, stir in half the coriander powder and pour into the pastry case.

Dust the tart with the remaining coriander powder and place in the oven. Cook for 5 minutes, then turn the oven off and leave the tart in it for 30–40 minutes, until just set. Remove from the oven and leave to cool.

serving
Cut the tart into 10–12 portions and serve with a scoop of the raisin ice cream.

lemon and pine kernel iced mousse with fromage blanc and black pepper sorbet

When planning a dessert menu, you should always include a light, refreshing pudding. This one is just that. It has an acidic freshness and several different textures. Pepper makes a natural ally for acidic fruit and, in this case, the fromage blanc. It seems to bring a much cleaner, fresher taste to the sorbet. You could experiment with different types of pepper. We have used cubeb pepper here, which has an aromatic flavour with a hint of orange, but grains of paradise, which is less peppery but very aromatic, could be used, or even a mild chilli. Reduced passion fruit juice also works well with this recipe and at the restaurant we top the sorbet with a peppercorn tuile.

Serves 6

*for the fromage blanc and black pepper
  sorbet*
100ml liquid glucose
100ml milk
100ml double cream
*12g cornflour, mixed to a paste with a little
  milk*
75g caster sugar
50ml water
500g fromage blanc
juice of 1/4 lemon
cubeb peppercorns, in a peppermill

for the lemon and pine kernel iced mousse
juice of 6 lemons
grated zest of 3 lemons
200ml double cream
100g caster sugar
30ml water
4–5 egg yolks (approximately 120g)
100g pine kernels, toasted until golden

for the lemon curd
juice and grated zest of 4 lemons
5 egg yolks
300g caster sugar
1 teaspoon cornflour
250g unsalted butter, diced

for the caramel craquant
200ml liquid glucose
200g caster sugar
50ml water
100g flaked almonds, toasted until golden

fromage blanc and black pepper sorbet

Put the glucose, milk, cream, cornflour paste, sugar and water in a thick-bottomed pan and bring to the boil, stirring all the time. Remove from the heat and leave to cool. Put the fromage blanc in a bowl and pour in the glucose mixture. Whisk in the lemon juice and coarsely grind in pepper to taste. Transfer to an ice-cream machine and freeze according to the manufacturer's instructions. Place in the fridge to soften slightly about 10 minutes before serving.

lemon and pine kernel iced mousse

Put the lemon juice and zest in a small pan and boil until reduced to 75ml. Remove from the heat and set aside. Whip the double cream until it forms soft peaks, then set aside in the fridge.

Place the caster sugar and water in a small saucepan and heat gently, stirring, until the sugar has dissolved. Bring to the boil and boil until it reaches the soft-ball stage (115°C on a sugar thermometer). While it is boiling, whisk the egg yolks in a freestanding electric mixer until thick, airy and very pale. When the sugar syrup is ready, slowly drizzle it on to the egg yolks with the machine running on high. Continue to whisk until cold.

Fold in the lemon juice, then the whipped cream and finally add the pine kernels. Place a 36 x 11.5 x 4cm metal cooking frame on a baking tray and pour in the mixture. Freeze until set; this will take at least 6 hours.

lemon curd

Bring the juice and zest to the boil in a saucepan. Whisk the egg yolks, caster sugar and cornflour together in a bowl. Pour the juice on to the yolks, whisk well and return to the pan. Cook over a medium heat, stirring constantly, until the mixture has thickened; do not let it boil or the eggs will scramble. Remove from the heat, cool down a little, then whisk in the butter bit by bit, letting each piece melt before adding the next. Pour through a fine sieve into a bowl and leave to cool. Store in an airtight container in the fridge.

caramel craquant

Place the glucose, caster sugar and water in a thick-bottomed saucepan and heat gently, stirring, until the sugar has dissolved. Bring to the boil and cook, without stirring, until it becomes an amber-coloured caramel. Immediately pour on to an oiled baking tray and sprinkle with the almonds. Put to one side until cold and very crisp. Break the caramel up, place in a food processor and pulse to a coarse powder. Store in an airtight container.

When needed, sprinkle the craquant in an even layer on a baking tray lined with a sheet of baking parchment the same size as the frame for the iced mousse. Place in an oven preheated to 200°C/Gas Mark 6 until it has melted and formed a single sheet of caramel. Remove from the oven and leave to cool. Just before it sets, cut it into strips the same size as the slices of iced mousse will be.

serving

Place a slice of mousse at the top of each serving plate and put a craquant slice on top. Place a teaspoon of lemon curd on the plate and drag it across to create a teardrop shape. Finally place a scoop of sorbet on top.

chocolate and star anise truffle cake with fennel ice cream

Fennel and chocolate may sound like a strange combination but it's the slight aniseed flavour of the fennel that makes it work so well. Do give it a try. We use fairly bitter chocolate at the restaurant, and we find it makes a good base for many sweetish vegetables, such as parsnips, beetroot and chicory – a warm parsnip tart with bitter chocolate ice cream, for example. However, the vegetables have to have a good, true flavour of their own in order not to be overwhelmed by the chocolate.

A shaved fennel and orange salad would make a good accompaniment to this dessert.

Serves 8

for the fennel ice cream
275g fennel, chopped
500ml milk
500ml double cream
8 egg yolks
185g caster sugar
50ml liquid glucose
25ml Ricard or Pernod

for the chocolate and star anise truffle cake
500ml double cream
75ml liquid glucose
75ml strong espresso coffee
1 teaspoon ground star anise
250g bitter chocolate (71 per cent cocoa solids), finely chopped
2 teaspoons Ricard or Pernod
bitter cocoa powder for dusting

fennel ice cream
Put the fennel, milk and cream into a heavy-based saucepan. Bring gently to just below the boil, then remove from the heat and leave to infuse for 2 hours, or even overnight. Then gently bring to the boil again. Meanwhile, whisk the egg yolks with the sugar and glucose until pale and creamy. Pour half the milk mixture on to the eggs, whisking to incorporate it, then pour this back into the saucepan. Cook over a gentle heat, stirring constantly with a wooden spoon, until the mixture thickens enough to coat the back of the spoon (it should register about 84°C on a thermometer). Do not let it boil or it will become scrambled. Remove from the heat immediately and pour through a fine sieve, pushing as much of the fennel through as possible. Then stir in the Ricard or Pernod and leave to cool. Pour into an ice-cream machine and freeze according to the manufacturer's instructions. Transfer to the fridge to soften slightly about 10 minutes before serving.

chocolate and star anise truffle cake
Whisk the double cream until it forms soft peaks. Heat the glucose, espresso and star anise until almost, but not quite, boiling. Pour on to the chopped chocolate and stir until melted. Leave to cool a little, then quickly fold in the double cream in 2 batches. Stir in the Ricard or Pernod and pour into a loose-bottomed 17cm round tin, 4cm deep. Chill for at least 4 hours. Remove from the fridge 30 minutes before serving.

serving
Remove the truffle from the tin and, using a hot knife, cut into 8 portions. Dust with cocoa powder and place on plates with a scoop of the fennel ice cream.

gorse flower ice cream with banana cake and caramelised bananas

On the hills that surround Cheltenham there are plenty of gorse bushes, which have flowers almost all year round. So when we have a quiet moment, off we go. For this recipe I first tried infusing the flowers directly in the custard mix. This achieved a nice light flavour, but I wanted to make it a little more powerful, so I dried the flowers for 2 days in the kitchen to intensify their flavour. I find they give a slight hint of coconut and banana to the ice cream – hence pairing it with this dessert.

Serves 6

for the banana cake
250g banana flesh, mashed to a pulp
175g demerara sugar
75g unsalted butter, melted and cooled
250g plain flour
10g baking powder
a pinch of salt
2 eggs
50ml extra virgin rapeseed oil

for the gorse flower ice cream
75ml milk
375ml double cream
100g gorse flowers, scattered over a tray and left in a warm place (such as an airing cupboard) for a day or so to dry out
8 egg yolks
200g caster sugar
25ml liquid glucose

for the caramelised bananas
1 vanilla pod
200g caster sugar
50ml water
30ml dark rum
30g unsalted butter
6 bananas, peeled and cut into 8cm lengths

for the banana wafers
100g banana flesh (you could use the trimmings from the caramelised bananas)
10g rice flour
50g caster sugar
30ml double cream or milk
30g unsalted butter, melted and cooled

preparing the banana cake
Mix the banana pulp and sugar together, then cover and leave out overnight (this concentrates the flavour of the bananas).

gorse flower ice cream
Place the milk, cream and gorse flowers in a heavy-based saucepan and bring gently to just below the boil. Remove from the heat and leave to infuse for 2 hours or even overnight. Then gently bring to the boil again. Meanwhile, whisk the egg yolks with the sugar and glucose until pale and creamy. Pour half the milk mixture on to the eggs, whisking to incorporate, then pour this back into the saucepan. Cook over a gentle heat, stirring constantly with a wooden spoon, until the mixture thickens enough to coat the back of the spoon (it should register about 84°C on a thermometer). Do not let it boil or it will become scrambled. Strain immediately through a fine sieve into a large bowl and leave to cool. Pour into an ice-cream machine and freeze according to the manufacturer's instructions. Transfer to the fridge to soften slightly about 10 minutes before serving.

caramelised bananas
Slit the vanilla pod open and scrape out the seeds. Put them in a heavy-based saucepan with the sugar and water and heat gently, stirring to dissolve the sugar. Bring to the boil and cook without stirring until it becomes a deep golden caramel. Immediately remove from the heat, add the rum and whisk in the butter, being careful as the mixture will spit.

Arrange the bananas in an ovenproof dish and pour the caramel over them. Leave to macerate for 1 hour, then transfer to an oven preheated to 80°C (or the lowest possible setting on a gas oven). Cook for about 30 minutes, until the bananas are soft, spooning the syrup over them every 10 minutes. They should have taken on a deep colour. Keep warm until needed.

banana wafers
Push the banana flesh through a fine sieve into a bowl. Mix in the rice flour, followed by all the other ingredients. Spread the mixture out as thinly as possible on a baking sheet lined with baking parchment. Bake in an oven preheated to 160°C/Gas Mark 3 for 7–10 minutes, until crisp and pale golden. Leave to cool, then break into pieces and store in an airtight container until needed.

baking the banana cake
Transfer the banana and sugar mixture to a mixing bowl and beat in the melted butter and the dry ingredients. Beat in the eggs one by one and then the rapeseed oil. Pour into 6 buttered and lined ring moulds, 7cm in diameter and 4cm deep, placed on a baking sheet (or you could use ramekins lined with baking parchment). Bake in an oven preheated to 160°C/Gas Mark 3 for 40–50 minutes, until the cakes are golden and a knifepoint comes out clean. Leave to cool for 5 minutes.

serving
Turn the cakes out of the moulds. Pierce with a roasting fork and drizzle a little of the banana cooking juices over them. Serve with the caramelised banana, a scoop of ice cream topped with a wafer, and a little of the cooking juices drizzled around.

fig tatin with browned butter ice cream and burnt orange syrup

This is one of our longest-standing desserts, although we do change the ice cream occasionally. We have served it with toasted almond ice cream, caramel and cardamom ice cream, spiced bread ice cream and a spiced red wine sorbet. The combination of hot and cold works so well – that's probably why it has been around for such a long time.

The best figs to use for this are black mission figs. Once cooked, they have a deep, intense figgy flavour with caramel overtones. The burnt orange syrup could be replaced with Maury Syrup (see page 20).

Serves 6

for the browned butter ice cream
200g granulated sugar
100ml water
400ml milk
400ml double cream
200g unsalted butter
10g cornflour
6 egg yolks
20ml liquid glucose

for the burnt orange syrup
100g caster sugar
25ml water
500ml orange juice

for the fig tatin
275g caster sugar
75ml water
75g unsalted butter
12 large ripe black mission figs
200g Puff Pastry (see page 26)

browned butter ice cream

Put the sugar and water in a large, heavy-bottomed saucepan and heat gently, stirring to dissolve the sugar. Raise the temperature and cook without stirring until the mixture becomes a deep golden caramel. Remove from the heat and add the milk and double cream, whisking constantly; be careful, as it will splatter. Return to the heat, bring to the boil and continue stirring until the caramel has dissolved.

Melt the butter in a frying pan until it turns golden. Immediately remove from the heat and strain into a bowl. Cool slightly and then whisk in the cornflour.

Whisk the egg yolks and glucose together in a bowl and add the brown butter and cornflour mixture. Pour in half the milk mixture, whisking constantly. Pour back into the pan with the other half of the milk mixture and cook over a low heat, stirring constantly with a wooden spoon, until the mixture has thickened enough to coat the back of the spoon (it should register about 84°C on a thermometer). Immediately strain through a fine sieve into a bowl and leave to cool. Pour into an ice-cream machine and freeze according to the manufacturer's instructions. Place in the fridge to soften slightly about 10 minutes before serving.

burnt orange syrup

Place the sugar and water in a heavy-based saucepan and heat gently, stirring, until the sugar has dissolved. Raise the heat and cook without stirring until it becomes a deep caramel colour; you need to catch it just on the verge of burning, so watch it carefully. Remove from the heat and whisk in the orange juice, then return to the heat and bring slowly back to the boil. Cook until reduced to a syrupy consistency, then leave to cool. If it is too thick, add a little water and bring to the boil again. If it is too thin, reduce a little more.

fig tatin

Put the caster sugar and water in a small saucepan and heat gently, stirring, until the sugar has dissolved. Raise the heat and cook without stirring until it turns a rich, deep amber colour. Immediately pull to the side of the stove and whisk in the butter, little by little. Leave to cool.

Butter 6 metal ramekins, 8cm in diameter and 4cm deep, and place a disc of baking parchment in the bottom of each one, just to make sure the figs don't stick. Next pour in a layer of caramel about 5mm deep. Leave until set hard.

Cut the figs into 6 wedges each; this will give you 72 wedges. Place a small knob of butter in the bottom of each ramekin on top of the hard caramel and arrange 12 wedges of fig pointing to the middle of the mould as tightly as you can. Roll out the puff pastry on a lightly floured surface and cut out six 10cm circles. Place a disc of puff pastry over the top of each Tatin and tuck in the sides all the way around. Pierce the pastry several times with the point of a small knife to allow the steam to escape. Place a heavy cast iron frying pan on the stove, large enough to hold all the moulds, and pour in a little oil. Place the moulds in the pan, pastry-side up. Cook on top of the stove until you see the caramel bubbling round the edges of the pastry. Place the pan in an oven preheated to 200°C/Gas Mark 6 and cook for 15–20 minutes, until the pastry is crisp and a deep golden brown. Remove from the oven and leave to rest for 4 minutes.

serving

Quickly turn the moulds over and allow the excess juice to drain off. Lift the tatins with a palette knife, place on the plates and remove the moulds. Pour the burnt orange syrup around and add a scoop of browned butter ice cream.

crab apple parfait
with green apple and haw sorbet

In the autumn when we take our dogs walking in the forest, we pick crab apples. They have a wonderful tart flavour, which is incredibly sour. The combination of crab apple parfait and green apple sorbet makes for a clean, fresh dessert. If you can't find crab apples or it is the wrong time of year, then substitute Bramleys.

If you have a little crab apple purée left after making the parfait, you can use it to help dress the plate. Sometimes we serve it with dried apple slices that have been soaked in syrup. We also sprinkle a little of the ground Caramel Craquant on page 148 on top of the parfait to add a different texture. You could even use a crumble topping that has been cooked in the oven till crisp.

Serves 6

for the green apple and haw sorbet
500g Granny Smith apples
150g caster sugar
50ml liquid glucose
200ml water
20g haw berries, crushed
5g haw tops
30ml lemon juice

for the crab apple parfait
400–500g crab apples, quartered and cored
30g unsalted butter
190g caster sugar, plus more to taste if necessary
30ml water
4 egg yolks
200ml double cream, whipped to soft peaks
lemon juice, if needed

green apple and haw sorbet
Place the apples in the freezer for 2 hours; this helps to fix the green colour of the sorbet. Meanwhile put the sugar, glucose, water, haw berries and tops in a small saucepan and bring to the boil, stirring to dissolve the sugar. Set this syrup aside to infuse for 2 hours.

Remove the apples from the freezer, cut each one into 6 and remove the core. Place in a liquidiser or food processor with the syrup and liquidise quickly, adding the lemon juice half way through. Push the mixture through a fine sieve and then pour into an ice-cream machine. Freeze according to the manufacturer's instructions.

crab apple parfait
Put the crab apples in a pan with the butter and 80g of the caster sugar and cook gently until very soft. Push through a fine sieve to make a purée, then leave to cool. Taste and add more sugar if necessary.

Place 100g of the remaining caster sugar in a small saucepan with the water and heat gently, stirring until the sugar has dissolved. Bring to the boil and boil until it reaches the soft-ball stage (115°C on a sugar thermometer). While it is boiling, whisk the egg yolks in a freestanding electric mixer with the remaining 10g caster sugar until thick, airy and very pale. When the sugar syrup is ready, slowly drizzle it on to the egg yolks with the machine running on high. Continue to whisk until cold.

Fold in the apple purée and then the double cream. Add the lemon juice if needed to bring the apple flavour out. Pour into metal ring moulds, 5cm in diameter and 5cm high, and freeze for 2–3 hours, until firm.

serving
If you have any extra crab apple purée, place a streak across each serving plate. Turn the parfait out of the moulds on to the plates and serve with a scoop of sorbet.

chicory parfait with juniper ice cream

This is a great marriage of flavours and is very quick and easy to make. The parfait is at a perfect soft set, so you can serve it straight from the freezer. We have used chicory essence in this recipe as you may find chicory root hard to obtain. If you don't like chicory, you could substitute very strong espresso coffee. Or you could serve it simply as a caramel parfait by omitting the chicory. The caramel version works well with about 10 crushed and ground cardamom pods added to the parfait mix.

Serves 6

for the juniper ice cream
500ml milk
350ml double cream
25 juniper berries, crushed
6 egg yolks
125g caster sugar
25ml liquid glucose
70ml gin

for the chicory parfait
200ml double cream
150g caster sugar
100ml water
6 egg yolks
40ml chicory essence
a little powdered Caramel Craquant
  (see page 148)
bitter cocoa powder, for dusting

juniper ice cream
Put the milk, cream and juniper berries in a heavy-based saucepan and bring gently to just below the boil. Remove from the heat and leave to infuse for 2 hours, or even overnight. Then gently bring to the boil again. Meanwhile, whisk the egg yolks with the sugar and glucose until pale and creamy. Pour half the milk mixture on to the eggs, whisking to incorporate, then pour this back into the saucepan. Cook over a gentle heat, stirring constantly with a wooden spoon, until the mixture thickens enough to coat the back of the spoon (it should register about 84°C on a thermometer). Do not let it boil or it will become scrambled. Strain immediately through a fine sieve into a large bowl and leave to cool. Mix in the gin, pour into an ice-cream machine and freeze according to the manufacturer's instructions. Transfer to the fridge to soften slightly about 10 minutes before serving.

chicory parfait
Whisk the double cream until it forms soft peaks. Cover and place in the fridge until needed.

Put the sugar and water in a small, thick-bottomed saucepan and heat gently, stirring to dissolve the sugar. Raise the heat and boil without stirring until it turns into a deep golden caramel. Meanwhile, whisk the egg yolks in a freestanding electric mixer until thick and white. Pour on the caramel in a slow, steady stream, whisking on high speed, then continue whisking until the mixture is cold. Fold in the chicory essence and then the double cream. Pour into 6 metal ring moulds, 5cm in diameter and 5cm deep, then cover and freeze for at least 6 hours. The parfait can be made a few days in advance.

serving
Remove the parfait from the moulds (this is easily done if you briefly wrap a hot cloth around each one first) and place on serving plates. Sprinkle with a little powdered craquant and then dust with cocoa powder. Serve with a scoop of the juniper ice cream.

pistachio and olive oil cake with roasted strawberries and rhubarb sorbet

There is something inherently summery about this dessert, with its green, red and pink. Rhubarb and strawberries are a classic combination and go well together in so many forms: trifles, jellies and crumbles, to name but a few. Obviously the best strawberries to use are British ones in season. The olive oil gives the cake a fruity flavour and a lovely, moist texture. I use a mild, fruity Provençal oil, but not virgin oil, as that would be too powerful. You could serve the cake with apricots, peaches or nectarines instead of strawberries.

Serves 10

for the rhubarb sorbet
1kg rhubarb, finely chopped
250g caster sugar
30ml liquid glucose
100ml water
1½ gelatine leaves
lemon juice, if needed

for the pistachio and olive oil cake
50g polenta
200g ground pistachios
50g plain flour
1 teaspoon baking powder
125ml olive oil
100g unsalted butter, melted and cooled
3 eggs
200g caster sugar
juice and grated zest of 1 lemon
juice of 1 orange
icing sugar for dusting

for the roasted strawberries
100g unsalted butter
70 small strawberries, hulled
100g caster sugar
a few grinds of the peppermill

rhubarb sorbet
Put the rhubarb in a bowl, sprinkle with the caster sugar and mix well. Cover and place in the fridge overnight. The next day, strain off the juices and set aside. Place the rhubarb in a saucepan with the glucose and water, bring to a simmer and cook for 5 minutes, until soft.

Cover the gelatine with cold water and leave to soften for about 5 minutes. Squeeze out the excess water, add the gelatine to the hot rhubarb and stir until dissolved. Place the mixture in a blender and blend until smooth. Add the rhubarb juices and blend again. Taste for acidity; if it is too sweet, add a little lemon juice. Strain through a fine sieve and leave to cool. Pour into an ice-cream machine and freeze according to the manufacturer's instructions. Transfer to the fridge to soften slightly about 10 minutes before serving.

pistachio and olive oil cake
Mix the polenta, ground pistachios, flour and baking powder together. Add the olive oil to the melted butter. Whisk the eggs and caster sugar together until pale, then slowly whisk in the oil and butter. Whisk in the pistachio mixture, then add the lemon juice, orange juice and lemon zest. Transfer the mixture to a greased and lined 23cm loose-bottomed cake tin and bake in an oven preheated to 160°C/Gas Mark 3 for 40 minutes. The cake should be slightly underdone in the middle, so that if you insert a skewer it will come out with a little of the mixture sticking to it – the cooling process will finish it off. Leave to cool for 10 minutes before removing from the tin.

roasted strawberries
Heat the butter in an ovenproof frying pan, add the strawberries and sprinkle with the sugar and ground black pepper. Transfer to an oven preheated to 200°C/Gas Mark 6 and cook for 3–5 minutes, until the strawberries are soft but not mushy. Drain off 50 strawberries and keep warm. Put the remaining strawberries and their juices into a blender and blend to a purée.

serving
Cut the cake into 10 slices and dust with icing sugar. Serve with a little of the roasted strawberry purée, the roasted strawberries and a scoop of rhubarb sorbet.

prune and burdock iced mousse with toasted almond ice cream

Burdock is used a lot in Japanese cooking but rarely in the West. We include the leaves and stalks in other dishes at the restaurant but for this one we use the root. If you don't feel like digging your own up, you can find frozen shredded burdock root in Asian markets or you can buy it dried from herbalists. This recipe requires dried burdock. To dry your own, peel it, cut it into smallish pieces and dry in a low oven until all the moisture has gone. It has a deep, warming flavour with very slight liquorice tones. So if you can't find any, use some ground liquorice powder instead.

The toasted almond ice cream is also great with chocolate or apricot desserts, greengages and caramel.

Serves 8

for the toasted almond ice cream
200ml milk
300ml double cream
100g flaked almonds
6 egg yolks
75g caster sugar
15ml liquid glucose
30ml Amaretto liqueur

for the prune and burdock iced mousse
25g dried burdock root, finely crushed
200ml water
75g caster sugar
4 egg yolks
250ml double cream
100g Marinated Prunes in Armagnac, chopped (see page 22)
40ml Armagnac
powdered Caramel Craquant, to serve (see page 148)

for the prune coulis
100g Marinated Prunes in Armagnac (see page 22)
100ml prune syrup, from the Marinated Prunes
25ml water

toasted almond ice cream
Put the milk and double cream in a heavy-based saucepan and bring slowly to the boil. Toast the flaked almonds under the grill until a deep golden brown. Add to the milk and leave to infuse for at least 2 hours; overnight would be better. Then return to the heat and slowly bring to the boil again. Whisk the egg yolks, sugar and glucose together until thick, then pour half the milk mixture on to the yolks, whisking constantly. Pour back into the pan and cook over a low heat, stirring constantly with a wooden spoon, until the mixture thickens enough to coat the back of the spoon (it should register about 84°C on a thermometer). Do not let it boil or it will become scrambled. Strain immediately through a fine sieve into a large bowl and leave to cool. Stir in the Amaretto, then pour the mixture into an ice-cream machine and freeze according to the manufacturer's instructions. Transfer to the fridge to soften slightly about 10 minutes before serving.

prune and burdock iced mousse
Put the crushed burdock and water in a saucepan and simmer very slowly until the flavour has been extracted and the water has reduced to about 2 tablespoons. Strain off the liquid and keep; discard the root. Put the burdock juice in a small saucepan with 25ml water and 65g of the caster sugar and heat gently, stirring, until the sugar has dissolved. Bring to the boil and boil until it reaches the soft-ball stage (115°C on a sugar thermometer). While it is boiling, whisk the egg yolks and remaining caster sugar in a freestanding electric mixer until thick, airy and very pale. When the sugar syrup is ready, slowly drizzle it on to the egg yolks with the machine running on high. Continue to whisk until cold.

Whisk the cream to ribbons that will hold their shape when the whisk is drawn through it. Fold the chopped prunes into the egg yolk mixture, then the double cream and finally the Armagnac. Pour into 8 metal rings, 6cm in diameter and 4cm deep, then cover and leave in the freezer for 3–4 hours or overnight, until set. Melt the caramel craquant as described on page 148. When it is almost set, cut it into 8 discs with a 6cm cutter to fit the top of the iced mousses.

prune coulis
Place all the ingredients in a blender and blend until smooth. Push through a fine sieve to remove any lumps.

serving
Remove the mousse from the freezer and turn out on to serving plates, then place a disc of craquant on top of each one. Place a scoop of ice cream on top or to one side and add a little prune coulis.

caramelised apricots with apricot kernel cream and apricot and basil sorbet

This is one of those desserts that you can just keep on eating. It's refreshing and incredibly moreish. I thought about serving apricots with a cream made from their kernels when we were stoning some for another dessert. It seemed a logical next step to pair them with the kernel, which has an intoxicating almond flavour. Apricots and almonds are a classic combination.

To finish this dessert, we serve it with a basil and apricot sorbet. Basil goes well with many acidic fruits, such as pineapple and pink grapefruit, and equally well with raspberries and strawberries.

Serves 8

for the apricot and basil sorbet
about 1.2kg very ripe apricots, stoned
  (you will need 900g apricot flesh)
250g caster sugar
50g basil, shredded at the last minute
juice of $1/_2$ lemon
2 apricot kernels, crushed

for the apricot kernel cream
750ml double cream
100ml milk
10 apricot kernels, crushed (use nutcrackers
  to extract the kernels from the stones)
3 gelatine leaves
125g caster sugar
powdered Caramel Craquant, to serve
  (see page 148)

for the caramelised apricots
100g unsalted butter
12 ripe apricots, cut in half and stoned
100g caster sugar

apricot and basil sorbet
Chop the apricots up a little, add all the other ingredients and stir well. Cover and place in the fridge overnight. The next day, liquidise the mixture until smooth, then push through a fine sieve. Pour into an ice-cream machine and freeze according to the manufacturer's instructions.

apricot kernel cream
Put 500ml of the double cream in a pan with the milk and the crushed kernels and bring to the boil. Remove from the heat and leave to infuse; 2 hours will be fine but 24 hours would be better.

Place a 36 x 11.5 x 4cm metal cooking frame on a baking tray, oil lightly and then line with a sheet of clingfilm, making the finish as smooth as possible.

Cover the gelatine with cold water and leave for about 5 minutes, until softened. Bring the kernel cream back to the boil and stir in the caster sugar. Squeeze excess water from the gelatine. Add the gelatine to the cream and stir until dissolved. Strain the mixture through a fine sieve into a bowl and cool in the fridge, stirring from time to time; you need to catch it just before it starts setting. If it sets, don't worry; simply warm it up a little, mix well and try to catch it this time. Whisk the remaining double cream until it forms soft peaks and fold it into the kernel mixture. Pour into the prepared frame and chill until set.

Melt the caramel craquant as described on page 148. When it is almost set, cut it into pieces the same size as the slices of apricot kernel cream will be.

caramelised apricots
Melt the butter in a large, cast iron frying pan, place the apricots in it, cut-side down, and cook for 2 minutes, until they are lightly coloured underneath. Sprinkle with the sugar, turn the apricots over carefully and cook over a high heat until they have caramelised. Remove from the heat and cool slightly.

serving
Cut the kernel cream into 8 slices and lay a sheet of craquant on top of each one. Serve with the caramelised apricots, a little of their juice and a scoop of sorbet.

caramelised puff pastry with mango, lime leaf cream and spiced red wine syrup

This dessert has been on and off our menu for many years. The flavour of the mango goes exceptionally well with lime leaves and lemon grass, as you would expect, but the addition of spiced red wine syrup takes it into a different league. Caramelised pineapple or poached figs would work well here, too. The figs could be poached in the syrup before you reduce it.

Serves 6

for the lime leaf cream
juice and grated zest of 1 lemon
10 lime leaves
2 lemon grass sticks, dried outer husks removed, inner part smashed with the back of a knife
600ml double cream
70g palm sugar (available from Asian shops)
1³/₄ gelatine leaves

for the spiced red wine syrup
100g granulated sugar
150g demerara sugar
25ml crème de cassis
350ml Cabernet wine
150ml port
2 star anise
¹/₂ vanilla pod
2 lime leaves
1 teaspoon coriander seeds, crushed
7 cardamom pods, crushed
5 white peppercorns, crushed
1 teaspoon fennel seeds
3 cloves
3cm piece of cinnamon stick

for the caramelised puff pastry
250g Puff Pastry (see page 26)
icing sugar
3 ripe mangoes
caster sugar for glazing

lime leaf cream
Put the lemon juice and zest in a saucepan and bring to the boil. Add the lime leaves, lemon grass, double cream and palm sugar and bring to the boil again, then pull to one side and leave to infuse for about 2 hours. Bring back to the boil, then pour through a fine sieve into a bowl.

Cover the gelatine leaves with cold water and leave to soften for about 5 minutes, then squeeze out excess water and add the gelatine to the hot cream, whisking until dissolved. Use clingfilm to line 6 individual tart tins, 10cm in diameter and 2.5cm deep. Pour the mixture into the tins, filling them half way, then place in the fridge to set for at least 4 hours, or overnight.

spiced wine syrup
Place all the ingredients in a medium saucepan and bring slowly to the boil, stirring to dissolve the sugar. Lower the heat to a simmer and cook until reduced to a syrup. Place a little of the syrup on a plate and place in the fridge. When it is cold, check the consistency: if you draw your finger through the syrup, it should leave a clear path. If it is too thick, add a little water to the syrup in the pan; if too thin, boil until reduced some more. Strain through a fine sieve and leave to cool.

puff pastry
Roll out the puff pastry into a long rectangle approximately 4mm thick. Brush with a damp, but not wet, pastry brush and then sprinkle heavily with icing sugar. Roll up from one short end, so it looks like a rolled-up newspaper. Place in the fridge for 2–3 hours, until firm, then cut across into 14 thin slices (you will only need 12 but it's useful to have a couple of extra ones in case they don't work). Roll out each slice as thinly as possible, keeping its round shape. Place on baking trays lined with baking parchment and return to the fridge for a good 2 hours.

Place in an oven preheated to 180°C/ Gas Mark 4 and bake for 15–20 minutes, until golden brown. Immediately remove from the oven, place another sheet of baking parchment over the top and roll the pastry completely flat with a rolling pin; it should be as thin as possible. Put to one side to cool.

mango
Peel the mangoes and cut the flesh from each side of the stone to give 6 halves. Slice the mangoes widthways, keeping the slices together. Spread out lightly to the size of the lime leaf creams, then lift up with a fish slice and place on a baking tray. Sprinkle with a good layer of caster sugar and glaze with a blowtorch until golden.

serving
Turn out each lime leaf cream on to a puff pastry disc and carefully place the mango on top. Cover with the remaining puff pastry discs and dust with icing sugar. Drizzle some of the red wine syrup on to 6 plates and top with the mango pastries (any leftover syrup will keep well in the fridge).

marjolaine with tonka bean ice cream

Marjolaine, an extravagant dessert consisting of meringue layers with buttercream, chocolate ganache and cream, was created in the early twentieth century by the great chef, Fernand Point. Called le roi (the king) by his peers, he died in 1955, leaving a major mark on the culinary world. This dish is my interpretation of his dessert, made a little lighter and more up to date. I serve it with a tonka bean ice cream. Tonka beans come from the tonka trees of South America and have a fantastic flavour, faintly reminiscent of vanilla and bitter almonds. You should be able to find them in good delis.

This is quite a complex dessert, with lots of different stages, but the great thing about it is that the majority of the work can be done two or three days in advance, and you can even assemble it a day or two before you need it.

Serves 12

for the tonka bean ice cream
4 tonka beans
750ml milk
375ml double cream
8 egg yolks
200g caster sugar
20ml liquid glucose

for the meringue
225g hazelnuts, toasted and skinned
115g flaked almonds, toasted
90g pistachios, toasted
30g plain flour
200g granulated sugar
8 egg whites
100g caster sugar

for the praline buttercream
290g caster sugar
5 egg whites
340g unsalted butter, diced
175g granulated sugar
15g hazelnuts, toasted and skinned
15g almonds, toasted and skinned
15g pistachios, toasted and skinned

for the ganache
200ml double cream
250g bitter chocolate (70 per cent cocoa solids), chopped
55g raisins, soaked in enough rum just to cover for at least 4 hours

for the whipped cream
100ml double cream
100ml soured cream
Tia Maria, to taste
30g icing sugar

for the chocolate glaze
200ml double cream
15ml liquid glucose
250g bitter chocolate (70 per cent cocoa solids), chopped
80g unsalted butter

tonka bean ice cream

Place the tonka beans in a small frying pan and heat until a lovely aroma of almonds hits you. Grind in a spice grinder or crush with a pestle and mortar.

Place the milk, cream and ground tonka beans in a heavy-based saucepan and bring gently to just below the boil. Remove from the heat and leave to infuse for 2 hours, or even overnight. Then gently bring to the boil again. Meanwhile, whisk the egg yolks with the sugar and glucose until pale and creamy. Pour half the milk mixture on to the egg yolks, whisking to incorporate, then pour this back into the saucepan. Cook over a gentle heat, stirring constantly with a wooden spoon, until the mixture thickens enough to coat the back of the spoon (it should register about 84°C on a thermometer). Do not let it boil or it will become scrambled. Strain immediately through a fine sieve into a large bowl and leave to cool. Pour into an ice-cream machine and freeze according to the manufacturer's instructions. Transfer to the fridge to soften slightly about 10 minutes before serving.

meringue

Finely chop the toasted nuts, then mix in the flour, followed by the granulated sugar. In a separate bowl, whisk the egg whites until stiff. Add the caster sugar and whisk until shiny. Fold the nut mixture into the egg whites. Line a large baking sheet (or 2 smaller ones) with baking parchment. Spread out the meringue on it in 4 rectangles, 12 x 36cm and 5mm deep. Place in an oven preheated to 200°C/Gas Mark 6 and bake for 15–20 minutes, until golden. Turn the oven off and prop the door open slightly. Leave the meringue in the oven until cool.

Put 175g of the caster sugar in a small, heavy-based saucepan with 50ml water and heat gently, stirring until the sugar has dissolved. Raise the heat and cook without stirring until the mixture becomes a golden caramel. Meanwhile, whisk the egg whites in a freestanding electric mixer with the remaining caster sugar until they form soft peaks. Pour on the caramel in a slow, steady stream, whisking on high speed. While the mixture is still warm, whisk in the butter bit by bit until incorporated. Put the granulated sugar in a heavy-based saucepan with 45ml water and heat gently, stirring to dissolve the sugar. Raise the heat and boil without stirring until the mixture becomes a deep golden caramel. Add the nuts and pour the mixture on to an oiled baking tray. Leave to set.

Break up the nut mixture, put it in a food processor and pulse until it resembles fine breadcrumbs. Add the nut mixture to the buttercream and mix well. Place in a container and cover. Keep in the fridge until needed.

ganache

Bring the double cream to the boil and pour it on to the chopped chocolate in a bowl. Whisk until smooth. Cool and then whisk a little more to make it lighter. Fold in the rum-soaked raisins and keep in the fridge until needed.

whipped cream

Whisk all the ingredients together until they form medium-stiff peaks.

chocolate glaze

Bring the cream and glucose to the boil, pour them on to the chocolate and stir until melted. Add the butter, stirring all the time until incorporated.

assembly

Trim one rectangle of meringue. Place in a 12 x 36cm mould, 4cm deep. Spread a 1cm-thick layer of the chocolate ganache over the meringue. Carefully put another layer of meringue on top and spread a 1cm-thick layer of buttercream evenly over this. Carefully push another piece of meringue on top. Spread a layer of the whipped cream on top of this, then cover with the final meringue. Carefully push down to make it level. Place in the fridge to set for about 4 hours, then remove from the mould and carefully place on a wire cake rack. Gently reheat the chocolate glaze and completely cover the marjolaine with it, making it as even as possible. Return to the fridge to set. This can all be done 1–2 days in advance.

serving

Remove the marjolaine from the fridge, trim both ends off and cut it into 12 slices. Serve with a scoop of tonka bean ice cream.

crème brûlée of chervil tubers with brioche ice cream and mandarin jelly

Chervil tubers are grown specifically for the tuber, not for the leafy herb that is used as a garnish. We use the tubers quite a bit when they are in season in the autumn, mainly with meat, fish and game. However, they have a natural sweetness and an almost honeyed taste with a hint of orange – hence pairing them with the mandarin jelly here.

The brioche ice cream makes a pleasantly rich addition. If you can't get hold of brioche, try croissants. We have also used spiced bread and liquorice.

Serves 8

for the crème brûlée of chervil tubers
400g chervil tubers, peeled
250ml milk
250ml double cream
3 egg yolks
3 eggs
125g caster sugar, plus 15g for glazing

for the brioche ice cream
600ml milk
400ml double cream
150g brioche, lightly toasted and cut into
    2cm cubes
8 egg yolks
150g caster sugar
50ml liquid glucose

for the mandarin jelly
1 litre mandarin juice
4 gelatine leaves
200g caster sugar
juice of ¹/₂ lemon
100ml water

crème brûlée of chervil tubers
Prepare 8 moulds. We use rings, as they are easier to unmould. Wrap clingfilm tightly around the base of 8 metal rings, 6.5cm in diameter and 5cm deep, making sure it comes half way up the sides of each one. Place in a roasting tin.

Cook the chervil tubers in a pan of boiling salted water until tender. Drain well and purée in a blender. Bring the milk and cream to the boil in a saucepan, add the chervil tuber purée and bring back to the boil. Meanwhile, beat the egg yolks, eggs and caster sugar together until pale. Pour the chervil mixture on to the eggs, mix well and then return to the pan. Cook gently for about 3 minutes, stirring constantly, until the mixture thickens enough to coat the back of the spoon. Push through a fine sieve and pour into the moulds. Pour enough boiling water into the roasting tin to come a third of the way up the moulds. Place in an oven preheated to 90°C (or the lowest possible setting on a gas oven) and cook for 1 hour, until set. Remove from the oven and cover the whole tin with clingfilm so no air escapes. Leave for 30 minutes, then carefully pour off the water and place the roasting tin in the fridge. Leave for at least 3 hours, until firm. If you make them the day before, the flavour will be more developed.

brioche ice cream
Put the milk and cream in a heavy-bottomed saucepan and gently bring to just below the boil. Remove from the heat, add the brioche and leave to infuse for 2 hours, or even overnight. Transfer to a blender and blend until smooth. Pour into a saucepan and gently bring to the boil again. Meanwhile, whisk the egg yolks with the sugar and glucose until pale and creamy. Pour half the milk mixture on to the egg yolks, whisking to incorporate, then pour this back into the saucepan. Cook over a gentle heat, stirring constantly with a wooden spoon,

until the mixture thickens enough to coat the back of the spoon (it should register about 84°C on a thermometer). Do not let it boil or it will become scrambled. Strain immediately through a fine sieve into a large bowl and leave to cool. Pour into an ice-cream machine and freeze according to the manufacturer's instructions. Transfer to the fridge to soften slightly about 10 minutes before serving.

mandarin jelly
Put half the mandarin juice in a saucepan and boil until reduced to 50ml. Soak the gelatine leaves in cold water for about 5 minutes, until soft, then squeeze out excess water. Add the gelatine to the saucepan, stirring until dissolved. Add the caster sugar and lemon juice. Strain this mixture through a fine sieve into a bowl containing the remaining mandarin juice and add the water. Stir well and pour into a plastic container. Chill for at least 4 hours, until set.

serving
Remove the clingfilm from the crème brûlées. Place on 8 serving plates, sprinkle with the 15g caster sugar and caramelise with a blowtorch until golden, being careful not to let the plates get too hot. Run a small knife around the inside of the rings and carefully lift them off. Serve with a scoop of brioche ice cream and a couple of spoonfuls of mandarin jelly.

acorn panna cotta with butternut ice cream, and paper and wattleseed tuiles

We pick the acorns for this ourselves. They are a glorious by-product of our mushroom picking, especially when there aren't many mushrooms about. I have read somewhere that in hard times acorns used to be ground and used as a polenta substitute in Italy, as were chestnuts – they are both in season at around the same time.

The acorns have a very deep flavour when roasted, with hints of mocha, chocolate, almonds and caramel. If you don't fancy using acorns, you could substitute chicory root, coffee beans or even wattleseeds. Wattleseeds can be ordered through Sambava (see My Suppliers, page 183).

Serves 6–8

for the butternut ice cream
1 butternut squash, weighing 750g–1kg
500ml milk and 500ml double cream
a pinch of ground cinnamon
1 vanilla pod, slit open lengthways
6 egg yolks
200g caster sugar
50ml liquid glucose

for the acorn panna cotta
60g acorns, shelled
700ml double cream
100ml milk
110g caster sugar
3 gelatine leaves

for the paper and wattleseed tuiles
200g caster sugar
200ml water
2 sheets of rice paper
1 dessertspoon wattleseeds

for the coffee extract
100g demerara sugar
50ml water
100ml strong espresso
5g extra bitter cocoa powder
50g dark chocolate (70 per cent cocoa
 solids), finely chopped

butternut ice cream
Cut the butternut squash in half lengthways and remove the seeds. Place the squash halves on a baking sheet, cover with foil and bake in an oven preheated to 200°C/Gas Mark 6 for 40–50 minutes, until soft. Remove the foil, return the squash to the oven and leave to dry out for 5 minutes.

While the squash is baking, make the custard base for the ice cream. Put the milk, cream, cinnamon and split vanilla pod in a thick-bottomed pan and bring to the boil. Whisk the egg yolks, caster sugar and glucose together, then pour half the milk on to the egg mixture, whisking constantly. Pour back into the pan and cook over a low heat, stirring constantly with a wooden spoon, until the mixture thickens enough to coat the back of the spoon (it should register about 84°C on a thermometer). Do not let it boil or it will become scrambled. Immediately strain through a fine sieve into a bowl and leave to cool.

When the butternut squash is ready, scoop out the flesh and place in a blender. Pour in the custard base and blend until smooth. Push through a fine sieve, then place in an ice-cream machine and freeze according to the manufacturer's instructions. Transfer to the fridge to soften slightly about 10 minutes before serving.

acorn panna cotta
Place the acorns on a baking tray and roast in an oven preheated to 150°C/Gas Mark 2 until they are deep brown; be careful not to let them burn or they will taste very bitter. Leave to cool, then grind to a coarse powder in a spice mill or coffee grinder.

Put the cream, milk, sugar and ground acorns in a thick-bottomed saucepan and gently bring to the boil. Pull to the side of the stove and leave to infuse for 40 minutes, to extract as much of the acorn flavour as you can.

Soak the gelatine in a little cold water for about 5 minutes, until soft and pliable. Remove and squeeze out all the water. Bring the acorn mixture back to the boil, then remove from the heat. Squeeze out excess water from the gelatine and whisk the gelatine into the acorn mixture, making sure it has dissolved. Strain through a fine sieve, pressing on the acorns to extract as much juice as you can. Leave to cool, then pour into 6–8 lightly oiled dariole moulds, about 130ml in capacity. Cover and place in the fridge for at least 4 hours, until set.

paper and wattleseed tuiles
Put the sugar and water in a pan and heat gently, stirring to dissolve the sugar. Raise the heat and boil for 3–4 minutes to make a syrup, then leave to cool.

Cut each sheet of rice paper into 3 or 4, or simply tear the pieces to give a more natural look. Pour the syrup into a shallow tray, place the rice paper in the syrup and then carefully lift it out, keeping the shape of the paper. Place on a nonstick baking tray or a tray lined with baking parchment, sprinkle with the wattleseeds and bake in an oven preheated to 85°C (or the lowest possible setting on a gas oven) for 3–4 hours, until crisp and rigid. Leave to cool, then slide a palette knife under the rice paper and lift it off the tray.

coffee extract
In a small saucepan, dissolve the demerara sugar in the water over a gentle heat. Raise the heat and cook without stirring until it becomes a deep golden caramel. Remove from the heat and stir in the coffee, but be careful as it will splatter. Whisk in the

cocoa powder, return to the heat and cook for 2 minutes. Cool slightly, then pour on to the chopped chocolate in a bowl and stir until smooth. Strain through a fine sieve and leave to cool.

serving
Dip the dariole moulds in hot water for 2–3 seconds, then gently pull the edge of the panna cotta away from the moulds and quickly turn it out on to serving dishes.

Serve with a scoop of butternut squash ice cream, a slash of coffee extract and a paper tuile.

greengage tarts with hazelnut frangipane and greengage sorbet

Greengages are a type of plum and taste just heavenly, with a delicious tartness. The unfortunate thing is that they have such a short season. So you could exchange them for Victoria plums for a slightly sweeter taste, or even use apricots instead. The frangipane could be made traditionally with ground almonds instead of hazelnuts, or with vibrant green pistachios.

Serves 6

for the greengage sorbet
150g caster sugar
50ml liquid glucose
250ml water
1.5kg ripe greengages, halved and stoned

for the hazelnut frangipane
125g unsalted butter
125g caster sugar
50g plain flour
125g ground hazelnuts
2 eggs

for the greengage tarts
1 quantity of Sweet Pastry (see page 16)
24 greengages, halved and stoned
50g unsalted butter
50g demerara sugar

greengage sorbet
Put the sugar, glucose and water in a pan and bring to the boil, stirring to dissolve the sugar. Boil for 3 minutes to make a syrup, then leave to cool. Liquidise the greengages in a blender, then add the syrup and continue to blend to a smooth pulp. Push through a fine sieve, pour into an ice-cream machine and freeze according to the manufacturer's instructions. Keep in the freezer until required but try to use within a couple of days, if possible.

hazelnut frangipane
Cream the butter and sugar together until pale and fluffy. Sift the flour and hazelnuts together. In a separate bowl, beat the eggs until pale. Beat a little egg into the butter mixture, then a little flour, and repeat until all the flour and eggs have been used. The mixture should be light, creamy and smooth. Keep in a cool place until needed.

greengage tarts
Roll the pastry out on a lightly floured surface to about 3mm thick, then cut out 6 discs, 13cm in diameter (you will probably need just over half the pastry; the rest can be wrapped in clingfilm and frozen for another day). Place in the fridge and chill for at least 30 minutes, or until needed. Place the pastry bases on a baking sheet lined with baking parchment, prick them all over with a fork and bake in an oven preheated to 160°C/Gas Mark 3 for 3 minutes, just to set the bases. Remove from the oven and leave to cool, then spread a 4mm-thick layer of frangipane over them, leaving a 5mm border. Return to the oven for about 4 minutes; the middle should still be a little uncooked.

Remove from the oven and place the greengages cut-side up on the tarts, one in the middle and the rest around. Place a little of the butter in the cavities where the stones were. Turn the oven up to 180°C/Gas Mark 4. Sprinkle the tarts with the demerara sugar and return to the oven for about 20 minutes, until the pastry is a deep golden brown and the greengages are just cooked. The frangipane will have caught some of the juices and soaked them up. Remove from the oven and leave to rest for 2–3 minutes.

serving
Serve the warm tarts with the greengage sorbet.

prune tarts with milk sorbet

I have happy memories of making this dessert with the help of my good friend, Tony Robson-Burrell, for the National Chef of the Year competition in 1996. The simplicity of the dessert, with the classic hot and cold theme, is the reason for its success. The rich milk sorbet adds a luxurious taste but it's also very good with lemon ice cream.

Serves 6

for the milk sorbet
1.2 litres full fat milk
2 gelatine leaves
500ml Carnation evaporated milk
200g milk powder
150ml double cream
250g caster sugar

for the orange syrup
125g caster sugar
250ml orange juice

for the prune tarts
$^1/_2$ quantity of Sweet Pastry (see page 16)
150ml single cream
grated zest of 1 orange
juice and grated zest of $^1/_2$ lemon
seeds from 1 vanilla pod
4 eggs, separated
10g cornflour
15g ground almonds
10g plain flour
80g caster sugar
50ml Grand Marnier
200g Marinated Prunes in Armagnac
 (see page 22)
icing sugar for dusting

milk sorbet

Pour the milk into a heavy-based pan, bring to a simmer and cook over a low heat until reduced by half. Cover the gelatine with water and leave to soak for about 5 minutes, until softened. Remove the reduced milk from the heat, squeeze excess water out of the gelatine and whisk the gelatine into the milk until dissolved. Whisk the Carnation milk with the milk powder and cream. Pour the reduced milk on to this, whisking constantly. Add the sugar and stir until dissolved, then leave to cool. Pour into an ice-cream machine and freeze according to the manufacturer's instructions. Transfer to the fridge to soften slightly about 10 minutes before serving.

orange syrup

Put the sugar and orange juice in a saucepan and heat gently, stirring to dissolve the sugar. Raise the heat and simmer until thick and syrupy, then leave to cool. If it is too thick, add a little more water; if it is too thin, reduce a little more.

prune tarts

Roll out the pastry on a lightly floured work surface and use to line 6 buttered loose-bottomed tart tins, 8.5cm in diameter and 2.5cm deep. Chill for 40–50 minutes, then prick the bases with a fork, line with baking parchment and fill with rice or baking beans. Place on a baking sheet and bake blind in an oven preheated to 180°C/Gas Mark 4 for 5–7 minutes, until light golden. Carefully remove the paper and rice or beans.

In a small saucepan, bring the cream, orange and lemon zest and vanilla seeds to the boil. Put the egg yolks, cornflour, ground almonds, flour and 50g of the caster sugar in a bowl and mix well. Stir the cream mixture into this, then return to the pan. Cook over a low heat, stirring constantly with a wooden spoon, until the mixture thickens. Stir in the lemon juice and Grand Marnier, then transfer the mixture to a large bowl.

Whisk the egg whites until stiff, adding the remaining caster sugar half way through. Fold the whites into the cream mixture, a third at a time. Roughly chop the prunes and fold them into the mixture. Divide between the tart cases, level them off with a palette knife and bake at 180°C/Gas Mark 4 for 10–12 minutes, until just set. Leave to rest for 2 minutes.

serving

Turn the tarts out of their tins and dust with icing sugar. Serve with a scoop of milk sorbet and some orange syrup.

rice pudding with meadowsweet and compote of cherries

Rice pudding is one of my favourite desserts, served hot, cold or in a mousse. Here I have used risotto rice, because the grains are bigger when cooked, and I have flavoured it with meadowsweet, which lends a lovely, subtle perfume. If you cannot get fresh meadowsweet, then use 15g dried flowers. Alternatively, omit it altogether, double the amount of orange zest in the rice pudding and serve it with Marinated Prunes in Armagnac (see page 22) instead of the cherry compote. But, trust me, the flavour of meadowsweet works so well with cherries. The cherries can also be cut in half after the compote has been made and semi-dried in a very low oven (about 80°C) for a different texture.

Serves 6

for the compote of cherries
juice of 1 lemon
grated zest of 1 orange
500ml red wine
1 meadowsweet head
3 cherry kernels, crushed
100g caster sugar
500g cherries, stoned

for the rice pudding
75g carnaroli risotto rice
350ml milk
150ml double cream
3 meadowsweet heads
pared zest of 1/2 orange, in wide strips
50g caster sugar, plus extra for glazing
1 1/2 gelatine leaves
1 teaspoon Grand Marnier

for the pastry cream
100ml milk
75ml double cream
40g caster sugar
1 egg yolk
5g cornflour

compote of cherries

Put all the ingredients apart from the cherries in a saucepan and bring to the boil. Simmer for 3–4 minutes, then add the cherries and cook for 4–5 minutes. Immediately remove the cherries and place in a bowl to cool. Boil the cooking juices until reduced by half, then leave to cool. Strain on to the cherries and leave to macerate overnight.

cooking the rice

Place the rice, milk, 75ml of the double cream, meadowsweet heads, orange zest and caster sugar in a saucepan and bring to the boil, stirring constantly. Reduce the heat to a simmer and cook for about 20 minutes, until the rice is soft and the mixture is thick and creamy. Remove from the heat.

Cover the gelatine with cold water and leave for about 5 minutes to soften. Squeeze out the excess water and add the gelatine to the hot rice, stirring until dissolved. Remove the meadowsweet heads and leave to cool.

pastry cream

While the rice pudding is cooking, make the pastry cream. Bring the milk and cream to the boil in a small saucepan. Put the sugar, egg yolk and cornflour in a bowl and whisk until well amalgamated. Pour on the milk and cream, whisking continuously. Pour the mixture back into the saucepan and cook over a low heat, stirring constantly, until it thickens. Remove from the heat and leave to cool.

finishing the rice pudding

Whisk the remaining double cream with the Grand Marnier until it forms thick ribbons. When the rice pudding and the pastry cream are cool, lightly mix them together and place in the fridge for about 1 1/2 hours, until almost set. Just before it sets, fold in the whipped cream and transfer to 6 oiled metal ring moulds, 6cm in diameter and 4cm deep. Cover and chill for 3–4 hours.

serving

Turn the rice pudding out of the moulds on to serving plates and sprinkle lightly but evenly with caster sugar. Glaze with a blowtorch until golden; be quick though, otherwise any protruding grains of rice will scorch. Serve with the cherry compote.

bitter chocolate fudge

We serve a choice of 12–16 petits fours at the restaurant and it has taken a few years to achieve the right balance and the correct recipes. They range from chocolates to jellies to brownies and little cakes, and make for a very dramatic presentation on the glass plates I designed and had made specifically for the purpose.

This recipe and the one below are our most popular chocolate petits fours. We have been making the fudge for years, and it is a favourite with many of our customers, and especially with my wife, Helen! I change the flavourings occasionally, sometimes adding orange and lemon zest, sometimes liquorice and sometimes even chilli.

250ml liquid glucose
250g demerara sugar
400ml double cream
250g bitter chocolate (64 per cent cocoa solids)
75g peeled pistachios
75g raisins

Put the glucose, demerara sugar and double cream in a large, heavy-based saucepan. Place on a moderate heat and bring slowly to the boil. Meanwhile, finely chop the chocolate. Sprinkle the chocolate into the boiling cream mixture, stirring until it dissolves. Turn the heat up and boil without stirring until it reaches 243°F on a sugar thermometer (this measurement must be accurate, hence this specific Fahrenheit reading – centigrade isn't precise enough), then pour the mixture into the bowl of a food mixer and beat at medium speed until it has cooled a little.

Add the nuts and raisins and beat one last time. Pour into a baking tray lined with baking parchment, cover and leave in the fridge to set. Cut into the desired shapes and store in an airtight container until needed.

chocolate truffles

As chocolate truffles tend to be very rich, I add lemon and orange juice and zest, which help cut through the richness and leave quite a clean taste in the mouth. You could add all sorts of different flavourings to the base mix, omitting the lemon and orange – maybe bergamot, chamomile or eucalyptus. You could then add whatever spirit you fancy. Try Baileys, or Tia Maria with 50ml strong espresso, or whisky and orange, or Sour Mash and salt. Play and enjoy.

300ml double cream
65g unsalted butter, diced
500g bitter chocolate (64–70 per cent cocoa solids), chopped
juice and grated zest of 1 lemon
juice and grated zest of 1/2 orange
30ml Cointreau
cocoa powder for dusting

Put the cream and butter in a small saucepan and bring to the boil, then remove from the heat. Put the chopped chocolate in a bowl and pour the cream over it. Stir until the chocolate has melted, then add the orange and lemon juice and zest, plus the Cointreau. Mix well, then place in the fridge to set just a little. Beat with an electric mixer until smooth and pliable. Pipe the mixture into cone shapes on a baking tray lined with baking parchment (alternatively you could pipe it out in a long sausage and cut it across, or even just put teaspoonfuls of it on the parchment). Leave to set in the fridge, then dust with cocoa powder. Store in the fridge.

wild food glossary

There has been a steady reawakening of my interest in wild food in the last six to seven years as I have grown to love the Cotswold countryside. I don't use wild food in all my cooking but it forms a useful addition to my repertoire.

One of the best things about gathering wild foods is that the supply is forever changing with the seasons. Nature also has a way of making matches, like morels with wild garlic, elderflowers with gooseberries, chestnuts with ceps. These seasonal pairings are just perfect.

It is vital to be sure that you can correctly identify anything you pick. There are many good field guides available, and these will provide a useful tool when you go out foraging. However, I believe that the best way to get to know wild foods is to find someone you trust to show them to you. There are many plants out there and very

few of them are poisonous, but you must be 100 per cent certain that you know what you are picking. Cow parsley, for example, can look like hemlock and fool's parsley. Cow parsley is safe but the other two, although very similar in appearance, are highly poisonous and sometimes fatal. This is why I think it is preferable to be shown wild food by an experienced forager. Furthermore, when you are with someone who knows what they are doing, they will show you how to pick without decimating the countryside.

There are plants that could be picked on a walk down the road but these are best avoided, as they will have been polluted by car exhausts, etc. By all means use them to help you learn to identify wild plants and thus broaden your knowledge.

What could be better on a warm sunny day, than going for a long, leisurely walk and coming back with a basket full of wild foods?

Tasting some finds with Marcus, Steve and Ryan during a day gathering wild foods.

acorns

We pick acorns from oaks in the autumn to use in our Acorn Panna Cotta (see page 166). When roasted, they have a deeply spicy, bitter flavour, which makes a great pairing with caramel.

alexanders

(smyrnium olusatrum)

Available from September to March, alexanders can be found by the sea and in estuaries. They belong to the same family as angelica and lovage, and are sometimes called black lovage because of the colour and shape of their seeds. It's no surprise, then, that lovage or indeed celery can be used as a substitute. Good as a soup or sauce ingredient in their own right, alexanders also add a wonderful flavour to a daube of beef.

alexanders

buckler-leaved sorrel

(rumex scutatus)

In season from May to July, this grows in pastures and near ancient walls and mounds. It has a good sharp flavour and can be eaten raw in a mixed green salad, wilted for use in a fish or game dish, or made into a lovely, fresh-tasting oil. Ordinary sorrel can be substituted, although it won't have the little hit of pepperiness.

burdock

(arctium lappa)

We use the roots and leaves, which can be found on roadsides, waste places, and generally along country walks. The root is best in the autumn and has a deep, spicy flavour when dried. Eaten fresh, it has a juicy, clean taste. If you slice it thinly and cook it in butter with a little water, the texture is similar to bamboo shoots. Fresh young burdock shoots, picked in April, have an agreeable slight bitterness.

burdock

chickweed

(stellaria media)

Chickweed can be found at any time of year in gardens and fields all over the country and indeed the world. It is very prolific and can be a pest in the garden. Use it as an addition to salads – or for soups or sauces, although you will have to pick a lot.

chickweed

cleavers

(galium aparine)

Cleavers grow all over the place – in hedges, gardens, fields, etc. – during spring and summer. The young tips have a clean taste like freshly podded peas. We use them raw in salads and dishes that need a little texture. Pea shoots could be substituted.

cleavers

crab apples

(malus sylvestris)

You can find crab apples in woods, hedgerows and commons – and in some gardens, if you are lucky. Traditionally they are used to make a wonderful sour juice and, of course, for jelly, but we use them in ice creams, mousses and parfaits, such as the one on page 154. You could even make them into a sauce to serve with suckling pig.

dandelion leaves

(taraxacum officinale)

These grow everywhere, all year round. Young spring dandelion leaves add bitterness to a salad. Wilted with a little orange juice, they make a good garnish for fish. The roots can be cooked and then roasted for desserts.

gorse flowers

(ulex europaeus)

Gorse bushes grow on heaths and dry, sandy hills. The flowers begin to appear in May. They are hard to pick because they are surrounded by thorns but it is worth the effort. Dried for 1–2 days and then used to infuse ice creams and brulées, they have a slight coconut and green banana flavour – see Gorse Flower Ice Cream with Banana Cake and Caramelised Bananas on page 151.

ground elder

(aegopodium podagraria)

Growing freely in gardens and fields, ground elder is best in the spring, when you can pick the young, tender shoots. Wilted like spinach, with a twist or two of black pepper, it can accompany fish – for example, in Monkfish Cheeks with Duck Confit, Crispy Duck Skin and Ground Elder Shoots (see page 104). Cooked and minced, it can be used in risotto, lending a bitter, earthy taste (see Roasted Zander with Snail and Ground Elder Risotto on page 82).

ground elder

hairy bittercress

(cardamine hirsuta)

This grows in gardens, ploughed fields and near walls. Pick from late September to May, and always look for evenly coloured leaves. Slightly bitter and peppery, it makes a good addition to salads or a garnish to counteract sweetness – with carrot purée, for example.

hawthorn berries

(crataegus monogyna)

Hawthorn trees are seen a lot in the countryside, with their lovely white blossom. Both the leaves and flowers can be added to salads. The berries are ripe from August to early November, and can be used in jellies, syrups and wine. We use them fresh or dried to add to an apple sorbet; the tannic flavour goes well with them.

hogweed

(heracleum sphodylium)

At its best from April to July, hogweed is very common in woods, hedges and grassy areas. The leaves are good for soups and purées, whilst the young stalks should be lightly peeled and cooked with a little butter and water.

hogweed

horseradish

(armoracia rusticana)

Horseradish is found from May onwards by the roadside and in fields and pastures. The leaves have a pleasant tang and can be eaten raw or wilted to serve as an accompanying vegetable. And of course the root can be used both cooked and raw to give a strong pungency to all kinds of meat dishes.

jack-by-the-hedge

(alliaria petiolata)

Also known as garlic mustard, this has a garlicky scent and flavour. It grows prolifically in hedgerows and by roadsides from March to May; I have even seen it in people's gardens as I walk to the gym. Belonging to the cabbage family, it makes a great vegetable and a wonderful sauce for fish. The white flowers, which have a peppery, oniony taste, can be added to salads.

jack-by-the-hedge

land cress

(barbarea verna)

Land cress grows wild all over the world, and is in season in the UK from February to May. I believe you can now get a cultivated strain. Use as you would watercress, for salads, sauces, soups, or as a garnish with a peppery kick.

meadowsweet

(filipendula ulmaria)

Meadowsweet flowers from early May until October in warmer summers. Look for it in damp woods, marshy areas and sodden fields. It has a wonderful sweet scent, which lends itself to desserts such as ice creams, brûlées and mousses. We have also used it successfully in a rice pudding (see page 170). The leaves can be used as well, although they are not quite as scented as the flowers.

meadowsweet

nettles
(urtica dioica)

The common stinging nettle grows practically everywhere, all year round, though it is best to pick it in spring for the young shoots. It makes a great soup, or can be treated like spinach and used in risottos, gnocchi and stuffings.

oxalis
(oxalis acetosella)

Also known as wood sorrel, oxalis grows from March onwards in damp areas and ancient woods, especially pinewoods. It is not good to eat in large quantities because of the presence of oxalic acid but a few leaves added to a salad, or used as a garnish for rich dishes that need a hit of lemon, are just perfect.

oxalis

pennywort
(umbilicus rupestris)

Pennywort is found in damp, mostly shaded, ground in spring and autumn. It doesn't really taste of much, but its texture is fabulous – crisp, yet releasing a hit of water. It makes a lovely garnish or addition to a salad.

pennywort

plantain leaves
(plantago major)

This very bitter plant is found on grassland everywhere but is at its best from spring to early summer. Use the youngest, most tender leaves to spruce up a salad that has a sweetness to it. The leaves can also be blanched and used as a garnish, glazed with a little maple syrup.

sea beet
(beta vulgaris maritima)

Sea beet grows near estuaries and on seashores from early April to December. Pick the younger, smaller leaves. They can be eaten raw for a crisp taste of the sea, with its wonderful natural seasoning. They are also good wilted with butter and treated like a superior spinach, and can even be used to help give a good base to a vegetable stock.

sea purslane
(halimione portulacoides)

Sea purslane, with its lovely salty flavour, can be found on salt marshes all year round. We prefer to use the young leaves raw for their crisp texture. The larger leaves can be quickly wilted and, with a little cream to bind, make a good accompaniment to fish dishes – see Meunière of Dover Sole with Parsnip Purée, Razor Clams and Sea Purslane on page 96.

silverweed
(potentilla anserina)

Look for silverweed in spring and summer, in fields, meadows and country lanes. The young leaves give an attractive colour to a salad. The roots, dug in autumn, have a sweet taste when cooked, resembling chervil tubers or parsnips. They are very small but if you can get enough of them they make a good purée with a little butter.

sweet cicely
(myrrhis odorata)

Sweet cicely grows in woods, hedges and some gardens, from February to May. A pleasant, aniseed-flavoured herb, it is great with broad beans or peas and also very good in salads. We even make a sweet cicely soup at the restaurant when we have enough.

wild garlic
(allium ursinum)

Also known as ramsons, or bear garlic, wild garlic is found in the spring in damp woods and by streams and fresh water.

One of my favourite plants, it has a subtler flavour than ordinary garlic. The leaves are delicious wilted to serve as a vegetable, or puréed or in a soup. Alternatively you can slice them finely and add raw to a salad. The flowers are also good in salads, while the stems work well in a risotto

woodruff
(galium odoratum)

Woodruff favours shady areas, such as dark, ancient woods, and is in season from March to June. Good as an addition to roasting root vegetables, it has a scent reminiscent of tobacco and new-mown hay. I use it a lot with apples and pears – a little in a pear ice cream can make it.

woodruff

yarrow
(achillea millefolium)

Look for yarrow in meadows, pastures and by the roadside from June to September. The leaves and flowers have a slightly peppery, lemony tang. I like to smother birds such as pigeon and chicken with butter and then sprinkle chopped yarrow over them before roasting. For a similar treatment with quail, see Roast Quail with Marinated Baby Artichokes and Cheltenham Beetroot on page 68.

yarrow

mushrooms
cep
(boletus edulis)

Known as penny bun in English and porcini in Italian, ceps are one of the kings of the mushroom world. They grow in coniferous, deciduous or mixed woodlands in autumn and early winter. When very fresh and in pristine condition, they are wonderful raw, in salads. Cooked they are as good as an accompaniment to roasted game as they are in a risotto, soup, mousse or sauce. Dried and reconstituted, they make an invaluable addition to stews. Ground dried ceps can be used to coat meat or fish (see Pork Dusted with Cep Powder on page 120).

ceps

chanterelle
(cantharellus infundibuliformis)

This spindly mushroom grows in most woods, but particularly deciduous and pinewoods, in the autumn. When thoroughly washed and sautéed, it makes a lovely addition to a game salad or an omelette. We use chanterelles to garnish many of our dishes in season.

chanterelle

girolle
(cantharellus cibarius)

Girolles can be found in beech, birch and pinewoods – we get a lot of ours from Scotland during early autumn. They are glorious sautéed with a little garlic and duck fat, useful as a garnish with meat and fish, and also make a lovely soup.

girolles

morel
(morchella esculenta)

Look for morels from February to May, in sandy, chalky areas, on scorched ground and even in retail-park planting areas laid to mulch. They need to be trimmed and washed several times in plenty of water, as they usually contain grit and sand.
I just love them, simply sautéed with a little butter or used in the classic dish, chicken with morels and Vin Jaune (a wine from the Jura area of France).

saffron milk cap

morels

saffron milk cap
(lactarius deliciosus)

I usually find these in pinewoods but have also found some by the roadside. In season from August to early October, they are an orangey colour with flecks of green. If you cut the stem and squeeze it lightly, a deep-orange milky liquid will appear.

Saffron milk caps make a delicious soup (see page 40). Alternatively, if you render a little bacon fat in a frying pan and then fry some saffron milk caps in it, you will have the most wonderful meal.

trompette noire
(craterellus cornucopioides)

With its deep black colour, this can look somewhat sinister – it comes as no surprise that it is also called trompette des morts (trumpet of the dead). The English name is horn of plenty. It grows in deciduous woods and beechwoods from early autumn to early winter, and can be treated in the same way as chanterelles.

trompette noire

my suppliers

Finding good suppliers is the starting point for any serious cook. The suppliers that I have listed below provide me with produce of outstanding quality and reliability. If you are lucky enough to live within close proximity to any of those listed here then do try and seek them out – some provide a mail order service. Wherever you live though, do make a point of seeking out the very best produce from the very best supplier – ask around, you will soon pick up names and recommendations and begin to build an invaluable address book that will help transform your culinary life.

mis en place

Unit 4 Quarry Bridge Works
Chesterton Lane
Cirencester
Gloucestershire GL7 IYD
01285 641144

My vegetable supplier.

the mountain food company ltd

Banc-y-ddol
Hebron
Whitland
Dyfed
01994 419555

Yun helps supply us with some of the wild foods we use, perfect for when I am too busy to get out, or for when I need foods from the sea. Thank you, Yun, for sharing your knowledge.

m.j. & j.a. watts

5 Suffolk Parade
Cheltenham
Gloucestershire GL50 2AB
01242 522151

My butchers who have been with me since the day I opened, always reliable. Thanks for teaching me and allowing me to teach you. Adrian – here's to the next 19 years.

island divers

Unit 26f3
Kyle Industrial Estate
Kyle of Lochalsh
Ross-Shire IV40 8AX
01599 530300

My amazing scallop and langoustine supplier. Madeleine – the quality astounds me. Wholesale, but may provide occasional mail order.

the cheese works ltd

5 Regent Street
Cheltenham
Gloucestershire GL50 1HE
01242 255022

Ben's shop in Cheltenham supplies us with our wide variety of cheese in prime condition.

Years of building a good working relationship together. My butchers have been with me since the day I opened.

hereford snails

L'Escargot Anglaise
Credenhill
Hereford HR4 7DN
01432 760750

Tony's snails have long been on our menu in different forms. He takes all of the laborious preparation away for us and provides them ready to cook to our recipe.

campbell environmental oil ltd

Swell Buildings Farm
Lower Swell
Stow on the Wold
Cheltenham
Gloucestershire GL54 1HG
01451 870387

Hamish Campbell came in to the restaurant one day to give us a sample of his virgin rapeseed oil to use. Thank you Hamish – this oil now has pride of place in the kitchen and is used in many of our dressings. This is a wonderful product from a man who cares as much about his oil as we do about our food.

sambava

Unit 2, Roseberry Place
Bath BA2 3DU
01225 426309

My spice man. I get some of my more unusual spices from James, such as wattleseed or black limes. Mail order service available.

g. baldwin and co.

171–173 Walworth Road
London SE17 1RW
020 7703 5550

My dried plant and root suppliers. I get things like dried burdock root and dried chamomile flowers. Mail order service available.

equipment

bodo sperlein ltd

Unit 1.05, Oxo Tower Wharf
Barge House Street
London SE1 9PH
020 7633 9413

A big thank you to Bodo for supplying us with some of the most interesting china used in this book. A man whose artistry knows no bounds.

thermomix

[Janie Turner]
UK Thermomix
Pinehill, Sunning Avenue
Sunningdale
Berkshire SL5 9PW
01344 622344

By far the best blender out there – blends, weighs and cooks: a must for the kitchen.

nickel-electro ltd

Oldmixon Crescent
Weston-Super-Mare
North Somerset BS24 9BL
01934 626691

The nickel electro water bath is used for precise poaching and cooking. Watch this piece of equipment – it's a must-have now, and I am sure it will be in most kitchens of the future.

index

acknowledgements

Thank you to my chefs, both past and present. I have been very lucky over the years to have had some great people working with me: Adrian Offley, 19 years ago; Derek Baker; Matt Topping; Craig Sherington; Robert Marshall-Slater; Clive Dixon; Laurent Chable; Arnaud Kaziewicz; Lisa Allen; Anthony Rush; Sam Miller. I am proud of you all.

Special thanks goes to my team at the time of writing this book: Marcus McGuiness, Steve Lyons, Ryan Hodson and to Helen's helpers, Ivana Mravcakova and Hannah Parker. And not forgetting our new arrival, Jason Eaves. Thanks guys, for all your help and for coming in on your days off.

Thanks to Yun at The Mountain Food Company Ltd, who helped with the location for the pictures and the supplies when I didn`t have time.

Thank you to Lisa Barber, my photographer, as big a perfectionist as I am, and to Cynthia.

And finally, to everyone at Absolute Press: Jon, thank you for your guidance, and for allowing me to have a free rein with this book and not pushing me in a different direction. Thank you to Meg and Matt for your wisdom and design. Thank you to Jane Middleton, my editor, for helping to organise some of my ramblings.

The biggest thank you of all is to everyone who has supported Helen and myself over the last 19 years.

picture credits
All photography © Lisa Barber except for following glossary photos: **© Dorling Kindersley:** *alexanders* (Derek Hall); *burdock* (Neil Fletcher); *chickweed* (Neil Fletcher); *ground elder* (Neil Fletcher); *hogweed* (Neil Fletcher); *jack-by-the-hedge* (Neil Fletcher); *meadowsweet* (Neil Fletcher); *oxalis* (Neil Fletcher and Matthew Ward); *woodruff* (Neil Fletcher and Matthew Ward); yarrow (Steve Gorton); *girolles* (Diana Miller); *morels* (David Murray); *saffron milk cap* (Neil Fletcher); *trompette noire* (Diana Miller). **© Roger Phillips:** *ceps*; *chanterelle*. **© Legambiente Arcipelago Toscano:** *pennywort*.